The Gramscian Challenge

Coercion and Consent
in
Marxist Political Theory

The Gramscian Challenge

Coercion and Consent
in Marxist Political Theory

JOHN HOFFMAN

Basil Blackwell

© John Hoffman

First published in 1984 by Basil Blackwell Publishers
Ltd., 108 Cowley Road, Oxford OX4 1JF.

Basil Blackwell Inc.
432 Park Avenue South, Suite 1505
New York, NY 10016, USA

British Library Cataloguing in Publication Data

Hoffman, John
   The Gramscian challenge.
   1. Communism
   I. Title
   320.5'315   HX73
   ISBN 0—85520—771—X

Typeset by Cambrian Typesetters,
Aldershot, Hants.
Printed and bound in Great Britain by
Billing and Sons Ltd., Worcester

To
ROWAN, FREDDIE and FRIEDA

Hark, in thine ear: change places; and, handy
    dandy, which
is the justice, which is the thief? . . . Get thee
    glass eyes;
And, like a scurvy politician, seem
To see the things thou dost not.
                            (*King Lear*, Act 4, Scene 6)

All things are relative, all things flow, and all
    things change.
                            (Lenin in 1905)

CONTENTS

PREFACE

The idea of writing a book like this arose in a somewhat roundabout way from the late Maurice Cornforth. Cornforth had in fact also suggested the topic of my earlier book on Marxist theory and praxis and when that work was complete, he put it to me that more needed to be done on the problem of democracy. Alas, I found the task of defining democracy much more burdensome than polemics over praxis! Although David De Grood of Bridgeport University, Connecticut, encouraged me to press ahead and helped me publish work I had begun on democracy (Hoffman, 1983), it became increasingly clear that to tackle this question, the more general concepts in political theory would also require specific attention. Indeed, one of the last pieces I showed Maurice Cornforth before his death at the end of 1980, was a projected outline for a book on 'Politics and the Will' and some of my thoughts on this subject have found their way into chapter 5 of this present work.

It was however the rise of Eurocommunism, as a theory as well as a movement, which convinced me that no serious analysis of concepts in Marxist political theory could be undertaken without critically engaging the prison writings of Antonio Gramsci. It was after I had given a lecture at the Marx Memorial Library on 'Hegemony and Dictatorship' that I thought of writing something specifically on the problem of coercion and consent. Martyn Stevens in London and Frank Cunningham of the University of Toronto assured me that this was a subject worth pursuing and Neil Harding kindly provided me with an opportunity to develop my ideas on 'The Coercion/Consent Analysis of the State under Socialism' at a conference which he organized in the late summer of 1981 on behalf of the Communist Politics Group of the Political Studies Association. I am grateful to David McLellan who acted as discussant on that occasion and to Ali Rattansi for his critical comments on my paper. I have also learnt a good deal from the discussions at seminars on this and later papers around this theme and I would particularly like to thank in this regard, John Rodger, John Foster and all their colleagues in the Department of Politics and Sociology at Paisley College of Technology.

In 1982 Jeff Sawtell, editor of the cultural magazine *Artery*, invited me to respond to Tony Benn's challenging lecture on 'Marxism and Democracy' (Benn, 1982). Ironically it was on the basis of a kind of Eurocommunist analysis of coercion and consent that Benn established his *critique* of Marxist theory and I showed Benn my critique of his critique and received a characteristically generous and friendly reply. The more I thought about Gramsci, Eurocommunism and the classical Marxist tradition, the more I realized that the question was more complex than I had earlier supposed. In my previous efforts to resolve the coercion and consent problem, I had assumed that classical Marxism analysed politics simply in terms of coercion, whereas Gramsci and those who built upon his work, had 'extended' the state in order to find a place for the question of consent and this had necessarily led to eclecticism, dualism and the like. It now became clear that this kind of argument seriously oversimplified the classical Marxist position for it meant demoting ideological factors in politics to a secondary role, apart from and external to the state's 'coercive essence'. This in turn made it impossible to find any relationship between political coercion and social coercion since if politics is conceived of as a monopoly of 'brute force', it appears to have no coercive counterpart within society as a whole. Crucial to my argument in this book is the contention that classical Marxism *does* present (albeit implicitly) a 'broad' view of politics and the state and this makes three things possible. A better appreciation of Gramsci's contribution to Marxist theory; an understanding that reducing politics to 'pure' force is just as untenable as reducing it to 'pure' consent and a way of integrating the economic insights of *Capital* into a political analysis of the coercion/consent problem.

A discussion with Danny Goldstick brought me sharply up against a further problem. If politics is defined broadly in a way which links coercion and consent together, what is it that gives consent its particular identity? Ben Fine also helped me with this question and whether either will be satisfied with my formulation of consent as the 'dialectical negation of coercion', this somewhat Hegelian sounding 'solution' to the problem does at least have the merit of emphasizing the distinction between the two without at the same time breaking up their unity.

Writing this book would not have been possible without a sabbatical term from the University of Leicester and I am particularly grateful to John Day, head of the Department of Politics, for facilitating arrangements and to Peter Savigear who kindly agreed to postpone his own study leave entitlement so that I could meet publishers' deadlines. The Research Board provided funds to visit other libraries in search of material and the University's own library staff have been extremely prompt and efficient with inter-library loans: to both, thanks are due. I am indebted to Christopher Hughes who recently retired from the Politics Department, for his reassurance that paradoxes in politics do exist and that all pupils of the 'mighty Hegel' should spare no effort in the attempt to resolve them while Jack Spence, currently senior pro-vice-chancellor, assiduously traced a quote for me from *Alice* about curiosity and I owe him an apology for not finding a place for it in my final draft! The late

Maurice Hookham read drafts of my earlier work and with his untimely death in 1981 I lost a friend and confidant who would have been of great help to me in preparing this book.

In addition to those mentioned above, I would like to thank the following for their interest and advice: Kate Clark, Julian Cooper, Ralph Faris, Mike Gane, Andras Gedo, Terry Johnson, Monty Johnstone, Mike Levin, Betty Matthews, Bert Ramelson and Dominic Strinati. On the domestic front — to which even cloistered academics retreat to write books — I am grateful to Rowan Roenisch for relaxing the stern, egalitarian (and usually honoured in the breach) norms of the household, while the task of keeping young children at bay gave me ample opportunity to reflect on the fact that a dialectical unity between coercion and consent seems so much easier to establish in theory than in practice! I know that Dallah Hoffman will be pained to find that although I have virtuously abstained from generic usages of the term 'man' in my philosophical observations, resolve has failed me with references to the individual and I can only plead that despite these linguistic lapses, my book is motivated by a sincere concern with human emancipation in all its forms.

Finally, I would like to thank the publishers for their encouragement and reiterate the customary disclaimer that the responsibility for the arguments which follow is essentially mine. In a work as controversial as this one, this is a point worth making and I am also conscious of the fact that many of the people I take to task are people I know and respect. Without the stimulus of their theories and commentaries, this book could not have been written.

John Hoffman
4 January 1984

LIST OF ABBREVIATIONS

References to the works of Marx, Engels, Gramsci and Lenin are not included in the bibliography at the back nor are they cited in the text according to date of publication. Instead the following abbreviations have been employed:

AD   Frederick Engels, *Anti-Dühring* (3rd edn), Moscow, Foreign Languages Publishing House, 1962.

C I   Karl Marx, *Capital*, vol. 1, London, Lawrence and Wishart, 1970.

C III   Karl Marx, *Capital*, vol. 3, Moscow, Progress Publishers, 1966.

CCPE   Karl Marx, *A Contribution to the Critique of Political Economy*, London, Lawrence and Wishart, 1971.

DN   Frederick Engels, *Dialectics of Nature* (3rd edn), Moscow, Progress Publishers, 1964.

FI   Karl Marx, *The First International and After*, Harmondsworth and London, Penguin and New Left Books, 1974.

G   Karl Marx, *Grundrisse*, Harmondsworth and London, Penguin and New Left Books, 1973.

LCW   V.I. Lenin, *Collected Works*, Moscow, Progress Publishers, 1960–1970.

LP   Antonio Gramsci, *Letters from Prison*, London, Jonathan Cape, 1975.

MECW   Karl Marx and Frederick Engels, *Collected Works*, London, Lawrence and Wishart, 1975—

MELAAS   Marx, Engels, Lenin, *Anarchism and Anarcho-Syndicalism*, Moscow, Progress Publishers, 1972.

MESW   Karl Marx and Frederick Engels, *Selected Works* one vol., London, Lawrence and Wishart, 1968.

OFPPS   Frederick Engels, *The Origin of the Family, Private Property and the State*, London, Lawrence and Wishart, 1972.

PC   Karl Marx and Frederick Engels, *On the Paris Commune*, Moscow, Progress Publishers, 1971.

SC   Karl Marx and Frederick Engels, *Selected Correspondence* (3rd edn), Moscow, Progress Publishers, 1975.

SPN   Antonio Gramsci, *Selections from the Prison Notebooks*, London, Lawrence and Wishart, 1971.

SPW I   Antonio Gramsci, *Selections from Political Writings 1910–1920*, London, Lawrence and Wishart, 1977.

SPW II   Antonio Gramsci, *Selections from Political Writings 1921–1926*, London, Lawrence and Wishart, 1978.

W   Karl Marx and Frederich Engels, *Werke*, Berlin, Dietz Verlag, 1961–1968.

1

THE POLITICS OF CONSENT AND
THE 'CRISIS OF MARXISM'

CLASSICAL MARXISM AND ITS ERRANT ISMS

The problem of coercion and consent in Marxist theory has
been posed sharply in recent years by the stark assertion
that classical Marxism, in emphasizing the coercive nature
of politics, has been correspondingly weak in analysing the
problem of consent. In a book written in the late 1960s
which was to set the tone for much of the controversy
around the question of the state in the following decade,
Ralph Miliband argued that Marxist political theory had
become 'stuck in its groove' with 'little capacity to renew
itself' (1969, p. 5) precisely because Marx and Engels had
never really departed from the view that the state was 'above
all' coercive in character. Miliband was concerned to tackle
the problem of power in post-war liberal capitalist regimes
and the question his book posed was this: if these are regimes
in which 'an economically dominant class rules *through*
democratic institutions, rather than by way of dictatorship'
(1969, p. 22), how are they to be understood by a theory
which appears to emphasize merely the repressive nature
of the state? What of states which enjoy significant popular
support, where an 'economically dominant class' rules
through consent? The very relevance of classical Marxism
to an understanding of the liberal capitalist world is called
into question.

The deficiencies of Marxist political theory became a

dominant theme of the Marx commentaries in the 1970s, from Lucio Colletti's complaint to the editor of the *New Left Review* that 'the development of political theory has been extraordinarily weak in Marxism' (1977, p. 331), to a recent work on *The Capitalist State* which finds classical treatments of the subject incomplete, incoherent and contradictory (Jessop, 1982, p. 1). (See also, e.g. Anderson, 1976, p. 114; Gunn, 1977, p. 15; McLellan, 1979, pp. 3—4; Miliband, 1977, p. 43; Perez-Diaz, 1978, p. 87). Three 'isms' in particular are levelled against traditional Marxist theory. *Instrumentalism* — the analysis of the state as an 'instrument' of a dominant class which, it is said, denies the state any autonomy or dynamic of its own. *Reductionism* — the concept of politics as a superstructure, an 'epiphenomenon' derived from an economic base, which accordingly smothers the specific role of the state in society and *catastrophism*, the assumption that relations between bourgeoisie and proletariat will increasingly polarize as an inevitable consequence of capitalist crisis, so that the need to allow for conscious political intervention from above or below becomes redundant. All three errant isms make the same critical point: by treating the state as an 'instrument', a 'superstructure' or the paralysed spectator of a capitalist crisis, classical Marxism lacks a proper theory of politics. 'We have to be frank about it,' declared Louis Althusser in 1977, 'there does not *really* exist any "Marxist theory of the State"' (1979, p. 234), and it logically follows, of course, if Marxism lacks a theory of the state, it also lacks a theory of democracy (Hunt, 1983, p. 106). This was indeed the major point of Santiago Carrillo's celebrated bombshell *'Eurocommunism' and the State* with its criticism of the 'frivolity and haste' with which 'highly respectable Marxists' have disposed of the concept of democracy (1977, p. 14) and it echoes the theme of the earlier Miliband critique. Classical Marxism is weak on democracy because, by over-emphasizing the coercive character of politics, it is also weak on consent.

Althusser made the same point in a slightly different way. In his unprecedently sharp attack on the classical tradition and its 'pathetic' formulas on the state in 1977, he argued that all attempts to tackle the question of politics and class struggle boil down to little more than 'a repeated warning to avoid all bourgeois conceptions of the state — a rather negative demarcation line and definition' (1979, p. 234). This accusation of 'negativity' reinforces all the other errant isms with which classical Marxism is arraigned and ties them in more closely with the problem of consent, for if the state is a mere instrument, tool, reflection or superstructure, then clearly it can do nothing *positive* for society and the support which capitalist regimes receive from wide sections of the population cannot be explained. Instrumentalism, reductionism and catastrophism are all negative conceptions which imply *coercion* and coercion and repression cannot possibly explain why, as Miliband puts it, 'many if not most of these regimes' have endured (1977, p. 43). At the heart of all classical Marxism's errant isms lies this problem of consent.

The centrality of this question to the various woes and isms diagnosed above in the traditional theory of the state is further evidenced by the immense revival of interest by Western Marxists in the writings of Antonio Gramsci, the Italian communist leader who was imprisoned by Mussolini and died in 1937. Althusser's reference to Gramsci (along with Lenin) as a theorist who groped unsuccessfully towards solving the problem of negativity in the Marxist classics (1979, p. 235) is strikingly atypical. Miliband, for example, while criticizing traditional Marxist analyses of domination as 'manifestly inadequate', heralds Gramsci's work as a 'signal exception' to classical deficiencies (1977, p. 42) and it has become commonplace, despite Althusser's strictures, to see Gramsci as the founder of a 'new science of politics'; the first Marxist to develop 'the elements of a full political theory within Marxism' (Hobsbawm, 1977, p. 208); a theorist whose work inaugurated a new chapter in the development of a Marxist theory of politics and the state (Mouffe, 1979a, p. 5). What has earned Gramsci these handsome tributes? His preoccupation with the problem of consent, his 'broad' view of the state as the 'entire complex of practical and theoretical activities with which the ruling class not only justifies and maintains its dominance, but manages to win the active consent of those over whom it rules' (Gramsci, *SPN*, p. 244). This celebrated and much quoted formulation brings us face to face with what is undoubtedly the key concept in Gramsci's thought — the concept of *hegemony*. Through his concept of hegemony, Gramsci focused on what he called 'intellectual and moral leadership' as opposed to dictatorship or domination (*SPN*, p. 57) and by posing, in the words of one of his French commentators, 'the question of consent in a way new to Marxism' (Buci-Glucksmann, 1982, p. 117), Gramsci, it is argued, was the first to tackle the great Achilles Heel of the classical tradition. His conception of hegemony, politics-as-consent, lies at the heart of his new science of politics and by focusing explicitly on the question of consent in the political process, serves to bring democracy back into Marxism (Mercer, 1980, p. 105).

To tackle the question of consent, it is necessary also to tackle the errant isms. Gramsci as the theorist of hegemony, began the process, declare his commentators, of ridding Marxist theory of its passivist instrumentalism, economistic reductionism and simplistic catastrophism: a veritable reconstruction of the entire conceptual framework of traditional Marxism (Mercer, 1980, p. 103). It is not simply that Gramsci added a concern with consent to an existing theory of the state as an instrument of coercion or merely 'expanded' the activities undertaken by a political super-structure. His concept of hegemony challenges the whole notion of the state as a class instrument and lays the basis for transcending the very base/superstructure 'metaphor' central to classical historical materialism (Buci-Glucksmann, 1982, p. 118; Showstack Sassoon, 1980a, p. 85). Tackling the problem of consent, in other words, requires a 'Copernican revolution' (Laclau and Mouffe, 1981, p. 16) in Marxist political theory in order to escape, as Buci-Glucksmann puts it, 'the problematic of the state as violence, the basis in fact of Stalinist theory and practice in this field' (1980, p. 12).

THE 'CRISIS' AND THE SCHIZOID MALADY

This last comment underlines the fact that what is at stake in this argument are not merely deficiencies within classical Marxist theory, but the whole future of Marxism itself. If it is true, as Colletti contends, that 'the political movement inspired by Marxism has been virtually innocent of political theory' (1977, p. 331), then the gravest practical implications follow. A political theory which neglects the question of consent will, at the very least, facilitate Communist leaderships which exercise power 'in the name of Marxism' but without 'any control by the masses over whom they rule' (Colletti, 1977, p. 332). The absence of an adequate political theory has, according to Colletti and Althusser, brought Marxism itself into crisis as the result of a paralysing rift between the emancipatory potential of its theory and the repressive actualities of its practice. The 'central test of *Capital* itself has not come to pass', declares Colletti, 'a socialist revolution in the advanced West. The result is that Marxism is in crisis today, and it can only surmount this crisis by acknowledging it' (1977, p. 340). Althusser made the same point even more dramatically. We are confronted, he told a conference organized by the far-left Italian *Il Manifesto* group, by 'the extreme difficulty . . . and perhaps even, in the present state of our theoretical knowledge, almost the impossibility of providing a really satisfactory explanation of a history which was, after all, made in the name of Marxism' (1979, p. 227). For Althusser, the roots of the crisis go back to the Stalin period in the 1930s: for others, they can be traced right back to the October Revolution itself (Claudin, 1979, p. 138).

What is clear is that this declaration of a 'crisis of Marxism' in the 1970s has brought sharply to a head the long festering doubts and dilemmas of that trend and tradition whose troubled logic defines it as a 'Western Marxism'. A Marxism, as Anderson has argued, born of pessimism and defeat, reflecting both the failure after the First World War of proletarian revolutions to succeed in the West and a growing disenchantment, particularly among the radical intelligentsia, with the policies of the Comintern and the new Soviet state in the East (Anderson, 1976, p. 92). The result: a Marxism confined to the universities and academies 'far from the life of the proletariat' and displaying as the most fundamental of its characteristics, the 'structural divorce' of its Marxist theory from political practice (Anderson, 1976, p. 92; p. 29). It must be said that this is a most curious and paradoxical fate for a Marxism to suffer, for how can Marxists *qua* Marxists content themselves with interpreting the world when, as the classical tradition affirms, the point is to change it? If, in some way or other, problems of theory are only soluble through practice and the 'dispute over the reality or non-reality of thinking which isolates itself from practice is a purely scholastic question' (Marx, *MECW* 5, p. 6), then a Marxist theory structurally divorced from practice becomes a Marxist *scholasticism*, less one might suppose a 'unity of opposites' than an outright contradiction in terms! It might well be asked whether so paradoxical a kind of Marxism is viable at all but what is clear is that this Marxist tradition, whose luminaries embrace Karl Korsch, the early Lukacs, Althusser and Colletti, Jean-Paul Sartre and the theorists of the Frankfurt School, stands vehemently opposed to what might be called 'existing Marxism': a Marxism deeply involved in that historical practice which it is apparently unable to explain. An 'official Marxism' which vindicates the living realities of existing socialism.

In the 1940s the liberal political scientist David Easton warned of a 'threatened eclipse of liberalism', a 'schizoid malady' resulting from liberalism's long history of 'divorcing theory from practice' (1949, p. 17). But if this divorce is a problem for liberalism, how much more so is it for Marxism whose basic epistemology consciously eschews all dualisms? What can be described as Western Marxism's theoretical opposition to practical Marxism has resulted in the striking selectivity of its doctrinal allegiances. The theme of much of its literature since the late 1960s — the period in which the End of Ideology gave way to the Rebirth of Critique — has been that of Marx against the Marxists! The defence of the theorist against betrayal by his practitioners. It was not just a question of demoting Joseph Stalin from a position of World Authority to that of Arch-Vulgariser for after 1956, with Khrushchev's denunciation of the 'cult of the personality', Stalin conspicuously disappeared as a 'classical' thinker in most, if not quite all, of the official Marxist world. Much more dramatic was the wedge which Western Marxists drove between Karl Marx and Frederick Engels, traditionally regarded as a reliable interpreter of his life-long friend. Why was the divorce necessary? If Western Marxism can be correctly characterized as a 'university' or a 'professorial' Marxism (Parkin, 1979, p. x; Feuer, 1978), then as Timpanaro has unkindly suggested, it must satisfy in advance 'the requirements of the most avant-garde elements of bourgeois culture' (1975, p. 74). Anyone whose writings might make Marxism appear naive, simplistic or out of date must be 'dumped' and since Engels devoted much of his energy to expounding and defending Marx's ideas in the periodical press of his day, he is the ideal candidate. Concerned as he was with what might be called the 'practical face' of Marxism and its links with working class organization, it is logical enough that he should be unmasked as con-taminator!

Nor is this paradox the only consequence of a defence of the theoretical Marx against his vulgarizing practitioners.

Even more curious was the effect that this argument had on the status of Marx himself within Western Marxism. As Anderson noted in his interview with Colletti, demoting Engels creates a 'sacred zone' around Marx (Colletti, 1977, p. 329). A stance of remorseless *critique* — against Engels, Lenin, the Marxism of the Second and Third Internationals, the philosophy of dialectical materialism and much else besides — coexists with the defence of a 'pure Marx' who stands above criticism. It is Marx's very inaccessibility to 'practical' judgement which protects him from the fate of his followers. Marx must be 'read', in Althusser's celebrated phrase, in a way which emphasizes just how complex and elusive his theory really is. If, as Timpanaro puts it, Marx is to be *de rigueur* in our cultural world, then his physiognomy must be that of an intellectual 'profound and subtle (and still uncomprehended)' (1975, p. 74). Theological metaphors are irresistible for it seems that once Marx is brought down to earth and able to communicate to 'the class which really matters' (Parkin, 1979, p. ix), his profundity is irretrievably destroyed. Rather like Kierkegaard's existentialist God whom we know only because he is unknowable, Marx's superiority emerges in Western Marxist eyes from the fact that nobody can really understand him!

But how long can such absurdities last? Althusser's *For Marx* (1966) had been fiercely critical of 'Stalinist dogmatism' (e.g. 1969, p. 30) and during the 1970s his attacks on existing socialism and official Marxism become increasingly vehement. But the crisis in the international communist movement is still ascribed to 'Stalinist practices' which rupture the 'Marxist and Leninist tradition' (1977a, p. 11), to a failure by communist party leaders to make use of the 'scientific means of understanding history' provided by Marx himself (1977b, p. 53). In his statement in Venice, the argument takes a dramatic turn. The problem is rooted within the theory itself. Even the 'theologized' Marx is a god with clay feet. Hobsbawm has argued that there is a crisis *in* Marxism rather than a crisis *of* Marxism (1983, p. 11) since while there has been a breakdown in consensus about what constitutes the main body of Marx's ideas, the ideas themselves are still valid, albeit as 'an instrument for analysing reality' (Hobsbawm and Napolitano, 1977, p. 95). But which ideas are these? For, as Colletti noted, Western Marxists had begun to challenge the 'central pillars on which Marx's theoretical edifice rests' (1977, p. 341). If the predictions of *Capital* are flawed and, as Colletti himself says, 'there are critical areas of uncertainty and confusion about the dialectic' (1977, p. 329), then it is not so much a question of disagreeing about Marxism but of deciding whether Marxism is worth disagreeing about.

Anderson interviewed Colletti in 1974. By 1976 he had begun to express growing doubts. In an Afterword to his *Considerations on Western Marxism* he commented self-critically that in that work the possibility that elements in the classical heritage were not so much incomplete as incorrect had not been taken 'with sufficient seriousness' (1976, p. 112). The *Il Manifesto* conference of 1977 on 'Power and opposition in post-revolutionary societies' took the 'crisis of Marxism' as its organizing theme and in July 1978, *Marxism Today*, the theoretical journal of the British Communist Party, carried the text of Althusser's contribution to the conference with a cover sketch of a Karl Marx, hospitalized, feverish and clearly running a very high temperature! It is revealing that Althusser who had done more than any other Western Marxist to encourage the search for a 'real Marx' freed from the vulgarities of his official interpreters, should now repudiate such an exercise as futile (1979, p. 231). Marxism *itself* contains 'difficulties, contradictions and gaps' which touch precisely on vital points of the present crisis (p. 232). The three 'very rough examples' Althusser offers — the presentation of surplus value in *Capital*, the enigmatic 'formulae' on the dialectic and the absence of a theory of the state — all relate to a common problem: the relationship of politics to economics, the class struggle and the movement of history. The absence of a 'real' Marxist theory of the state simply dramatizes the overall weakness of Marxist political theory in general (1979, pp. 234–6).

If then, as we have presented the Western Marxist argument, the question of consent lies at the heart of the errant isms of classical political theory, the wider implications of this critical change should now be clear. The problem of consent not only challenges Marxist politics: it threatens the whole future of Marxism and is central to that long smouldering schizoid malady which has erupted into self-destructive proportions.

A EUROCOMMUNIST SOLUTION TO THE 'CRISIS'?

In reporting the argument that the problem of coercion and consent has brought Marxism into a state of 'crisis', the point has also to be made that the projected solution to this 'crisis' is less than reassuring. For this is not the first time a 'crisis of Marxism' has been declared. Lenin in 1899 noted the argument by Russian supporters of the German 'revisionist' Eduard Bernstein that an 'intolerant', 'negative' and 'primitive' Marxism needs to yield to a Marxism which is 'democratic' and commented angrily: 'To talk about a "crisis of Marxism" is merely to repeat the nonsense of the bourgeois hacks who are doing all they can to exacerbate every disagreement among the socialists and turn it into a split in the socialist parties' (Lenin, *LCW* 4, p. 176).

Althusser himself is conscious of this historical precedent and in somewhat 'Leninist' tones, characterizes the 'crisis of Marxism' which erupted at the turn of the century as a 'crisis' engineered by the enemies of the labour movement which 'led to the "bankruptcy" of the Second International, its desertion to the camp of class collaboration' (1979, p. 225). Yet, how does the 'crisis of Marxism' associated with Bernstein at the turn of the century differ from the 'crisis' proclaimed by Althusser in 1977? The parallels between the two are most interesting. Bernstein, it is worth recalling, did not see himself as in any sense an 'enemy' of Marxism and in his *Premises of Socialism and the Tasks of Social Democracy* (1899) he argues that 'the further development and elaboration of the Marxist doctrine must begin with criticism of it' (1961, p. 25). Once we acknowledge what is mistaken within Marx – his critique of utopianism, theory of dialectics, theory of value, theory of history and analysis of capitalist crisis – we will then be able to see why it is 'Marx who finally carries the point against Marx' (1961, p. 27)! There seems to be an unmistakeable echo of these 'mistakes' in the 'difficulties, contradictions and gaps' spotted by Louis Althusser. Althusser suggests stoically that Marxists should not shrink from the notion of 'crisis' since despite the earlier crisis which culminated in the collapse of the Second International, 'Marxism survived' (1979, p. 225). But we have to pose the question, *Which* Marxism survived? The Marxism of Bernstein which declared Marxism in crisis or the Marxism of Lenin which rejected the whole notion of a 'crisis of Marxism' out of hand? Yet, despite what would seem to be an unpromising historical precedent, Althusser, like Colletti before him, insists that the crisis must be acknowledged. Out of a dubious and negative phrase, to be exploited by our enemies, there must emerge something dynamic and positive: 'instead of stating that "Marxism is in crisis", we can say: "At last the crisis of Marxism has exploded! At last it is in full view! At last something vital and alive can be liberated by this crisis and in this crisis" ' (1979, p. 229). But how and why? If the 'crisis of Marxism' denoted 'collapse and death' in the period before the First World War, why should it provide the opportunity to liberate 'something alive and vital' some 70 years later?

In Marxism, more so perhaps than in any other theory, the notion of 'crisis' denotes a malaise which is not merely symptomatic, but profound. Althusser himself made the point which has become an integral part of the 'crisis of Marxism' argument – that the 'crisis of Marxism' parallels

a 'crisis of capitalism' (McLennan, 1983, p. 15; Laclau and
Mouffe, 1981, p. 17; Altvater and Kallscheuer, 1979, p. 104).
Does this parallel invite the presumption that the 'crisis of
Marxism' is a crisis in the same sense as the 'crisis of capitalism'?
Marxists would normally take a 'crisis of capitalism' to
imply that the entire system is obsolete and needs to be
radically replaced by a new one. If the 'central pillars' and
'keystones' of Marx's own theoretical edifice have become
similarly problematic, does not the declaration of a 'crisis
of Marxism' imply the demand for a new kind of theory
altogether? Or the return to a theory even more 'classical'
than the one to be superseded?

It is significant that at the very time schizoid maladies
were erupting into a 'crisis of Marxism', a new trend of
communism was becoming apparent, a *Euro*communism,
a communism to provide a practical answer to the long
standing dilemmas of the Western Marxist tradition. We
have already encountered the argument that behind the
'crisis of Marxism' lie the deficiencies of political theory
and central to these errant isms: the problem of consent. What
is the outstanding characteristic of this 'new' communism?
Its self-presentation as a democratic communism pursuing
a 'democratic road' to a democratic 'model' of a socialist
society, free from the coercive realities of existing systems.
A communism based on consent: the search for a 'third
way' (Mercer, 1980, p. 101; Showstack Sassoon, 1982,
p. 9) between 'Stalinism' and social democracy, between
those who reject Marxism in theory and those who claim to
have implemented Marxism in practice. An organizational
vehicle capable of tackling the central problem of Western
Marxism, the schizoid divorce of its theory from practice,
with a new science of politics, firmly repudiating the
traditional instrumentalist, reductionist and economistic
neglect of consent. As a practical political trend, Eurocommunism embodies in party programmes and policy
statements many of the doubts and dilemmas, the fears
and the frustrated aspirations confined in the past to the

seminar room and lecture theatre. Indeed, the development in the mid-1970s of the British 'Communist University' as a forum for Western Marxist argument and debate provided just such a convergence between theory and practice, as did Eurocommunist party congresses (the Twenty-Second Congress of the French Communist Party in 1976, for example) in which critiques of official Marxism were embodied in programmatic forms.

The revival of interest in the writings of Antonio Gramsci, noted above, has had therefore a wider practical significance. If Gramsci is seen as the greatest representative of Western Marxism, he was also the 'least typical' (Anderson, 1976, p. 67). While most of the Western Marxists were academic philosophers, the *Prison Notebooks* were written by a revolutionary working class leader: if he suffered 'intellectual contradictions and uncertainties' (Anderson, 1976, p. 25), they were the doubts and dilemmas of a practical politician. Gramsci's preoccupation with the problem of consent, of hegemony, is seen by Western Marxists as a 'starting point for a necessary engagement with the current "crisis of Marxism" ' (Mercer, 1980, p. 103; see also, Jessop, 1980, p. 25). Predictably, although as we shall see, problematically, Gramsci has been acclaimed the father of Eurocommunism (Bridges, 1978, p. 25): the founder of a new science of politics and a new political trend. A communist leader who sought to resolve in practice the theoretical maladies of Western Marxism.

It is from Gramsci's *Prison Notebooks* that I take the formulation of the problem central to this book: the question of politics in terms of coercion and consent. It is a question raised sharply by those who claim that the 'old' theory of politics with its errant isms has plunged Marxism into crisis. A new politics centred around a new political trend with Consent as its mast-head, points the way out of the classical cul-de-sac. But is this really so? The new communism uncannily echoes trends in the past. It is not only the analogy with Bernstein's Marxist criticism of Marx which is compelling;

Salvadori has noted the presence of strong 'Kautskyist' themes in some contemporary Western communist thought (1979, p. 13) and the uncomfortable precedents alluded to by Althusser provoke the following question. Is Eurocommunism with its rediscovered emphasis on 'democracy' and 'consent', an emphasis which it shares perfectly with Bernstein and the later Kautsky, less an *answer* to the 'crisis of Marxism' than one of its more paradoxical victims? Callinicos has suggested that the tragic fate of two of Eurocommunism's most respected proponents, Althusser and Poulantzas, is a personalized symptom of a wider impasse (1982, pp. 23–24) and even those who regard the 'crisis of Marxism' as a 'commonplace', still await the solution to the old question of 'what is to be done?' (Jessop, 1980, p. 23). Does the Eurocommunist Emperor really have any clothes? For the reflection of theoretical doubts and dilemmas in practical political movements may serve only to further *exacerbate* them, bringing not hope and renewal, but collapse and despair. Eurocommunism is certainly an expression of Western Marxism's crisis, but is it an answer?

THE PROBLEM AS CHALLENGE

If, as seems likely, Eurocommunism is symptomatic of a new 'revisionism', then this makes consideration of the problem of coercion and consent within the framework of classical Marxist political theory, all the more important. For what are we to say of the errant theoretical isms and the coercive practical realities which are alleged to characterize 'existing Marxism'? Is the classical tradition, because of its emphasis on politics-as-coercion, unable to tackle the problem of consent?

The question of politics as a blending of coercion and consent may seem to be a new one for Marxism, raised explicitly for the first time in the *Prison Notebooks* of Antonio Gramsci, but it is a very old question for political thought. Pateman has argued that the conceptual contrast is rooted in the classical liberal notion of society as a voluntary scheme whose autonomous members acknowledge only those obligations which are self-imposed (1979, p. 2). Gramsci, for his part, was to trace the 'dual perspective' right back to Machiavelli's Centaur, half-animal and half-human and itself an allegory rooted in ancient political wisdom (*SPN*, pp. 169–170). Gramsci's 'compelling ancestor', as Anderson calls him (1976, p. 67) was a political theorist from the Renaissance period; his hegemonic Communist Party a New Prince. The problem of coercion and consent in Marxist political theory is therefore also a problem of assessing the degree of continuity which Marxist theory can be said to enjoy with the concepts and traditions of the past. No less than the argument about 'crisis', this problem of continuity imposes an important challenge.

As far as Lenin was concerned, Marxism must seek to combine openness with coherence. As the direct and immediate continuation of past theories (*LCW* 19, p. 23), Marxism must be open but since it is 'cast from a single piece of steel' (*LCW* 14, p. 326), it must also be coherent. Too little dialogue with the past and Marxism becomes a 'hidebound, petrified doctrine' (*LCW* 19, p. 23): too much 'loan and dialogue', to echo Anderson (1976, p. 56), and the very specificity of Marxism as an independent theory with its own logic and structure, is placed in doubt. Indeed, Marxism is plunged into 'crisis' with proliferating doubts about its 'keystones' and 'central pillars' precisely because this problem of continuity has become acute. If Marxists are to 'take democracy seriously', declares Hunt, then socialist revolution must be understood as the 'realisation of the democratic project initiated by the bourgeois revolutions of the eighteenth and nineteenth centuries' (Hunt, 1980, p. 17). Yet this is precisely the formula employed by Karl Kautsky in his attack on Bolshevism in 1933 (Salvadori, 1979, p. 365) and explicitly repudiated by Marx in his *Grundrisse* where he comments on the 'foolishness' of those socialists 'who want to depict socialism as the realization of the ideals of *bourgeois* society articulated by the French revolution' (*G*, p. 248). Socialism, argues Carrillo, 'must recover for itself the democratic and liberal values, the defence of human rights, together with respect for dissenting minorities' (1977, p. 98), but is this Eurocommunist 'recovery' anything other than a (somewhat belated) endorsement of Bernstein's celebrated formulations of 1899? Socialism as the 'legitimate heir' of liberalism (1961, p. 149), a liberalism 'organized' for, as Bernstein put it, 'when one examines closely the organisations that socialism wants and how it wants them, he will find that what distinguishes them above all from the feudalistic organisations, outwardly like them, is just their liberalism, their democratic constitution, their accessibility' (1961, p. 154). Here indeed is 'continuity' with the past but what has happened to Marxism?

The question of continuity involves dangers, certainly, but also a challenge. The legitimate concern about the identity of Marxism as, in Gramsci's words, 'a new, independent and original conception' (*SPN*, p. 398) cannot be an argument against dialogue with the past. Coherence requires openness if it is not to degenerate into 'hidebound petrification' for, as Lenin put it, 'the genius of Marx consists precisely in his having furnished answers to questions already raised by the foremost minds of mankind' (*LCW* 19, p. 23). If communism is a 'fully developed' naturalism and humanism, then this can only be because it 'is the riddle of history solved' (*MECW* 3, p. 297). Coherence requires openness and openness requires coherence: this, in essence, is the challenge to which this book seeks to respond. The young Marx defiantly defines his communism as 'the *genuine* resolution of the conflict between man and nature and between man and man — the true resolution of the strife between existence and essence, between objectification and self-confirmation, between freedom and necessity, between the individual and the species' (*MECW* 3, p. 296). Is it too much to hope that the classical Marxist tradition should also be able to resolve the 'strife' between coercion and consent? Laslett was to declare in 1956, in a discussion on the 'death of political philosophy' that 'Marxists are quite simply not interested in the perennial debates which exercised the political philosophers in the past, and their immensely successful political following in the twentieth century has apparently found little occasion to present them with philosophical problems of the political sort. They have got on without it and they have frightened everybody else' (1956, p. viii). Yet, if this was true during the cold war when, it has been said, communism was left to the communists and radicals were generally isolated (Partridge, 1967, p. 39), what of the situation in the 1960s when the End of Ideology (as noted above) gave way to the Rebirth of Critique? Here a revival of interest in Marxist political theory was accompanied by the assumption that the classical Marxist tradition had little or nothing to offer (Wolfe, 1974, p. 131). Dialogue tended to involve a process of grafting Marxism onto existing bodies of theory, past and present, with eclecticism rather than synthesis the inevitable result. Galvano della Volpe's important work on Rousseau in 1964 (English edn, 1978) is a classic case in point. Openness was pursued in a way which imperilled coherence.

The challenge posed by the problem of coercion and consent then is this. It is an old question which requires a new answer: a 'liberal' problem which needs to be tackled in a *Marxist* way. It is an issue, as we shall see, bristling with metaphysical pitfalls, abstract ahistoricism and perplexing paradox. It is the kind of challenge to which only a Marxism which involves 'the most radical rupture with traditional ideas' can successfully respond.

2

THE PROBLEM IN MARX AND ENGELS

ABOVE ALL COERCIVE?

What makes the question of coercion and consent a problem in Marx and Engels is that classical Marxist definitions of politics and the state appear to place their main emphasis on the centrality of coercion. Tucker expresses a widely held view when he says that 'the state is seen in classical Marxism as fundamentally a repressive force' (1973, p. 132). As far as Miliband is concerned, the presentation of politics in the *Communist Manifesto* as the 'organised power of one class for oppressing another' (*MECW* 6, p. 505) stands as Marx's 'primary view' (1973a, p. 163) and there can be little doubt that comments of this kind abound in the classical writings, whether we think of *Civil War in France* where the state is depicted as 'a public force for social enslavement . . . an engine of class despotism' (*PC*, p. 69); Marx's jottings on Bakunin which refer to the need for the proletariat to employ '*coercive* measures, that is, government measures' (*MELAAS*, p. 147) or Engels's pithy definition of the state as 'a special repressive force' (*AD*, p. 385). Why is it improper for socialists to speak of a 'free state'? Because, Engels tells Bebel, even under socialism, the state is only necessary 'to hold down one's adversaries by force' (*SC*, p. 339). A social movement becomes *political*, comments Marx, when it assumes a form 'possessing general, socially coercive force' (*SC*, p. 255): in an exhaustive account of Marx's views on politics and bureaucracy, Draper locates the 'essence' of the state in 'institutionalized forcible coercion' (1977, p. 263; p. 250). If we ask what it is that differentiates authority in a community which has *yet* to develop a state from politics proper, the answer can only be — organized coercive force (Draper, 1977, p. 240; p. 242). Evans in his useful study on *Karl Marx* agrees (1975, p. 110). If, as Jessop argues, Lenin is guilty of an 'all too one-sided emphasis on the repressive role of the state' (1982, p. 20), it has to be said that, if this is a problem, it is a problem for the whole classical Marxist tradition. After all, when Lenin acclaims as 'a splendid and extremely profound definition', the view of the state as 'a special coercive force', he is quoting the maxim of Engels and his *State and Revolution* (from which this comment is drawn) (*LCW* 25, p. 397) is peppered with similar quotations from the political writings of Marx. Are we to conclude, therefore, that for Marx and Engels, the state was 'above all' the coercive instrument of a ruling class (Miliband, 1969, p. 5) and that, accordingly, this is a conception of politics which is too negative and narrow to tackle the crucial question of consent?

The question is rather more complicated. If there is widespread agreement that an emphasis on politics-as-coercion is a prominent and even predominant strand in classical Marxism, the argument is also advanced that Marx embraced another and quite different view of the state. The most frequently cited sources of this claim are Plamenatz (1954) and Sanderson (1963) who found alongside Marx's view of the state as organized coercion, a theory of the state 'as a parasite on the whole of society' (see also, McLellan, 1983, p. 148) and it is this 'other' theory, it is argued, which should caution us against discussing the Marxian state purely in terms of class oppression (Sanderson, 1963, p. 951; p. 955). Miliband gave this argument a qualified endorsement in 1965 (1973a, p. 163; but see Miliband, 1983, p. 58) and Richard Hunt has claimed that the two rival concepts, the parasite state and the class state, can be found side by side within individual passages in Marx and Engels's political writings (1974, p. 128). In Tucker, we encounter the problem of an unresolved tension, if not outright contradiction, between the state as alienated social power and the state as organ of class rule (1973, pp. 129–31). Maguire has even argued for *three* concepts of the state in Marx: a 'servile' state (a mere instrument of civil society); a 'dominant' state and a 'pretentious' state in which servility aspires to domination (1978, p. 13)!

Now this line of argument clearly implies that Marx's view of politics is not nearly as narrow as it might at first appear. It hints at a wider conception of the state which Jessop, echoing the formulations of Poulantzas (1973), characterizes as the factor of social cohesion in the social formation (1982, p. 16) and it is a point which has an important bearing on the problem of consent. If the state in Marx and Engels is conceived both as a social power ('a factor of social cohesion') and an organ of class coercion, then 'space' is provided for precisely those ideological and cultural dimensions apparently absent from the coercive definitions noted above. In so far as Marx and Engels suggest that the state has a role to play as a socially necessary institution, they anticipate, argues Jessop, Gramsci's subsequent analysis of 'hegemony': the exercise of moral and intellectual leadership aiming at winning the 'active consent' of the dominated (1982, p. 17). This 'broad' hint makes it possible to break with what Poulantzas has called the 'ideologically contaminated' schema of the state 'as the tool or instrument of the dominated classes' (1973, p. 273), since the 'other' theory of politics, the state as a cohesive factor with economic, ideological and political functions, lays the basis for an end to 'reductionism' and the development of the conception of the 'relative autonomy' of the capitalist state (Poulantzas, 1973, p. 187; 1973, part iv, *passim*).

If however, there is more to Marx than the mere conception

of politics-as-coercion, the problem is this. Where Marx does make room for a broader view, able to encapsulate the question of consent, this seems simply to contradict his narrower definitions of politics-as-coercion. While Western Marxists in the Althusserian/Poulantzian tradition locate the broader view in Marx's later writings, and particular emphasis is placed upon the analysis of Bonapartism in the *Eighteenth Brumaire*, whereas 'exegetists' like Richard Hunt and Maguire find a 'dominant/parasite' state in Marx's earliest writings, both sets of commentators are agreed on the absence of a 'homogeneous Marxism' (Hall, 1977, p. 18); on the presence of 'discontinuities and disjunctions, incompleteness and indeterminacy' (Jessop, 1982, p. 1) in Marx's theory of the state. There *are* fertile hints for a broader conception, an ideologically oriented view of politics in classical Marxism, but these coexist in a state of disharmony and tension with an instrumentalist emphasis on coercion. Where this coercion is emphasized, the theory is negative and narrow; where 'space' is made for a consideration of the question of consent, incoherence and inconsistency is the result. The state still stands as the great stumbling block of classical Marxism.

THE EARLY WRITINGS AND THE BIRTH OF NEGATIVITY

How are we to evaluate the argument that either Marx's theory of politics is negative or it is inconsistent? How did Marx (and Engels) come to develop a view of the state which so many consider to be narrow, instrumentalist or (at best) downright contradictory? How did the errant isms of the classical tradition arise? This is a question well worth posing because it has been argued by the exegetists that Marx's earliest conceptions of the state, as presented, for example, in his articles of the *Rheinische Zeitung* 1842–3, are both broad in scope and ethical in orientation (Hunt, 1974, p. 38; Draper, 1977, p. 32). If we compare these early formulations with the kind of 'classical' definitions presented, for example, in the *Poverty of Philosophy* (1847) or the *Communist Manifesto* (1848), an emphasis on coercion would appear to have replaced a stress on consent; breadth, it seems, has given way to narrowness, a positive approach to negativity, an autonomist view of the state to crude class instrumentalism. How is such a transformation to be explained? Did the 'classical' Marx simply jettison his earlier views or is the relationship between a youthful 'breadth' and an older 'narrowness' somewhat more complicated? Even if we accept that the broader view also appears in Marx's later writings, this still leaves open the question as to how and why Marx should have developed a seemingly narrow view of politics-as-coercion when this apparently contradicts the perspectives presented elsewhere?

The young Marx was steeped, as has been frequently noted, in the traditions of the French Revolution and the Enlightenment. He consciously identified his standpoint with what he called the 'ever new philosophy of reason' (*MECW* 1, p. 202) as a philosophy which extended back to Heraclitus and Aristotle, embracing in the sweep of its development, Machiavelli and Campanella, Hobbes, Spinoza and Grotius, Rousseau, Fichte and, of course, Hegel. This philosophy, particularly in its 'recent' form, looks upon the state, declared Marx grandly, 'as the great organism, in which legal, moral and political freedom must be realised, and in which the individual citizen in obeying the laws of the state only obeys the natural laws of his own reason, of human reason' (*MECW* 1, p. 202). At the heart of this 'great organism' (we must presume) lies consent. The individual, in obeying the state, obeys his own reason so that, as Rousseau puts in in the *Social Contract*, men defend their persons and their goods with a 'collective force', under which each, uniting himself with all the others, 'remains as free as before' (1968, p. 53). Clearly there is a place for coercion within this 'collective force' but only, if somewhat paradoxically, as the necessary expression of the 'general will' (Rousseau, 1968, p. 64).

If Rousseau's conceptions of politics underlie Marx's political philosophy during the years 1842–3, they do so as part of Marx's commitment to the Young Hegelian ideal of the 'rational state'. Like Arnold Ruge and the other Hegelian radicals of his day, the young Marx held the view that Hegel's defence of monarchy, bureaucracy and the principle of representation by estates gravely compromised his own Hegelian ideals (see McGovern, 1970, pp. 435–6; O'Malley, 1970, p. x). Hence in the pages of the *Rheinische Zeitung*, the radical paper he briefly edited, he attacked censorship and anti-peasant legislation as practices perverting the community-based ideal of the rational state. What has happened, Marx protests, is that a mere *part* of the state, the 'government', has usurped the wider role of the state and, in the case of laws preventing peasants from collecting firewood, government has degraded the structure of the state into 'an instrument of the forest owner' (*MECW* 1, p. 245). Every citizen becomes the victim of 'vexatious bullying' and in permitting forest owners even to levy their own fines, the government is prepared to allow a 'material problem' to be handled in a 'non-political way' i.e. without any connection with 'the whole of the reason and morality of the state' (*MECW* 1, p. 262). Here is just that perversion which Rousseau had feared when he spoke of government continually exerting itself against the sovereign people (1968, p. 131) for, as Marx says a few months later, it is a negation of political life when a 'bargain' is struck between government and the private interests of landed property or industry: a violation of that popular 'self-representation' which is distinguished from other expressions of state life 'by the universality of its content' (*MECW* 1, p. 306).

These passages are of great interest because they indicate that the young Marx does not merely have an ethical view of the state as an expression of 'universality', a general will, but that, alongside this view, there stands a coercive, instrumentalist conception of politics. It is true that this coercive instrumentalism is in conflict with what Marx sees as the concept of the modern state (*MECW* 1, p. 241), a perversion of its rational ideal. Richard Hunt, noting the passage cited above in which Marx speaks of the degradation of the state to an instrument of private interest, criticizes the 'rash inference' of those who see in this kind of sentiment the inception of Marx's theory of government as an 'organ of class domination' (1974, p. 39). It is certainly true that for the time being, *partisan* coercion does contradict Marx's 'ideal' state in which the coercive activities of ruling, judging, taxing and administering are seen as 'free creations of the spirit' and 'dissolved at every moment in the unity of the whole' (*MECW* 1, p. 296). Nevertheless Marx's reference to the state as 'a servant of the forest owner' does establish the existence of a coercive instrumentalism, which, although presented as the perversion of an ideal, clearly anticipates his later position (Maguire, 1978, pp. 11–12).

Indeed, when Marx comes to write his critique of Hegel's *Philosophy of Right* in the summer of 1843, there is a significant shift in his view of politics. Whereas previously he had spoken of the illegitimate acts of government as 'non-political', contrary to the spirit of politics as the interests of the community as a whole, now the term 'politics' tends to be used (although not always, see McGovern, 1970, p. 449) in a *pejorative* way. Thus Hegel is criticized for confusing the state 'as the whole of the existence of the people' with the 'political state' (*MECW* 3, p. 78) which, Marx tells us, merely represents 'the nature of the modern State as it is' (*MECW* 3, p. 63) and is unacceptable because it presupposes a fixed 'antithesis' between state and civil society. Private property predominates (*MECW* 3, p. 100), and the police, judiciary and administration act not as the deputies of civil society itself, 'in and through whom it administers its *own* general interest', but rather as the 'representatives of the state for the administration of the state over and against civil society' (*MECW* 3, p. 50). The 'political state', declares Marx, 'rules without really ruling' and in a 'true democracy', it will necessarily be *'annihilated'* (*MECW* 3, p. 30). This is not, as some have suggested (Carrillo, 1977, p. 144; Lefebvre, 1972, p. 135; Avineri, 1968, p. 38), a position equivalent to Marx's later thesis of the 'withering away' of the state, for 'true democracy', as presented in 1843, is still a form of the *state*, albeit one which 'passes for the whole' as the 'self-determination of the people' (*MECW* 3, p. 30). Nevertheless what is of immense significance here, as we shall see, is Marx's reference in the *Critique* to the 'political state' as 'a theological notion' (*MECW* 3, p. 119): 'an abstract state form', 'the *religious sphere*, the *religion* of national life, the heaven of its generality over against the *earthly existence* of its actuality' (*MECW* 3, p. 31). This abstraction of the political state, says Marx, counterparts 'the abstraction of private life' as it has developed in modern times (*MECW* 3, p. 32).

In the *Jewish Question* the distinction between a 'true state' and a 'political state' completely falls away. The term 'political' is employed pejoratively throughout so that while Marx sees political emancipation as 'a big step forward' (*MECW* 3, p. 155), it is not 'real, practical emancipation'. 'Human' emancipation is only accomplished when social power no longer stands outside the individual as *political* power (*MECW* 3, p. 168) and the 'abstract citizen' is re-absorbed into the real man. *All* states are now theological notions. This is especially true of the democratic state and there is therefore no further reference to a 'true democracy' which avoids the religiosity of the 'political state'. Since, as Marx puts it, 'the existence of religion is the existence of a defect, the source of this defect can only be sought in the *nature* of the state itself' (*MECW* 3, p. 151), even if this 'theological' nature only stands revealed when the political state exists 'in its completely developed form' (*MECW* 3, p. 150). Whereas in the *Critique* the 'true state' had been identified as an 'actual political society' (*MECW* 3, p. 113), now Marx argues that the 'political character of civil society' has been 'abolished' as the political spirit is withdrawn from society and is gathered up and established as 'the sphere of the community, the *general* concern of the nation, ideally independent of those *particular* elements of civil life' (*MECW* 3, p. 166). The democratic state perfects this process of separating the general from the particular so that to the idealism of the state with its 'abstract, artificial man', there corresponds the materialism of civil society with its man of egoism (*MECW* 3, p. 167). 'Man', the member of civil society, is 'the basis, the precondition, of the *political* state' (p. 166) and although in theory, political rights are superior to the power of money, 'in actual fact politics has become the serf of financial power' (*MECW* 3, p. 171).

These passages are of remarkable importance. On the one hand, politics is conceived of as an instrument of financial power and yet, on the other, it is presented as 'an illusory sovereignty' (*MECW* 3, p. 154) — an abstract community as 'spiritual' in relation to civil society as heaven is to earth. It is precisely at this point in the development of Marx's political thought that we can see what has happened to those 'broader', universalistic conceptions of his 'youth'. They have not simply been rejected: they have been *absorbed* so that they invest the partisan, 'instrumental' character of the state with an apparent or illusory communality. By implication, we can see therefore what happened to the question of consent: it has not been jettisoned. It has been 'carried over' and integrated into the coercive instrumentalism of the 'political state'. The rational state, the state as the 'great organism' which superintends the whole has not disappeared from Marx's theory but now stands as 'a theological notion': an ideal unmasked as illusion.

Marx's *On the Jewish Question* is dated as autumn 1843. In the autumn of the same year, the young Frederick Engels (although the two were not to begin collaborating until the following September) had reached substantially the same conclusion. Initially a champion of general civil and human rights (*MECW* 2, p. 365), Engels had come to the position that since 'principles can only develop from interests', the revolution 'will be social, not political' (*MECW* 2, p. 374). Curiously enough, Engels's last wholly sympathetic reference to democracy appears to have been written in May 1843 and this is the same month in which Marx, writing to Arnold Ruge, makes his final, positive reference to democracy's 'human world' (*MECW* 3, p. 139). In November 1843, Engels takes up the themes of the *Jewish Question* with a blistering attack on democracy as 'an untruth, nothing but hypocrisy (theology, as we Germans call it) . . . the appearance of liberty, and therefore the reality of servitude' (*MECW* 3, p. 393). The 'spiritual' and the 'material' stand together. Because the appearance of liberty is anchored to the reality of servitude, politics must be identified with hypocrisy. As Marx comments in the following year, the modern state and the modern commercial world are 'intimately riveted together' as the contradiction between 'public and private life,' between general and particular interests (*MECW* 3, p. 198).

What follows from this analysis is of critical importance. For Marx and Engels do not present the state simply as the servant of private (at this stage, commercial) interests. The state stands as the servant of the private *in the name of the public*. It is an instrument of the 'particular', to be sure, given the fact that the slavery of civil society provides the natural foundation on which the modern state rests (*MECW* 3, p. 198). But it is more than this. It is the instrument of the particular *expressed as the general*, the servant of individual interests presenting themselves in universal terms. If such 'theology' seems absurd, it is an absurdity which, in Colletti's words, embodies 'the whole inverted logic of modern society', in which the 'general interest' of the community sanctifies and legitimates the 'disunity' among 'men' (Colletti, 1975, pp. 36–7). It is an absurdity rooted in real life. As Colletti adds, 'Paradox reigns, therefore: the general will is invoked in order to confer absolute value on individual caprice; society is invoked in order to render social interests sacred and intangible; the cause of equality among men is defended, so that the cause of inequality among them (private property) can be acknowledged as fundamental and absolute. Everything is upside down' (1975, p. 37). If the particular and the general, private property and the 'social state' contradict each other, this does not make them 'separate' attributes, each of which fosters a separate and independent theory of the state. The 'ideological' and the 'instrumental' are 'intimately riveted together' within a *single* theory of politics, paradoxical perhaps, but unified nevertheless. If a 'servile' state appears to vie with a 'dominant' one or the state as a class instrument coexists uneasily with the state as social power, that, for Marx, is a consequence not of theoretical inconsistency, but of the nature of politics itself.

The two sides, partisan instrumentality and universal pretension, ideology and force, coercion and consent are indissolubly fused together in what Marx called in his *Draft Plan for a Work on the Modern State* (November 1844), 'the self-conceit of the political sphere' (*MECW* 4, p. 666). Thus when Marx speaks in 1844 of the state as 'the active, conscious and official expression' of the present structure of society (*MECW* 3, p. 199) — a comment echoed in the polemic against Proudhon (*MECW* 6, p. 175) — it is clear that particular class interests can *only* be served if they are projected in this 'active, conscious and official' (i.e. universalistic) way. The very principle of politics requires belief 'in the omnipotence of the will' (*MECW* 3, p. 199), in the absolutism of its scope, so that when Marx, in *The Holy Family*, speaks of the ruling bourgeoisie acknowledging the state as 'the *official* expression of its own *exclusive* power and the *political* recognition of its own *special* interests' (*MECW* 4, p. 124), this only appears as a 'narrow', 'instrumentalist' conception because insufficient weight is given to Marx's italicized references to the 'official' and 'political' character of this class power. The state is not just an expression of bourgeois interests: it is an expression of these interests in 'official' terms i.e. as representing the interests of society as a whole. If such representation is illusory, this is because it is tied to the 'slavery of civil society' which, in appearance, is 'the greatest freedom' (*MECW* 4, p. 116). Illusion is as much a part of the state as this deceptive freedom is a part of civil society. What Marx now calls 'emancipated slavery' requires a '*modern spiritualistic-democratic representative state*' (*MECW* 4, p. 122), but such a state can only 'represent' particular interests if it does so in general, 'spiritualistic' terms. This, in a word, is what politics is all about.

If we take the two passages in *The German Ideology* (1845) in which, according to Richard Hunt, there is theoretical inconsistency, we can now see why, for Marx, the parasitical and the servile, the instrumental and the ideological, form part of the same definition. In the first of these passages where, we are told, two different theories coexist without an attempt to relate them (1974, p. 128), Marx and Engels refer to the 'common interest' assuming 'an independent form as the *state*, which is divorced from the real individual and collective interests'; an illusory community always based on real ties and especially 'on the classes, already implied by the division of labour, which in every such mass of men separate out and one of which dominates all the others' (*MECW* 5, p. 46). A contradiction here between the state as 'an illusory community' based on real ties and the state as representative of a dominant class? Certainly a contradiction in the sense that 'everything is upside down' and 'paradox reigns' but if there is illogicality, it is, as far as Marx is concerned, born not of theory but of practice! The *reality* of politics is such that a state cannot represent a dominant class unless this class domination is re-presented in an 'illusory form'. Every class aiming at domination, Marx comments further down the passage cited by Hunt, 'must first conquer political power in order to represent its interest in turn as the general interest' (*MECW* 5, p. 47). A class unable to present its particular interests in general terms, would be unable to rule: it would be unable to convert its social power into a power which could be properly called *political*.

The same point has to be made with regard to the second passage from *The German Ideology* which Hunt cites. At one point, he argues, we find the class state in pure form (1974, p. 128) for here Marx and Engels comment that to 'modern private property corresponds the modern state, which, purchased gradually by the owners of property by means of taxation, has fallen entirely into their hands through the national debt . . .' (*MECW* 5, p. 90). Yet this is followed, says Hunt, by the comment that 'through the emancipation of private property from the community, the state has become a separate entity, alongside and outside civil society' (*MECW* 5, p. 90) and here we now encounter Marx's independent parasite state 'in apparent contradiction to the preceding sentences' (1974, p. 128). Yet this contradiction is indeed 'apparent' because the modern state can only 'correspond' to private property (i.e. serve its interests) because this property has become 'emancipated' from the community and confronts the state 'as a separate entity'. As Marx puts it in the sentence sandwiched in between the two comments excerpted by Hunt: 'By the mere fact that it is a *class* and no longer an *estate*, the bourgeoisie is forced to organise itself no longer locally, but nationally, and to give a general form to its average interests' (*MECW* 5, p. 90). Unless the modern state exists a 'separate entity, alongside and outside civil society', it cannot be a *class* state since only by giving a general form to average interests, is it able to 'correspond' to private property. Unless, in Hunt's terminology, the state is 'parasitic', it cannot be servile.

Here in the 'classical' Marx is Rousseau's 'collective force' with which 'men' defend their persons and goods, but with this difference. The development which Rousseau *feared* — the division of society into rich and poor (1968, p. 68) — was, for Marx, an inexorable reality. Hence the 'general will', 'laws as they might be', the 'ideal state' could never be more than a 'corrupt equality': 'an appearance and an

illusion' (Rousseau, 1968, p. 68). In this phrase is demonstrated both the continuity and the discontinuity between
Rousseau and Marx. As far as the latter is concerned, the
state never loses those 'spiritual nerves' which pervade the
whole of nature (*MECW* 1, p. 306), for Marx, as I have tried
to show, did not simply throw overboard, reject or discard
his earlier view that politics concentrates society's interests
as a whole. Rather, it must be said, he *transcended* it, carried
it over, translated this political idealism into materialist
terms. 'Wholeness', universality and community remain
essential elements in Marx's theory of the state: it is true
these 'rational ideals' now appear as class-engendered
illusions but illusions, nevertheless, which are intrinsic to
political reality itself.

What I have called the 'birth of negativity' in Marx's
political thought needs to be analysed more carefully than
the proponents of the 'two states' theory would allow. Of
course, from the *Jewish Question* onwards, Marx sees politics
as an obstacle to human emancipation and allows it only a
transitional role. Revolutions are political, Marx says in
1844, because they are necessary to dissolve the old order,
but once the organizing activity of the new socialist society
begins, the political cloak has to be thrown away (*MECW*
3, p. 206). As Marx expresses the same idea in more 'mature'
vein a few years later, once 'the old civil society' gives way
to an association which exludes classes and their antagonism,
'there will be no more political power properly so-called'
(*MECW* 6, p. 212). If this is a negative view, it is also a
positive one for it *absorbs*, as I have argued above, Marx's
earlier formulations of the state as community; if it is narrow,
it is also broad since it emphasizes the 'spiritualistic-
representative' character of the state as an institution which
offers '*in appearance* the greatest freedom' (*MECW* 4, p. 116).
The classical conception of politics may be 'instrumentalist'
but it is also ideological for the state, in Marx, can only
serve class interests as an 'illusory community'. These new
insights lay the basis for understanding a very old problem

— the paradox of the 'perfected state'. They point beyond a world where 'everything is upside down' for as Engels comments in 1844–5, in the 'hypocritical servitude' of bourgeois society, the right to freedom is recognized 'in outward form'. The 'principle of freedom is affirmed, and the oppressed will one day see to it that this principle is carried out' (*MECW* 4, p. 474). It is not a question of rejecting the 'positive' heritage of the past: it is a question of carrying it forward onto a new plane. Human emancipation, if we may be allowed to express the matter perversely, *is* political emancipation but a political emancipation shorn of its class engendered illusions.

THE SPECIAL INSTRUMENT OF COERCION

It should be clear therefore that Marx does not merely view politics as coercion. 'Mixed up' with this coercion is *consent*, a sense of community, a belief in brotherhood, a universal citizenship. In other words, when we examine the way in which Marx did develop a coercive concept of politics, what transpires is the fact that this is a coercion of a most peculiar kind. It is a coercion which is concentrated in the hands of the state, generalized in its scope and presented ideologically as a force for the 'common good'. It is public and official, organized and 'legitimate' i.e. it claims to act in the interests of society as a whole. This, in a word, is what makes such coercion 'political'.

From this it must follow that political coercion cannot be reduced to mere 'physical force'. Politics involves a physical force with an ideological character, a coercion which commands consent and this is a point which commentators sympathetic to a coercion-oriented view of politics often miss. Draper, for example, is somewhat taken aback that Engels, after describing the state as a body of armed men, prisons and 'coercive institutions of all kinds, of which gentile society knew nothing' (*OFPPS*, p. 230), should also comment that 'the state presents itself to us as the first ideological power over man' (*MESW*, p. 627). As far as Draper is concerned, this suggests that 'while the essence of the state is class domination based on means of forcible coercion, there is much more to the state than an essence' (1977, p. 263) and he therefore follows a line of argument common among the Marx commentators that 'in addition' to an emphasis on the coercive nature of the state, Marx 'also' stressed its ideological character. Yet, what the development of Marx's political theory demonstrates as it transcends its Hegelian origins, is that the state's coercive 'essence' already implies an ideological dimension, for there can be no 'class domination' unless there is domination *on behalf of* a class. An institution presenting particular interests in general terms. The 'two factors' are inextricably fused for coercion, without ideology, cannot be political coercion at all. This is why Marx and Engels invariably speak of the state as an 'organized' coercion, a 'public' force, an 'official' expression of class rule: a 'negative' coercion which receives its 'positive' endorsement from society at large. A state which, as Draper says, 'maintains itself exclusively by the naked application of forcible suppression' is not only 'precarious and expensive' (1977, p. 263): it cannot, and this is the point which Draper misses, serve the general interests of a ruling class. Bereft of even an illusory communality, it would be unable to function as an instrument of class domination. Marx not only has a broad view of politics, he also has a *synthetic* one.

But it might be thought that while Marx's broad view of politics as coercion fused with consent is relevant to the modern liberal democratic state, it cannot apply to explicitly authoritarian political systems and that where parliamentary procedures, civil liberties, competing political parties and a 'free' suffrage are absent, the concept of the state as 'pure' coercion still stands. Yet if this were so, why is it that it is precisely in Marx's analysis of Bonapartism as an 'exceptional', avowedly *illiberal* political order, that many of his commentators find that he appears to move furthest away from a conception of politics in 'instrumentalist' terms? When Marx refers to the 'perfected' liberal state, he appears to see only organized coercion, but when he analyses illiberal, exceptional and authoritarian state-forms, the independent effectivity of politics and ideology comes into play and 'space' is created for rule by consent! In fact, as we shall see, Marx saw all state-forms as the special instruments of class rule. The distinction between the Bonapartist state and the liberal polity is not a distinction between politics-as-coercion and politics-as-consent. What differentiates them is something quite different. It is the degree to which the ruling class directly controls its own state: the extent to which, during 'exceptional' circumstances, a bourgeoisie is prepared to have a state acting on its behalf while freed from the normal, routinized political and legal constraints associated with the parliamentary order.

Although Althusserian Marxists tend to see a 'break' with 'instrumentalism' only in Marx's political writing after 1848–9 (Hall, 1977, p. 41; Rattansi, 1982, p. 104), in fact Marx had already raised the problem of Bonapartism in 1845. In *The Holy Family* he touches upon some of the complexities involved in a situation in which the bourgeoisie have yet to secure a state which is the 'official recognition' of their 'own exclusive power': where their rule is still relatively indirect. But what is clear even from Marx's analysis of the first Bonaparte, is that while the state may have an 'exceptional' degree of autonomy and is treated by Bonaparte 'as an *end in itself*' (*MECW* 4, p. 123), it is still an instrument of class rule. Napoleon may demand the sacrifice of bourgeois interests whenever they conflict with his own political dreams, but he had, says Marx, already discerned 'the essence of the *modern* state', the free movement of private interest, and had 'decided to recognise and protect this basis' (*MECW* 4, p. 123). Even the exceptional state has to preserve the general interests of the bourgeoisie.

It is of course a highly abnormal situation when, as Marx

says of the French bourgeoisie after 1851, 'its own interests dictate that it should be delivered from the danger of its *own rule*' (*MECW* 11, p. 143) — that in order to preserve 'its social power intact, its political power must be broken'. Logically, Marx argues, bourgeois interests find their 'pure political expression' in the parliamentary regime. Why then does the bourgeoisie itself demand that its own 'bourgeois parliament must, first of all, be laid to rest'? That, in order to continue exploiting other classes, it too must be condemned to 'similar political nullity' (*MECW* 11, p. 143)? The answer to this Bonapartist paradox cannot be found unless the relationship between the 'normal' parliamentary form and the 'exceptional', authoritarian state is properly understood. If the liberal democratic republic is, for Marx and Engels, 'the *logical* form of bourgeois rule' (*SC*, p. 350), it is also a potentially dangerous one. The desire to be freed from the logical form of its own rule arises in situations where, as in the case of the first Napoleon, the bourgeoisie are too weak or, as in the case of his nephew, the proletariat is too strong. But the movement from one state-form to the other is only possible because in both sets of circumstances, the state acts as the generalized expression, an ideologically charged instrument, of bourgeois class rule.

Miliband is right therefore to argue that the notion of 'relative autonomy', of the state acting 'on behalf of' the bourgeoisie rather than 'at its behest' (1973b, p. 83; 1977, p. 74), is central to Marx's political theory, even in the case of the liberal state-form. Hence the celebrated formula of the *Communist Manifesto*, so often characterized as narrowly instrumentalist, is much more 'broadly ideological' than is often assumed, for consider the implications of asserting that the executive of the modern state is but 'a committee for managing the common affairs of the whole bourgeoisie' (*MECW* 6, p. 486). Politics is clearly a separate sphere which embodies the general interests of the bourgeoisie because, as individual members of their class, they are divided among themselves. A 'general form' has to be given to 'average

interests' (*MECW* 5, p. 90). While the individual law injures
the capitalist, 'the whole fabric protects his interests' (*MECW*
4, p. 514) and hence, and this is the crucial point, the
bourgeoisie *need a state* because, as individuals, they cannot
directly rule themselves. Nor do they really want to. Buying
and selling, investing and accumulating are economic
activities which have seemingly been withdrawn from the
state's sphere of operation. The bourgeoisie, says Engels,
'turns the power of government against the proletariat and
keeps out of its way as far as possible' (*MECW* 4, p. 564),
and this makes it entirely understandable that a division
of labour should be involved between a class and its political
representatives.

   This 'division of labour' is not just a characteristic of the
exceptional form of the state where the 'extra-parliamentary
mass of the bourgeoisie' turn to adventurers like Bonaparte:
it is a general feature of political rule (*MECW* 5, p. 60).
Even the gulf between parliamentary representatives and
the class they represent is real: a situation in which 'according
to their education and their individual position' the two may
be separated as widely 'as heaven from earth' (*MECW* 11,
p. 130). When Engels comments that 'normally' the state of
'the most powerful, economically dominant class' is also
'the politically dominant class as well' (*OFPPS*, p. 231),
this should not be taken to mean that the capitalists 'govern'
as well as rule i.e. hold political office while accumulating
profits in a way which gives them a decisive veto power
(Block, 1977, p. 16; Miliband, 1969, p. 55). Wealth employs
its power indirectly, says Engels, if all the more surely
(*OFPPS*, p. 231). There can be no 'automatic translation'
of class power into state power (Miliband, 1977, p. 67)
since the very directness of the bourgeoisie's involvement
in the economy yields particularistic interests which
undermine a capacity to act disinterestedly on behalf of the
class as a whole (Draper, 1977, p. 232).

   In short, the *Manifesto*'s 'instrumentalist' formula
presumes something which its critics invariably overlook —

the irreducibly *specific* character of the political sphere. This is not something which Marx discovers after 1848–9, as Hall thinks (1977, p. 39); it is a view of the state which Marx inherits from the Enlightenment and takes for granted in all his political writings. Just as Rousseau in the *Social Contract* distinguishes between the particular interest and the general interest, between the 'will of all' as a mere collectivity of particular interests and the 'general will' which makes each individual 'an indivisible part of the whole' (1968, p. 61), so Marx, in presenting the state as 'a great organism' (*MECW* 1, p. 202), naturally assumes that the whole is irreducible to its parts. The 'idealism of the state' necessarily transcends its materialistic particulars. Marx rejects a 'simple reductionism' (Block, 1977, p. 11) because even where the state serves the bourgeoisie as 'the political idealism of its daily practice' (*MECW* 4, p. 123), this still presumes a gulf between the two. Engels was to describe the USA as providing proof that 'the bourgeois republic is the republic of capitalist businessmen, in which politics is simply a business like any other (*SC*, p. 427). It also provides proof, as Engels's lively descriptions show, of the state's 'relative autonomy' for 'the divergence of interests' even within the same class stratum necessitates the formation of political parties to represent these interests, the 'jumbling' together of which provides the splendid soil for the corruption and exploitation of the government 'that flourish over there so extensively' (*SC*, p. 416). Class instrumentality in no way contradicts parasitism and domination from on high!

We are now in a position to understand why the bourgeoisie should turn against the 'logical form' of its own rule. Even the 'purest' form of bourgeois rule presents itself as the representative of society as a whole and it is precisely these pretensions to universality which make the parliamentary regime a stable expression of bourgeois interests in 'normal times' but highly vulnerable to proletarian challenge in periods of crisis. If, in the parliamentary regime, 'every interest, every social institution' is 'transformed into general ideas' (*MECW* 11, p. 142) and these ideas are assumed to be as general in practice as they are in theory, then what is to prevent radical pressures from 'extending' liberal institutions in a socialist direction? The representatives who 'constantly appeal to public opinion' (*MECW* 11, p. 142) are only the reliable servants of the bourgeoisie when they articulate a general will that goes no further than giving a 'general form' to capitalist interests. The less 'illusory' the state becomes as a 'community', the less able it is to service these interests with an 'official expression'. When, as Marx puts it, the bourgeoisie comes to stigmatize as 'socialistic' what it had previously extolled as 'liberal' (*MECW* 11, p. 142–3), this ironic process of authoritarian transmutation, at the heart of Marx's analysis of Bonapartism, cannot be understood unless the contradictory logic of the state as the generalized expression of particular class interests, is grasped in *all* its forms. It is out of the conflict between universalist pretension and class reality embryonically present in the 'pure form' of the bourgeois state, that the need for an 'exceptional' solution logically arises.

Under Bonaparte, Marx tells us, the bourgeoisie, by rebelling out of enthusiasm for its purse against its own politicians, now 'submits to the superior command of an alien will' (*MECW* 11, p. 185). But although the state would seem to have made itself completely independent (p. 186), Bonaparte's mission is still to safeguard 'bourgeois order' and he is therefore the representative of a class whose political power 'he has broken' and 'daily breaks it anew' (*MECW* 11, p. 194). None of this contradicts Marx's view of the state as a special instrument of coercion: on the contrary, what it demonstrates is why this coercion, in exceptional circumstances, should appear so 'special', for what Bonaparte does is to underline, in a dramatic way, its 'generalized' character. A coercion implemented through the bourgeoisie's 'natural' representatives — parliamentarians, newspaper editors, and party politicians — 'normally' sensitive to capitalist pressures, yields to the coercion of an adventurer who mobilizes the peasantry, priests, army and lumpen proletariat in order to ensure that the political community *remains* an illusory one and thus arrests the slide from liberal into socialist rule. If this generalized coercion has now to be 'abstracted' from the 'political will' of the bourgeoisie, from its 'normal' representatives, this is only possible because this 'political will' had *already* been abstracted from the *individual* interests of the bourgeoisie and from those of society at large. Even without their 'normal' representatives, the bourgeoisie still rule. Napoleon I might despotically suppress 'the liberalism of bourgeois society' but French businessmen are able to shake Napoleon's power by an artificially created famine which delays the opening of his Russian campaign (*MECW* 4, p. 124). Napoleon III has his autonomy constrained by the fact that he protects the material power of the bourgeoisie whose interests, it should be noted, 'dictate' that it should be delivered from the danger of its own rule (*MECW* 11, p. 143). Of course, adventurers like Bonaparte are tempted by the heavenly aspirations of a political idealism to go beyond the materialist needs of the bourgeoisie, as in 1859, when, according to Marx, he alienates the business and financial community and rules 'henceforth by the sword alone' (Draper, 1977, p. 458). But this is an exceptional situation which proves the rule for Bonaparte can only survive for another decade by placating bourgeois interests. It was, after all, the bourgeoisie who 'invited Bonaparte to suppress and annihilate its speaking and writing section' in order to pursue its private affairs with 'full confidence' (*MECW* 11, p. 173), and this business 'confidence', as Block shows (1977, p. 17), acts as a formidable constraint on state autonomy.

The movement, therefore, between the differing state-forms can only be understood in terms of their common and contradictory logic of representation. Marx admirably captures this continuity within change when he shows how Napoleon 'perfected' the machinery of state, severing the '*common* interest' from society and transposing it into a 'higher, *general* interest' (*MECW* 11, p. 186), for is not this process of snatching social activity away and putting government activity in its place a characteristic of *all* states, however liberal, whatever the degree of their authoritarian autonomy? Parkin comments a trife unkindly that 'Present-day Marxists have indulged in much huffing and puffing in trying to discard the classical or vulgar concept of the state, only to have ended up with a thinly disguised version of the same thing' (1979, p. 128). The most Bonapartist state still functions as a particular kind of 'executive committee', given the fact that it is answerable in the last resort to its bourgeois constituency. This unity within distinction is missed if 'instrumentalist coercion' is counter-posed to 'ideological autonomy' and insufficient attention is paid to the question of what it is that makes political coercion so 'special'. Coercion and consent are both intrinsic to Marx's view of politics which, in all its forms, is constituted by a synthesis of the two.

This conception of the state as a special instrument of coercion could only have been developed by Marx through the analysis of a capitalist society. Only under capitalism does the state appear to cut itself adrift from everyday social life as an 'abstract' community alongside civil society's war of all against all. '*Political life* in the modern sense is the *scholasticism* of national life' (*MECW* 3, p. 31). Yet, should we conclude from this, as Western Marxists tend to argue, that there cannot be a general theory of the state in Marxism (Mercer, 1980, p. 120), that Marx's conception of the state 'as such' is only the modern state and that Engels and Lenin were wrong to attribute its characteristics to 'the state in general' (Colletti, 1975, p. 45)? An interesting argument, but a *non sequitur*. A distinction needs to be made between the conditions in which a theory can be conceived and the conditions to which such a theory can then apply (for a more general discussion, Hoffman, 1975, pp. 125–34). The great merit of capitalism, in Marx and

Engels's eyes, is that as the society in which 'all that is solid melts into air' and all 'that is holy is profaned', it compels 'man' 'to face with sober senses, his real conditions of life, and his relations with his kind' (*MECW* 6, p. 487). By 'perfecting' the dualism between state and civil society, capitalism makes it possible to grasp the nature of politics, *all* politics, as a special instrument of class rule. It is clear even in *The German Ideology* (1845) that the conception of the state as an illusory community was intended to apply generally. If such an insight can only arise when politics is concentrated into a seemingly autonomous sphere above and beyond the material world, it cannot be coherently sustained unless it forms the basis of a general theory of the state. There may be formidable complexities involved in trying to relate this view of politics to societies like feudalism where, according to Draper, economic and political power are fused in the same hands (1977, p. 472), but the point about generality still stands. Unless the state is understood as an instrument of coercion which commands consent, then the interrelationship of its differing forms cannot be grasped and this point is relevant not only to the capitalist state but also, as we shall see, to the transitional state under socialism.

INSTRUMENTALITY AND THE PROBLEM OF COHESION

We have argued that for Marx, the state acts on behalf of a class expressing its particular interests in a 'general form'. This process of abstraction involves (a) generalizing the specific interests of the individual members of a ruling class in order (b) to project these interests in the form of an 'illusory community' in the name of society as a whole. The first 'level' of abstraction cannot be sustained unless it is linked to the second. Hence we are now in a position to see why the role of the state 'as a factor of cohesion', binding the different levels of society together so that a given mode of production can be 'reproduced', does not contradict the character of the state as a special instrument of coercion. Coercion can only be fully 'political' if it commands the support, not only of individual members of a dominant class, but of society at large. The state's 'cohesiveness' is an intrinsic dimension of its specialized instrumentality.

In *Anti-Dühring*, Engels notes that, with the division of society into classes, 'the state, which the primitive groups of communities of the same tribe had at first arrived at only in order to safeguard their common interests (e.g. irrigation in the East) . . . from this stage onwards acquires just as much the function of maintaining by force the conditions of existence and domination of the ruling class against the subject class' (*AD*, p. 205). This passage poses a problem. It implies that the state historically acted to safeguard 'common interests' *before* it functioned in the interests of a ruling class: two separate and contradictory activities, it might be thought, one of which utilizes coercion, while the other promotes consent.

A similar problem arises with a passage from *The German Ideology* where Marx and Engels speak of the division of labour as implying a contradiction between individual and common interests: 'this common interest does not exist merely in the imagination, as the "general interest", but first of all in reality, as the mutual interdependence of the individuals among whom the labour is divided' (*MECW* 5, p. 46). Jessop refers to this passage in order to argue that, for Marx and Engels, an institutionally separate state emerges to manage the common affairs of a gentile society *before* the development of class antagonisms (1982, p. 17). State management of the 'common interest' appears necessary because of the mutual interdependence of individuals in societies where labour is divided: the maintenance of 'cohesion' as a function separate from and in contradiction with the state's class based coercive instrumentality.

In both passages, the problem is in fact a purely termino-logical one. As Draper points out, what Engels refers to as the 'state' safeguarding common interests is not, strictly speaking, a state but what Draper calls its 'protopolitical predecessor' (1977, p. 245) turning into its opposite. By not providing another name for this 'pre-state', Engels under-emphasizes the sharp *dis*continuity which exists between the two and which he stresses elsewhere when he speaks of the gentile constitution being *replaced* by the state as an institution whose specific identity derives precisely from its coercive, class character (*OFPPS*, p. 229). Similarly, with Marx and Engels's reference above to the 'common interest' and the division of labour. Strictly speaking, the two are incompatible for, as *The German Ideology* itself makes clear, the development of the second signals a rupture with the first. The division of labour 'only becomes truly such' (*MECW* 5, p. 44) when a division between material and mental labour appears and society *divides* along class lines. When labour is thus divided (as opposed to simply being co-operatively shared out), the 'mutual interdependence' referred to above ceases to express an authentic 'common interest' and is projected 'in the imagin-ation' by ruling class ideologists as an illusory general will. If the problem of characterizing the transition from one institution into its opposite makes for terminological difficulties and inexactitudes, the thought, as Draper puts it, 'is entirely clear' (1977, p. 245). The state arises historically not as the embodiment of a social harmony based on mutual interest, but as 'the admission' that with the division of labour along class lines, 'society has involved itself in insoluble self-contradiction and is cleft into irreconcilable antagonisms which it is powerless to exorcise' (*OFPPS*, p. 229).

Yet, if this is so, how is it possible for the state to act both as a factor of cohesion *and* as an instrument of coercion when these appear to be contradictory roles? Three points in particular here deserve consideration. The first turns on the element of continuity noted above: the fact that with the birth of a ruling class, the exercise of a social function now forms the basis, as Engels puts it, of political supremacy (*AD*, p. 248). The 'general interest' is historically rooted in the 'common interest', even if, at the same time, it mystifies the latter. This serves to sustain an *illusion* of communality, given the fact that those who control the means of material production also control the means of mental production and have an important 'intellectual force' at their command (*MECW* 5, p. 59). Secondly, when a new class wins power, it can only do so when the whole mass of society confronts the old order. Initially, therefore, Marx and Engels argue, 'its interest is as yet mostly connected with the common interest of all other non-ruling classes' and its victory benefits 'many individuals of other classes' (*MECW* 5, p. 61). It is only as the particular interests of this new ruling class are entrenched at the expense of the rest of society, that this 'common interest' generalizes itself into an increasingly illusory form. While thirdly, and this is a simple point which it is easy to overlook, the fact is that for Marx and Engels, a class-divided society is still a society. It is a divided *whole*. When Marx comments that 'proletariat and wealth are opposites; as such they form a single whole' (*MECW* 4, p. 35), he naturally adds that 'it is not sufficient to declare them two sides of a single whole'. If this declaration is not sufficient, it is important nevertheless. Without this 'unity' between 'opposites', capitalism could not exist for workers have to be maintained, kept alive, housed, educated, provided with transport, hospitals, networks of communication, etc. or they could not be exploited at all.

A state can only survive for any length of time when it discharges 'its social functions' (*AD*, p. 248) and no social order, capitalist or otherwise, could be sustained without them. Under capitalism, just as 'in the despotic states', writes Marx, 'supervision and all-round interference by the government involves both the performance of common activities arising from the nature of all communities, and the specific functions arising from the antithesis between the government and the mass of the people' (*C* III, p. 384). These 'common activities' are described in the *Civil War in France* as the 'legitimate functions' of the old governmental power to be wrested from an authority usurping pre-eminence over society itself (*PC*, p. 73) and elsewhere Marx refers to the 'social functions' of a communist society which are analagous to 'present state functions' (*MESW*, p. 331). Yet, although these functions or 'common activities' are necessary even in societies without a state, it does not follow that when performed in class-divided societies, these activities contradict the partisan instrumentality of the state, for without them, capitalism could not function as a social formation. The 'common interests' of the bourgeoisie cannot be represented without representing at the same time what Marx calls pejoratively the 'general interest' of society as a whole. The first is placed in jeopardy when the second is not fulfilled, for unless the state's 'spiritual nerves' foster the wider cohesion of society, legitimacy will be eroded and a stable regime undermined. The interests of classes cannot be opposed unless they *also* have interests in common.

It should be noted of course that the performance of 'common activities' in class-divided societies invariably intertwines with what Marx calls 'the specific functions arising from the antithesis between the government and the mass of the people' (*C* III, p. 384). Public welfare services can be administered in a way which subsidizes private interests and 'common' highways may just happen to pass through the residential areas where workers live (Hoffman, 1983, p. 139; Mandel, 1978, p. 154). Policies generating social cohesion may also create the same problems for a ruling class as all other expressions of the 'general interest' do when normality passes into crisis and expectations for a 'fairer' society increasingly obstruct continued capital accumulation and profit levels. Yet, whatever the degree of their 'reformism', either as a response to or pre-emptive move against pressures from 'below', the enactment of common measures must be regarded as an integral part of the state's generalized coercion. It helps to sustain the illusion of an overall 'common interest' and is essential to the functioning of any institution which has pretensions to govern.

Again, this is a point which Draper fails wholly to assimilate. He argues that while the basic task of the state is forcible coercion, it has other 'subsidiary' tasks which are characteristic of any organizing authority in a society. These he defines as 'non-class tasks' carried out *'inevitably in class distorted ways, for class ends, with class consequences'* (1977, p. 260). Yet, if the means are 'class distorted' and the ends 'class biased', what has happened to the 'non-class' character of these subsidiary tasks? A failure to grasp, as noted above, that classes have to have interests in common in order to be divided, inevitably means that Marx's concept of political coercion is broken up into a 'material' force and a 'spiritual' generality and loses its coherence and consistency. Precisely the same problem arises with Draper's discussion of what he calls 'auxiliary' or 'force-substitute' methods of control exercised by the state. They certainly make for a fascinating catalogue which Draper carefully documents with numerous excerpts from Marx and Engels's writing. They include strident moralism, media falsification, corruption, hypocrisy, racism and bribery (Draper, 1977, pp. 264–70), but none ought to be described as 'force-substitute' methods for all help to engender that very quality of illusoriness, of theological generality which makes the coercion of the state so special. Far from substituting for political coercion, such methods invest it with its necessary specificity. They make it essentially what it is.

If, as Western Marxists contend, the classical Marxist theory of politics is narrowly instrumentalist, it also implies an active, autonomous role for the state: a broad view embracing both coercion and consent. Individual members of the bourgeoisie cannot be coerced unless the class 'as a whole' supports 'its' state; society at large cannot be 'disciplined' by the law unless the state secures recognition as a 'public force' apparently acting in the common good. The 'consensual' elements, the 'space' for which is provided by the ideological character of the state, do not have a separate presence in Marx's theory, as so many commentators imply. On the contrary, they form an essential part of the way in which Marx analyses the class character of the state. Politics stands as a 'general, socially coercive force' (*SC*, p. 255) and in neither the parasitism of the Bonapartist executive, the liberal republic of businessmen nor of the state's performance of 'common activities' can the coercive and the consensual, the instrumental and the ideological, the class-biased and the socially cohesive be separated out. Marx's broad definition is, as we have noted above, a synthetic one.

THE PROBLEM AS PARADOX

The young Marx, I have argued, took as his starting point the 'ever new philosophy of reason'. The Enlightenment concept of the state as a rational community is not so much cast aside as it is critically reworked into an analysis of the state as a class instrument of coercion which defends the interests of the particular in the name of the general. But how is this possible? How is it possible for a coercion to exist which commands consent? The concept of politics in Marx appears as a paradox in which two seemingly antithetical attributes are fused together.

The problem of the 'two levels' of the Machiavellian Centaur, as we have seen, is a very old one. Some notion of consent as describing the relation of subjects with their government has, as Femia observes, been present 'throughout virtually the whole history of political speculation' (1981, p. 36). The dualistic dilemmas, so graphically portrayed in Plato's *Republic* (see e.g. 1955, p. 263), are thoroughly exacerbated by the liberal tradition which presents consent as the voluntary and deliberate act of individuals who alone can decide to become members of a commonwealth (Locke, 1924, p. 179). As Pateman has commented, the question of obligation to the state now takes on a particularly 'subversive' form and raises the fundamental problem of *'how and why any free and equal individual could legitimately be governed by anyone else at all'* (1979, p. 13). Free and equal individuals are to consent voluntarily to enter into a relationship of political obligation when this obligation necessarily requires *obedience*, a subordination to the will of others (1979, pp. 13—14). Truly, as Bosanquet called it, a 'paradox of self-government' (1920, p. 51). Classical liberals, like Hobbes and Locke, saw this as a problem and sought to reconcile coercion and consent through what Pateman calls a 'hypothetical voluntarism' (1979, p. 163) in which consent was merely inferred as in Locke's famous example of the 'citizen' walking down the highway. If classical liberals at least sought to provide fictional solutions to an apparently insoluble problem, contemporary liberal thinkers have tended to conceptualize it out of existence, suggesting that the question of whether citizens really do consent to the authority of those elected to office is no longer relevant (Plamenatz, 1968, p. 170; Femia, 1981, p. 37; Pateman, 1979, p. 14; p. 142).

A solution to the problem, argues Pateman, lies in Rousseau's concept of a 'participatory political association' in which citizens freely create relationships of authority for themselves (1979, p. 134; p. 136). Yet, while it may be said that Rousseau tackled the problem of coercion and consent, in Marx's words, without 'even the semblance of compromise' (*SC*, p. 148), it is difficult to see how he can be said to have resolved it. On the contrary, Rousseau presents the 'paradox of self-government' in its most devastating form. On the one hand, force, says Rousseau, is a 'physical power; I do not see how its effects could produce morality' (1968, p. 52); on the other hand, what bestows 'justice on civil contracts' is the fact that 'whoever refuses to obey the general will shall be constrained to do so by the whole body, which means nothing other than that he shall be forced to be free' (1968, p. 64). Pateman complains that Rousseau, by extending his formula of 'forcing people to be free' to dissident minorities, 'contradicts the basic principles of his theory' (1979, p. 160). In fact, it would be truer to say that in speaking of the murderer as one 'who consents to die' (1968, p. 79) and of the citizen who consents even to those laws 'that are passed against his will' (p. 153), Rousseau courageously grapples with the paradoxical realities of the state. As long as the 'participatory association' is a *political* one, this problem remains. *Libertas* is inscribed on the doors of the prisons (Rousseau, 1968, p. 153) and an institution which is fundamentally coercive, claims consent as a legitimating attribute of its political identity. The idealist T.H. Green tries to avoid the paradox by arguing that 'Will not Force is the Basis of the State' but even he is driven to contemplate gloomily the fact that without this force, 'the wild beast in man will not otherwise yield obedience to the rational will' (1941, p. 217): the celebrated general will which forces people to be free. One of his admirers, L.T. Hobhouse was to insist that 'liberty itself only rests upon restraint' (1964, p. 77), but how is this paradox to be explained? How is it that when people are coerced, they can also be said to consent?

Perhaps it is not surprising that Marx should have been somewhat sceptical and he invariably, as we have seen, characterizes the consensual aspects of politics as hypocritical, theological or abstract. Yet none of these epithets should be taken to imply unreality because, if the state's self-conceit and communal pretensions are not to be taken at face-value, they exist all the same. Class interests can only be organized politically when they are presented as a 'public force'. The absurdity of the state is perfectly evident, but can it be explained? By portraying politics as a coercion which commands consent, Marx emphasizes its paradox. Does he have a solution?

It has to be said that this problem is not really *analysed* by Marx and Engels in their political writings. Coercion and consent are always presented together in a political, if paradoxical, synthesis. Yet if this problem is to be tackled at its roots, an analysis is essential for if we are to explain how two logically contradictory attributes identify within the state, each has to be looked at separately in order to understand how such an absurdity arises. We turn to consider the work of the first Marxist who sought to develop a sustained and coherent investigation of the problem in analytically discrete terms.

3

'MACHIAVELLI'S CENTAUR': GRAMSCI'S CHALLENGE TO CLASSICAL MARXISM

'HEGEMONY' – A NEW CONCEPT?

I have already noted the importance of Gramsci in the eyes of those who argue that he inaugurated a new chapter in Marxist political theory by tackling the problem of consent within a 'new science of politics'. We are now in a position to evaluate this claim, for where precisely do Gramsci's celebrated 'formulae' on politics stand in relation to the classical Marxist tradition and in particular, to the work of Lenin as the Marxist who most directly influenced him? Clarity on this matter is made all the more important by the tendency of many of the Gramsci commentators to present Marx and Engels's theory of the state in purely instrumentalist and negative terms (e.g. Bobbio, 1979, p. 23; Adamson, 1980, p. 165; Mouffe, 1979a, p. 10). In fact, as argued above, the classical Marxist view of politics embraces both coercion and consent, even if these aspects are synthesized into a single definition rather than related to one another as discrete factors.

Gramsci's contribution to Marxist theory centres, as we have seen, upon his conception of hegemony and it is through this concept that, as Buci-Glucksmann puts it, he 'posed the question of consent in a way new to Marxism' (1982, p. 117).

It is worth recalling that whereas Althusser was somewhat dismissive of Gramsci's political theory at the Venice Conference of 1977, in his earlier *For Marx* he speaks highly of the *Prison Notebooks* where, he says, we find not only some completely original insights into the problem of superstructures, but 'as always with true discoveries, there are *new concepts*, for example, *hegemony*' (1969, p. 114).

What then is so new and original about Gramsci's concept of hegemony? This question deserves some attention, given the extent to which Gramsci's roots within the classical Marxist tradition (and its Leninist component) are so often understated. The notion of hegemony, as Anderson observes, had a long prior history as 'one of the most central political slogans in the Russian Social-Democratic movement, from the late 1890s to 1917' (1976–7, p. 15) and was taken by Axelrod, Martov and Lenin to refer to the role of the working class as a *leading* force in the fight for democracy. The concept was central to Lenin's *What is to be Done?* (1902) with its analysis of the party as 'a vanguard fighter for democracy', able to react to 'every manifestation of tyranny and oppression . . . no matter what stratum or class of the people it affects' (*LCW* 5, p. 423). This position is reaffirmed after the defeat of 1905: the proletariat must be 'the leader in the struggle of the whole people for a fully democratic revolution'. It is revolutionary 'only insofar as it is conscious of and gives effect to this idea of hegemony of the proletariat' (*LCW* 17, p. 232).

Hegemony for Lenin implied (a) the organized and disciplined proletarian leadership of (b) a broadly based movement extending to all classes and strata so that the vanguard party acts as a 'tribune of the people' (*LCW* 5, p. 423). Although the term is seldom used, it could well be argued that the idea itself is deeply embedded in earlier Marxist perspectives. Its roots are to be found in Marx's concept of the proletariat as a class with 'a universal character' which 'cannot emancipate itself without emancipating all the other spheres of society' (*MECW* 3, p. 186), in the conception of the proletarian movement as the 'self-conscious, independent movement of the immense majority' (*MECW* 6, p. 495). Proletarian leadership in the 1848 revolution is deemed vital, given the abysmal failure of the German bourgeoisie to act as 'a class speaking for the *whole* of modern society' (*MECW* 8, p. 162). From these and numerous other comments in Marx and Engels's political writings, there can be little doubt that Lenin's concept of the proletariat as *hegemonic* when it becomes the 'ideological leader of the democratic process' (*LCW* 8, p. 79) is part and parcel of the classical Marxist tradition. (For Gramsci's recognition of this point, see Buci-Glucksmann, 1980, p. 177).

It has been said that Gramsci's concept of hegemony was 'the logical conclusion to his total political experience' (Bates, 1975, p. 351), but if the idea requires proletarian leadership of an alliance with the peasantry on behalf of society as a whole, then it is difficult to see how the concept was anything more than 'potentially present' (Showstack Sassoon, 1980b, p. 53) in his earlier writings. Gramsci's comment that the Turin Communists posed concretely the question of the 'hegemony of the proletariat' i.e. of 'the social basis of the proletarian dictatorship and workers' State' (*SPW* II, p. 443) is somewhat misleading because it is only towards the end of the period of the factory council occupations in Turin (spring of 1920) that Gramsci accepts the need for a revolutionary party (Hoare and Nowell Smith, 1971, p. x1). Moreover, right up until his arrest by the fascists in 1926, Gramsci still expressed reservations about the Comintern strategy of a 'united front' with the socialists and it is precisely this strategy which provides the essential point of reference for the elaboration of hegemony in the *Prison Notebooks* (1929—35). Our problem remains: if Gramsci's concept of hegemony was in its developed form 'borrowed from Lenin' (Buci-Glucksmann, 1980, p. 175), what is it that makes the idea distinctively 'Gramscian'?

It might be thought significant that whereas the term was

generally used by Lenin to denote proletarian leadership within the *democratic* revolution, Gramsci, in 1926 for example, referred to the proletariat mobilizing the majority of the working population 'against capitalism and the bourgeois State' (*SPW* II, p. 443). Yet, as Anderson notes, the documents of the Comintern in the 1920s also refer to the struggle for hegemony in this wider context (1976–7, p. 18) and it is clear from Marx and Engels's own writings that proletarian leadership was seen as imperative for *all* phases of the struggle. Lenin himself had stressed the need for the party to 'realize its full hegemony' under socialism (Buci-Glucksmann, 1980, p. 180).

Not surprisingly, therefore, the analysis of hegemony in the *Prison Notebooks* reflects many of the themes evident in the positions of Lenin and the Comintern. For example, Lenin's insistence that renouncing hegemony leads to reformism (*LCW* 17, p. 233) is echoed in Gramsci's critique of 'economism' where he stresses the importance of making 'sacrifices of an economic-corporate kind' if hegemony is to be secured (*SPN*, p. 161). Comintern strictures of a 'narrow corporatism' which the proletariat must transcend in acting as 'the guide of the whole working class and exploited population' (Anderson, 1976–7, p. 18) find their counterpart in Gramsci's reference to the need for 'intellectual and moral unity', the need to pose questions on a ' "universal" plane' if a social group is to secure hegemony (*SPN*, pp. 181–2).

In emphasizing Gramsci's 'debt' to Lenin, the Comintern and the wider classical tradition, it is relatively easy to establish his Marxist 'credentials' as against those who see Gramsci as a 'Crocian', a reformist and a social democrat in the modern sense of the term (see Davidson, 1972, pp. 453–4; Femia, 1981, pp. 198–200). What is much more difficult is to see what is so distinctive, innovative or original about his concept of hegemony: why it should be widely regarded as the basis for a 'new science of politics' and a challenge to classical Marxism.

HEGEMONY, CULTURE AND THE BOURGEOISIE

It is commonly argued that in at least two aspects, Gramsci's hegemony offered something new. The first of the distinctively Gramscian attributes relates to the *extension* of the concept from the proletariat to the bourgeoisie so that hegemony becomes a feature of class rule in general. The second revolves around what is said to be the particularly cultural, moral and intellectualist emphasis that Gramsci injects into the notion. Neither of these aspects, it is contended, can really be found within classical Marxism.

The first of these claims, that Gramsci innovatively extended the concept of hegemony, is widely held indeed (Femia, 1981, p. 25; Anderson, 1976–7, p. 20; Buci-Glucksmann, 1980, p. 165; Simon, 1982, p. 22; Mouffe, 1979, p. 181; Gibbon, 1983, p. 341). There can be no doubt that hegemony was central to Gramsci's analysis of politics and he considered it the 'essential ingredient' of modern Marxism (*LP*, p. 235). The state is often characterized by Gramsci as 'hegemony protected by the armour of coercion' (*SPN*, p. 263) and to these two aspects, there corresponds 'two major superstructural "levels"' (*SPN*, p. 12), civil and political society. Hegemony is at the heart of Gramsci's concept of the intellectual (*SPN*, p. 13), the party (*SPN*, p. 16) and the formation of that 'historical bloc' by means of which an ascendant class roots its political leadership in the realm of production (*SPN*, p. 366). The 'war of position', as the gradualist dimension within revolutionary struggle, demands 'an unprecedented concentration of hegemony' (*SPN*, p. 238) and where this hegemony is deficient, social transformations take the form of a 'passive revolution' (Showstack Sassoon, 1980b, p. 207). Certainly, Gramsci regarded the notion of hegemony as a fundamental axiom of political science and hence relevant to all forms of political rule, but does it follow from this, as Anderson has argued, that Gramsci thereby pioneered 'a wholly new theoretical field of Marxist enquiry' (1976–7, p. 20)?

Here we need to be careful. While it is true that Lenin generally used the term to apply to proletarian leadership within the specific context of a bourgeois revolution, this fact in itself suggests that the term had a wider applicability, for why did Lenin regard proletarian leadership as so essential in the struggle for democracy? Precisely because in Tsarist Russia, as in Marx's Germany of 1848, the bourgeoisie appeared too weak to provide the kind of revolutionary leadership which their historical counterparts like the French Jacobins had been able to display. In this sense, the Bolsheviks are, for Lenin, 'the Jacobins of contemporary Social-Democracy' (*LCW* 9, p. 59). Lenin not only quotes with approval the reference in the *Neue Rheinische Zeitung* to 'the whole of French terrorism' settling accounts with absolutism and feudalism in a 'plebian way' (*MECW* 8, p. 161), but his analogy between communists and Jacobins directly echoes a similar comment by Marx (*MECW* 6, p. 545). If there is a parallel between the proletariat as 'the progressive class of the twentieth century' and the bourgeoisie as the progressive class of the eighteenth (*LCW* 9, p. 60), then an extension of the concept of hegemony from one to the other is logically implied, particularly given Lenin's reference to the bourgeoisie as a class whose historic achievements represented 'progress from the standpoint of the world development of society' (*LCW* 29, p. 486; see also, e.g., *LCW* 23, p. 38). Indeed, Marx's earliest reference to the proletariat as a force for 'universal' emancipation derives from his contrast between the German bourgeoisie which lacks 'the breadth of soul' to identify itself with the 'soul of the nation' and the situation in France where 'every class' is '*politically idealistic* and becomes aware of itself at first not as a particular class but as representative of social requirements generally' (*MECW* 3, pp. 185–6). In *The German Ideology*, Marx and Engels regard each 'new class' as hegemonic in so far as it achieves domination on a 'broader basis than that of the class ruling previously' (*MECW* 5, p. 61). It is true that Marx, like Gramsci (Showstack Sassoon, 1980b, p. 119), is aware that the bourgeoisie cannot sustain its universalistic claims once its particular interests become apparent, but the point about the 'political idealism' of hegemony is a general one. It is clearly not confined just to the proletariat.

We come to the second aspect of Gramsci's concept of hegemony which is held by commentators to be distinctive and innovative: the injection into the theory of a sense of 'intellectual and moral direction' (Mouffe, 1979b, p. 181) so that Femia can argue that 'the key *cultural* emphasis the word conveys in Gramsci's usage has no place in Lenin's theory of revolution' (1981, p. 25). (See also Adamson, 1980, p. 172; Anderson, 1976–7, p. 20.) Yet is this really so? How does Lenin's case for the party newspaper as a 'collective organiser', 'agitator' and 'propagandist' (*LCW* 5, p. 22) differ from Gramsci's view of the *Ordine Nuovo* as the organ of 'proletarian culture'? In *What is to be Done?* Lenin argues that the party must be 'guided by the most advanced theory' (*LCW* 5, p. 370) and take up actively the 'political education' of the working class (p. 400). Since this education must involve an 'exposure' of oppression 'as it manifests itself in the most varied spheres of life and activity — vocational, civic, personal, family, religious, scientific, etc.' (*LCW* 5, p. 401), the 'materialist analysis and the materialist estimate of *all* aspects of the life and activity of *all* classer, strata and groups of the population' (*LCW* 5, p. 412), it is difficult to see in what sense it can be said that Lenin's concept of hegemony lacks the 'cultural emphasis', the 'intellectual and moral direction' conveyed by Gramsci's usage of the term?

There appears therefore to be no 'limit' placed on the range of ideas relevant to the 'political idealism' of a hegemonic class within classical Marxism. One can only assume that the 'active, conceptive ideologists' who 'make the formation of the illusions of the class about itself their chief source of livelihood' (*MECW* 5, p. 60) would be unlikely to neglect cultural and moral questions, while the proletariat, for its part, if it is to abolish the rule of all classes, requires the production on a mass scale of 'communist consciousness' (*MECW* 5, p. 52). It is interesting that Gramsci, in his analysis of hegemony, should draw upon Engels's 'thesis' of the German proletariat as the heir of classical German philosophy (*SPN*, p. 357), for this same thesis is vigorously evoked by Lenin in *What is to be Done?* (*LCW* 5, p. 371). Even more significant is Gramsci's affirmation that 'the theorisation and realisation of hegemony carried out by Ilich [Lenin] was also a great "metaphysical" event' (*SPN*, p. 357) for, as Gramsci rightly recognized, the concept of hegemony in classical Marxism was not simply a narrow, 'instrumentalist' doctrine, but had implications of a far-reaching theoretical and philosophical kind (*SPN*, p. 365).

Neither Gramsci's 'extension' of hegemony nor the cultural and moral emphasis he places upon it, is sufficient to explain why he can be said to have posed the question of consent in a way new to Marxism. We have already noted the argument that the errant isms of the classical tradition are suffused with repressive overtones which have brought Marxism to a state of 'crisis' but there can be no doubt that hegemony in Marx and Engels, as in Gramsci, is tied to the question of *consent*. After all, the proletarian movement could hardly be characterized as the 'movement of the immense majority' (*MECW* 6, p. 495), if this did not imply winning mass *support*.

During the 1848 revolutions, Marx and Engels called the *Neue Rheinische Zeitung*, the 'Organ of Democracy' even though it seemed at the time to some of their critics in the Communist League that this meant sacrificing the immediate interests of the working class for the sake of broad, popular 'consent'. Engels recalled in 1895 how the *Communist Manifesto* had already proclaimed the importance of winning universal suffrage and argued that the history of the last 50 years has taught us that where 'it is a question of a complete transformation of the social organisation, the masses themselves must also be in it, must themselves have grasped what is at stake, what they are going in for, body and soul' (*MESW*, p. 664). If there is a role for people from other classes to bring 'real cultural elements' into the proletarian movement, this, declare Marx and Engels in 1879, in no way contradicts the battle-cry of the First International that the emancipation of the working class must be achieved by the workers themselves (*SC*, pp. 306–7). Lenin is adamant that socialism can only be reached *through* democracy (*LCW* 9, p. 28) and he endorses the classical Marxist opposition to Blanquism and the notion of a seizure of power by a minority (*LCW* 24, p. 49; Johnstone, 1983). The Paris Commune could only stand in Marx and Engels's eyes as 'the true representative of all the healthy elements of French society' because it was at the same time 'a government of the people by the people' (*PC*, pp. 79–80), while Buci-Glucksmann in making her case for the 'closeness' of Gramsci and Lenin, evidences the latter's commitment to winning a political majority (Buci-Glucksmann, 1980, pp. 192–4; *LCW* 32, p. 471).

We will have occasion to return to these matters in chapter 6, but for the moment it is enough to assert that the 'rediscovery' of Antonio Gramsci serves to demonstrate the importance and not the neglect, of consent in classical Marxism. The famous 'antinomies' centred around Machiavelli's Centaur, the levels of force and consent, authority and hegemony, violence and civilization, the individual and the universal moment, agitation and propaganda, tactics and strategy, etc., all reflect a *broad* view of politics and the state which Gramsci shared with Lenin, Marx and Engels. It is certainly true, as we shall see, that Gramsci sought to analyse the 'two levels', the problem of coercion and consent, in discrete terms but it cannot be said that the presence of these 'antitheses' in themselves constitute a 'new and fundamental dimension' (Mouffe, 1979b, p. 181) within Marxist political theory. Gramsci's claim to originality must be sought elsewhere.

CROCE AND THE METHODOLOGICAL DISTINCTION

Gramsci's challenge to the classical Marxist tradition, I wish to argue, arises not from the *fact* that he poses the question of politics in terms of a 'dual perspective' with its two fundamental levels (*pace* Boggs, 1976, p. 114), but from the way in which he analytically relates them. In other words, it is not the existence of the two levels which is innovatory: it is the fact that they are *analysed*.

Gramsci's position represents therefore a significant advance because as long as the 'dual perspective' is presented only as a synthesis — a coercion fused with consent — it cannot be properly examined. Buci-Glucksmann says of Lenin and Gramsci that under socialism, 'Hegemony *qualifies* the proletarian dictatorship' (1980, p. 182), but for classical Marxism, it can be said that hegemony is intrinsic to all political processes. It is the *quality* which endows the coercion of the state with its specifically political character. A coercion, as we have seen, which commands consent. But if we are to understand why the two are united in synthesis, is it not necessary that they should be analytically taken apart? How else can we resolve the political paradox?

Gramsci's analysis of the two levels poses a challenge, but it also gives rise to a problem. For how are the factors to be analysed without at the same time dissolving the synthetic identity of the state into the coercive, on the one hand and the consensual, on the other? We have already seen just such an 'analytical' presentation by those commentators who see in Marx's theory a contradictory amalgam of consensual communality and brute force; yet this kind of 'analysis' can in no way resolve the paradoxical problem of coercion and consent since it merely appears that the theological absurdities of the state arise out of the logical inconsistencies of Marx and not from the curious character of political reality! Gramsci's challenge to the classical tradition then is this: is it possible actually to analyse the question of coercion and consent in a way which *transcends* the problem rather than simply adds to its traditional mystification?

The development of Gramsci's political theory cannot be understood without some consideration being given to his relationship with Croce — the grand old man of Italian philosophy whose liberal idealism had decisively influenced Gramsci as a student in Turin (as Gramsci conceded, Jacobitti, 1975, p. 298) and who was even to claim the communist Gramsci as his philosophical disciple (Femia, 1981, p. 62). Gramsci's early political writings betray the full weight of Crocean 'dualisms' for in Gramsci's initial response to the Russian Revolution, the cultural and spiritual aspects of politics are separated from, and clearly superior to, coercive power. The Revolution is a proletarian 'act', replacing 'authoritarianism by liberty' and generating 'an atmosphere of absolute spiritual freedom' in which 'the whole of the Russian proletariat' consents to the new form of society (*SPW* I, p. 29). It is their revolutionary idealism which has enabled Lenin and the Bolsheviks to triumph: a revolution against *Capital* which requires the suspension of 'the canons of Marxist historical criticism' (*SPW* I, p. 35).

Few commentators appear to dispute that these early writings convey 'an idealist problematic' (Showstack Sassoon, 1980b, p. 30) and are firmly under the spell of Crocean liberalism (Femia, 1981, p. 4). What is more contentious is the question of how far these early formulations with their sharp cleavage between power and morality, coercion and consent, influence Gramsci's later writings and in particular, the analysis he developed in prison. We have already noted how the young Marx had also been preoccupied with his own version of Gramsci's 'free voice of universal consciousness' (*SPW* I, p. 29) and had integrated his early 'ethical-political' interests into a 'new' materialist theory of politics which stressed the coercive character of this 'illusory community'. How far did Gramsci travel down

the same road? Showstack Sassoon has argued that the
themes of the young Gramsci became 'integrated into a new
concept of politics' (1980b, p. 31), but to what extent did
the later theory reveal traces of the earlier 'problematic'?

There can be no doubt that Gramsci's overriding preoccupation with the problem of analysing politics in terms
of civil and political society, hegemony and dictatorship,
coercion and consent, derives from the impact of Croce.
In the *Prison Notebooks* Croce is praised for having 'drawn
attention energetically' to the question of cultural and
intellectual facts in historical development; the function
of intellectuals in civil society and the state and to the
moment of hegemony and consent as the necessary form
of the 'historical bloc' (*SPN*, p. 56). Yet however 'Crocean
in tendency' (Fiori, 1970, p. 106) Gramsci thought his
earlier positions, in the *Prison Notebooks* he is deeply
critical. Croce is to be transcended in the same way that
Marx had transcended Hegel (*SPN*, p. 402). The Crocean
heritage is one which has to be reworked before it can be
taken over. It is true that Croce had rightly (in Gramsci's
eyes) sought to maintain a distinction between hegemony
and dictatorship where Gentile, as the theorist of fascism
and the corporate state, treats force and consent as though
they were indistinguishable (*SPN*, p. 271), but Gramsci
is far from satisfied with the way in which Croce's analysis
proceeds. Croce's reformist prejudices are responsible for
the fact that in his historical writings he 'excludes the
moment of struggle; the moment in which the conflicting
forces are formed'; 'the moment in which one ethical-political
system dissolves and another is formed by fire and steel'.
The whole of his politics is absorbed into 'the moment of
cultural or ethical-political expansion' (*SPN*, p. 119). As the
theorist of the 'liberal, democratic regime' (*SPN*, p. 271),
Croce is guilty, as Gramsci puts it elsewhere, of 'an arbitrary
and mechanical hypostasis of the moment of hegemony, of
political direction, of consent in the life and in the development of the State and civil society' (Anderson, 1976—7,

p. 47). Croce may have sought to maintain the distinction between coercion and consent, but he does so in a way in which hegemony is simply abstracted from force.

In a passage much quoted by his commentators, Gramsci insists that the distinction between civil and political society (and hence by implication all the other 'antinomies' as well) is 'merely methodological', whereas liberals and syndicalists present it as though it was 'organic': 'in actual reality civil society and the State are one and the same' (*SPN*, p. 160). This means, says Showstack Sassoon, that actual institutions like state and church 'occupy two spaces at the same time' (1980b, p. 112) since the two moments of class supremacy are never 'completely separated'. Texier, in his reply to Bobbio, defends the distinction as 'useful and necessary' but reaffirms its methodological character as 'a practical canon of research in which it is radically impossible to separate these moments' (Texier, 1979, p. 51). For Buci-Glucksmann, the coercive function of the state is 'inseparable from a certain adaptive and educational role' (1980, p. 93) and Gramsci's view of the state 'in its integral meaning' as 'dictatorship and hegemony' (*SPN*, p. 239) assumes a combination of the ideological and the coercive. Gramsci's critique of the Crocean position is made perfectly plain. If fascists like Gentile ignore the distinction, liberals like Croce are guilty of treating the distinction as though it was 'organic' and hence separate hegemony from the 'aspect of force and economics' (Hoare and Nowell Smith, 1971, p. 207). In other words, if the two moments are to be distinguished analytically, in the real world they are to be found only in synthesis. In actual society they are 'one and the same'.

Gramsci's Modern Prince is the political party which provides 'the first cell' for the development of hegemony: it is the organization through which the collective will 'begins to take concrete form' (*SPN*, p. 129). Hence, says Gramsci, the party is 'the mechanism which carries out in civil society the same function as the State carries out, more synthetically and over a larger scale, in political society'

(*SPN*, p. 15). As the nuclear generator of hegemony, its activities are, however, by no means all 'consensual'. With the party, as with the state, coercion and consent appear to intertwine. It is difficult to deny, Gramsci comments, that all political parties carry out a certain 'policing function' and what is relevant is the question of whether this policing function is 'progressive', i.e. raises the 'backward masses to the level of the new legality', a new civilization; or whether such a policing function is 'regressive' and merely functions 'to conserve an outward, extrinsic order which is a fetter on the vital forces of history' (*SPN*, p. 155). Likewise, with the state: in as much as the state tends to create a new type of civilization, it must be conceived of as an 'educator'. The law, with its 'repressive and negative' (*SPN*, p. 247) activities, serves as the 'instrument for this purpose' (*SPN*, p. 246). It would seem, therefore, in both party and state the distinction between coercion and consent is merely a 'methodological' one since in the actual working of these institutions, both the negative and the positive, the 'ethical' and the repressive would appear to be involved.

This 'unity' between the two 'opposites' is however more problematic than it first appears. For the implication of Gramsci's analysis above is that coercion creates freedom, repression morality and violence engenders civilization in the case of a 'progressive' party and state, whose discipline, as Gramsci puts it elsewhere, involves not 'a passive and servile acceptance of orders' but 'a conscious and lucid assimilation of the directive to be fulfilled' (Showstack Sassoon, 1980b, p. 169). But what of 'regressive' political institutions which function to 'maintain a legality which has been superseded' (*SPN*, p. 155) and whose discipline is mechanical and 'bureaucratic'? Gramsci speaks of every state as 'ethical' and 'cultural' 'in as much as one of its most important functions is to raise the great mass of the population cultural and moral level' (*SPN*, p. 258), but where does this leave those parties and states which hold back 'the vital forces of history' in order to 'conserve an outward, extrinsic order' (*SPN*, p. 155)? It would seem that in the case of 'regressive' political institutions, repression is devoid of its educative qualities, violence is severed from civilization and coercion becomes an end in itself — *divorced from consent*. This argument has two consequences. Consent and morality are taken only, as it were, at 'face value', as an expression of society's real needs, even though these needs correspond 'to the interests of the ruling classes' (*SPN*, p. 258) and hence the problem of an illusory or 'metaphysical' expression of this morality or universality falls away. If consent is presented abstractly, so too is coercion. At least in regressive circumstances, it merely evokes 'a passive and servile acceptance of orders'. An abstractly conceived *brute* force counterparts a moralistically conceived 'civilization'.

Gramsci is certainly conscious of this 'organic' separation as a problem. In asserting the unity between 'spontaneity' and 'discipline', he makes the telling point that ' "pure" spontaneity does not exist in history: it would come to the same thing as "pure" mechanicity' (*SPN*, p. 196). Yet, if 'pure' spontaneity is an untenable abstraction, a free floating 'pure' consent devoid of coercive structure, how can it be correct to argue, as Gramsci does, that spontaneity must be united with 'conscious leadership' as a precondition for 'real political action' *as opposed to* 'an adventure by groups claiming to represent the masses' (*SPN*, p. 198)? Do not opportunistic 'adventurers', reactionary states and 'bureaucratic' political parties *also* unite the consensual with the coercive, the spontaneous with the structured, simply by virtue of the fact they too are political? Gramsci comments that during what is called a 'crisis of authority', a ruling class loses its consensus and exercises 'coercive force alone' (*SPN*, p. 276) and this takes us to the nub of the problem. For the implication in the argument above is that while the distinction between civil and political society, coercion and consent *should* be 'merely methodological', in fact it turns out to be 'organic'. Institutions exist and political practices occur in which consent has been separated from coercion and since force is portrayed in a purely physical form, consent, for its part, no longer has a role to play as the theological, hypocritical expression of its coercive opposite.

One of Gramsci's commentators is conscious of the fact that the relationship which Gramsci postulates between his antinomies is 'by no means simple' and that what is involved is 'a complex and reciprocal interaction dialectically conceived' (Williams, 1960, p. 587; see also, Showstack Sassoon, 1980b, p. 112; Hoare and Nowell Smith, 1971, p. 207). But if the relationship between coercion and consent is dialectical, and we will return to this problem in chapter 7, then clearly it cannot be 'mechanical' or 'organic' since, as Gramsci himself has commented, 'pure' mechanicity, like 'pure' spontaneity simply does not exist. Yet, in his fascinating notes on education, Gramsci lays stress on the importance of a 'mechanical repetition of disciplined and methodical acts': 'Would a scholar at the age of forty be able to sit for sixteen hours on end at his work-table if he had not, as a child, compulsorily, through mechanical coercion, acquired the appropriate psycho-physical habits?' (*SPN*, p. 37). But if such coercion is purely 'mechanical', how is 'great scholarship' to emerge? Gramsci places education in the context of work and a legal order which 'men' must respect 'through spontaneous assent, and not merely as an external imposition — it must be a necessity recognised and proposed to themselves as freedom, and not simply the result of coercion' (*SPN*, p. 34). The imperative mood here is all revealing, for to say that 'men' *must* assent spontaneously implies that 'pure' coercion is possible and *ought* to be avoided. The notion of 'mechanical coercion', like 'pure' spontaneity, is an untenable abstraction so that it is simply not possible to move to a higher state of 'freedom' through a 'mechanicity' which does not exist! If consent is to be linked *dialectically* to coercion, the 'ethical-political' to the moment of force, more is required than a mere amalgamation of the two. The character of each as 'an arbitrary and mechanical hypostasis' has to be tackled.

The abstract character of Croce's *idealist* conception of the 'ethical-political' is not dialectically transcended merely by placing it alongside its 'mechanical' opposite. The coexistence of two arbitrary abstractions still renders their distinction 'organic'.

LEADERSHIP VERSUS DOMINATION

In a passage in the *Prison Notebooks* in which Gramsci pays tribute to Croce for having stressed the importance of cultural and intellectual facts in historical development, he also refers to Lenin as a theoretician who has given 'new weight — in opposition to the various "economist" tendencies — to the front of cultural struggle, and constructed the doctrine of hegemony as a complement to the theory of the State-as-force' (*SPN*, p. 56). But who was responsible for this narrowly coercive view of the state which Lenin had been concerned to broaden? Gramsci probably had in mind the following: (a) those who formulated the left sectarian 'class against class' approach as expressed in Comintern policies after 1929; (b) the earlier 'theory of the offensive' developed by the Hungarian Bela Kun, defended by the Italian communist leader Bordiga and roundly condemned by the Comintern in 1921; and (c) Trotsky's theory of 'permanent revolution' which Gramsci sharply criticizes in the *Prison Notebooks* (e.g. *SPN*, pp. 236–8). This third point is of particular interest here because it helps to explain why Gramsci developed his 'organic' rather than 'methodological' view of hegemony.

One of the key 'texts', as Gramsci was well aware (Buci-Glucksmann: 1980, p. 177), for the development of Lenin's concept of hegemony was his *Two Tactics for Social Democracy* (1905). Here Lenin had argued that proletarian leadership was essential for a revolution which, in the Russian context, had *first* to be democratic *before* it could take on a socialist character (*LCW* 9, pp. 28–9). It was this notion of 'stages' rather than the concept of an 'uninterrupted revolution' which was the real bone of contention between Lenin and Trotsky (Geras, 1975, p. 6; Knei-Paz, 1978, pp. 148—9 and chapter 4 (vi) *passim*). Lenin's concept of a transitional 'dictatorship of the proletariat and the peasantry' was vigorously attacked by Trotsky as an 'idyll of quasi-Marxist asceticism', bound to collapse utterly when capitalists sabotage the 'minimum' programme and peasants oppose the social measures necessary to make it a reality (1971, pp. 330—331). Given Lenin's view that Trotsky lacked a clear conception of the transition from democracy to socialism (*LCW* 15, p. 371), it is not difficult to see why Gramsci should have regarded Trotsky as weak on hegemony and at least one of those responsible for a one-sided emphasis on politics-as-coercion (see also, *SPN*, p. 301 and Spriano, 1979, pp. 66—7). It is certainly revealing that Trotsky should have referred in 1907 to the state's monopoly of 'brute force' (1971, p. 399) for this is rather different to the concept of the state's monopoly of 'legitimate' force which Max Weber thought he had taken from Trotsky (Blackburn, 1976, p. 18). If the one is paradoxical, the other is the kind of 'organic' abstraction which Gramsci was anxious to avoid and which he believed that Lenin had opposed in his 'doctrine of hegemony as a complement to the theory of State-as-force' (*SPN*, p. 56).

Yet Gramsci's interpretation of Lenin's arguments in *Two Tactics* (which he warmly endorsed) had a theoretical consequence which was the very opposite of what was intended. In opposing those who, as Gramsci told his sister-in-law, 'usually thought of' the state in purely coercive terms (*LP*, p. 204), Gramsci was led to present a distinction which ought to have been merely methodological, in a way which was dramatically 'organic'. In what is perhaps one of the best known passages in the whole of the *Prison Notebooks*, Gramsci speaks of the 'two ways' in which the supremacy of a class manifests itself, as 'domination' (i.e. coercion) and 'intellectual and moral leadership' (i.e. consent): 'A social group can, and indeed must, already exercise "leadership" before winning governmental power (this indeed is one of the principal conditions for the winning of such power); it subsequently becomes dominant when it exercises power, but even if it holds it firmly in its grasp, it must continue to "lead" as well' (*SPN*, p. 58). Certainly this expresses a 'broad' view of political power that is securely rooted, as we have seen, in the Marxist classics, but the 'organic' separation which it implies between 'leadership' and 'domination' constitutes a sharp break with tradition. It not only contrasts with the position of Lenin (Bobbio, 1979, p. 40). In one of the translations of *The German Ideology*, we find Marx and Engels referring to the fact that 'every new class achieves hegemony only on a broader basis than that of the class ruling previously' (Arthur, 1977, p. 66) but it is clear from other translations that the term 'hegemony' here is merely a synonym for domination (*MECW* 5, p. 61). Political ideas are, of course, important for Marx and Engels but at 'the ideal expression of dominant material relations' (*MECW* 5, p. 59), i.e. an integral part of domination. Why then did Gramsci present 'leadership' and 'power' as 'organically' distinct? It appears that he based his argument on a curious misreading of Lenin.

Lenin in *Two Tactics* and elsewhere took hegemony to mean ideological leadership around the struggle for democracy and since the democratic path is a *precondition* for the victory of socialism (*LCW*, 9, p. 29), Gramsci appears to have inferred the following. Hegemony (democracy) as a condition for socialism (dictatorship of the proletariat) = leadership as a condition for domination. Anderson indeed supports this inference by arguing that Gramsci's distinction between 'leadership' and 'domination' is merely a restatement of 'the classical Russian distinction between "dictatorship" and "hegemony"... in a slightly new terminology' (1976—7, p. 21). He quotes Trotsky's comment: 'the hegemony of the proletariat in the democratic revolution was sharply distinguished from the dictatorship of the proletariat'

(1976–7, p. 17). But this is a much less 'Gramscian' distinction than Anderson supposes. Hegemony in the democratic revolution implied for Lenin 'the democratic dictatorship of the proletariat and peasantry' (*LCW* 9, p. 127) and hence the relevant contrast was not between hegemony and dictatorship but between *one kind of dictatorship and another*. The call for a 'democratic dictatorship' was designed, as Anderson himself notes, to give a 'governmental formula' to this hegemonic strategy (1976–7, p. 16). There is nothing in Lenin's *Two Tactics* to suggest that in the struggle for this 'democratic dictatorship' the exercise of leadership is a 'separate' factor which must *precede* the winning of power. On the contrary: a 'proletarian imprint' on events, Lenin writes, will only be secure when the revolution is carried to a 'real and decisive victory' (*LCW* 9, p. 18; p. 53). Leadership is intrinsic to the struggle for power and can only said to have been 'won' or decisively 'exercised' when the revolution succeeds and a new form of the state (i.e. dictatorship) is secured.

Gramsci's celebrated 'cleavage' leaves us with a puzzle. If exercising leadership is a process 'organically' distinct from that of winning power, are we to assume from this that political struggle only becomes *coercive* at the point when state power is won? Given the fact that Gramsci resisted what Femia calls 'a parliamentary road' to power and accepted the necessity for violent opposition to the capitalist order (1981, p. 205), the passage contrasting leadership with domination should, as Anderson suggests (1976–7, p. 45), be interpreted to mean that both coercion *and* consent are involved in political struggle in all its phases. When Gramsci writes that 'a social group dominates antagonistic groups, which it tends to "liquidate" ' while it 'leads kindred and allied groups' (*SPN*, p. 57), this simply distinguishes between the 'consensual direction' of friends and the necessity to coerce enemies (*SPN*, p. 168).

If this interpretation frees Gramsci's thesis from imputations of 'reformism' (Hoare and Nowell Smith, 1971, p. 207) and brings 'leadership' and 'domination' rather closer together, the basic problem still remains. If enemies are coerced while allies consent, then the two aspects are still not analysed in a way which *fuses* them into a single political process but continue to have 'organically' separate identities. We can certainly take Anderson's point that the concept of 'leadership' has a 'consensual tenor' (1976–7, p. 44) in so far as the proletariat is striving to win support for its cause, but can we conclude from this that the formation of alliances in class struggle is an activity *free from coercion*? For Lenin, the proletariat's alliance with the peasantry (many of whom are petty bourgeois in character) turns on fraternal relationships with a potential adversary. A temporary 'singleness of will' also requires 'the duty of keeping a strict watch "over our ally, as over an enemy"' (*LCW* 9, p. 85). Hence it would seem that if ideological leadership is brought to the fore, domination is never very far below the surface.

It is true that in this work I have generally used 'politics' and 'state' interchangeably and I shall continue to do so for reasons which I will expand at the end. It is however worth noting at this juncture that *political* coercion is a process which extends beyond *state* coercion since it embraces the activities of those striving to *win* and not merely sustain state power. Winning state power, therefore, consummates the wider struggles of pressure groups, parties and movements and denotes the *successful* exercise of that 'general, socially coercive force' which Marx considered essential to politics (see also, Burlatsky, 1978, p. 50; Miliband, 1969, p. 1). The party in its struggle to seize power exercises political coercion in embryonic form. For Lenin, this coercion is not only expressed in strikes and armed struggle against a class enemy: it is also implied in relations with allies and extends into disputes within the party itself. *What is to be Done?* pledges to fight those even within the socialist movement ('revisionists', 'economists', etc.) who unwittingly facilitate 'the ideological enslavement of the workers by the bourgeoisie' (*LCW* 5, p. 384). Ideologies not merely 'lead', they also 'dominate' and where they retard the growth of the movement (*LCW* 5, p. 386), they must be fought. There is an unmistakeably coercive edge to the ideological struggles waged by Lenin's Bolsheviks against those guilty of 'disruptive boycotts' (*LCW* 8, p. 126), those who refuse to submit to the majority decision of the Party congress and whose lack of loyalty leads to 'discord, vacillation and strife' (*LCW* 8, p. 438).

But what of the 'compact group' of vanguard fighters who are imbued with a conception of 'party honour' (*LCW* 5, p. 367) and who have combined 'by a freely adopted decision' for the purpose of fighting every kind of ideological misdemeanour (*LCW* 5, p. 355)? Here, at least, it might be thought that we encounter consent *without* coercion, leadership with no domination. Yet essential even to the party member is the 'universal and unreserved recognition' of party *discipline* (*LCW* 8, p. 438) and this discipline demands the acceptance of a collective coercion which circumscribes individual consent. Lenin's writing on the party abounds with military analogies as when he argues that each member of the factory committee (of the party) is 'obliged to submit to all its orders and to observe all the "laws and customs" of the "army in the field" which he has joined and from which in time of war he has no right to absent himself without official leave' (*LCW* 6, p. 244). Though it is certainly arguable that Lenin's emphasis on the importance of a factory 'schooling' (*LCW* 8, pp. 391–2) echoes the sentiments of Marx (*MECW* 4, p. 37), this conception of party discipline proved to be highly controversial at the 1903 Congress of the RSDLP and it is revealing that Trotsky, in fiercely opposing Lenin's views, counterparted his own abstract view of coercion with a 'spontaneist' view of consent (Knei-Paz, 1978, pp. 190–1).

For Lenin, therefore, there is a fusion of leadership and domination not only in the wider political processes, but within the party itself. But what of Gramsci? Gramsci may, in the passage commented upon earlier, have spoken of the

domination of enemies and leadership of friends (*SPN*,
p. 57), but his own analysis of relationships in the party
is by no means free of an implied coercion. Gramsci vigorously
distinguishes between the leadership as 'the principal cohesive
element' and a mass element 'composed of ordinary, average
men, whose participation takes the form of discipline and
loyalty, rather than any creative spirit of organisational
ability' (*SPN*, p. 152). This clearly differs from Lenin's
conception of a party of professional revolutionaries, but it
differs only because *within* the party, Gramsci makes an
'organic' distinction between the party 'generals' with their
'cohesive, centralising and disciplinary powers' and the
party rank and file who are only 'a force in so far as there is
somebody to centralise, organise and discipline them' (*SPN*,
p. 152). For Lenin, on the other hand, the consenters and
the coercers change places since he emphasizes the need to
'*decentralise responsibility to the Party* on the part of its
individual members, of every participant in its work'. This
decentralization, he adds, is 'an essential prerequisite of
revolutionary centralisation and an *essential corrective
to it*' (*LCW* 6, p. 249). Although Gramsci sees a role for
coercion even inside the party, the relationship he postulates
between leadership and mass seems mechanical and abstract
and appears to allow for no mechanism through which the
'educators' are to be 'educated'. The masses are a pure
passivity who, in the absence of a 'cohesive force' from
above, would 'scatter into an impotent diaspora and vanish
into nothing' (*SPN*, p. 152). It has to be said that in this
'organic' juxtaposition of two abstract conceptions, the
'cohesive force' of an active coercion and the passive consent
of an 'impotent diaspora', there is a curious, if somewhat
inverted, echo of the positions of Trotsky. Gramsci's attempt
to 'complement' a narrow view of the state through an
analysis of leadership *and* domination led him to make
repeatedly, at every level of his theory, just that 'organic'
distinction between civil and political society, consent and
coercion which he had been so anxious to avoid.

Even when he comes closest to a view of the party as 'self-discipline', his analysis betrays the Crocean influence of an 'ethical-political' moment mechanistically spliced apart from the 'moment of force'. He speaks, for example (*SPN*, p. 267), of the state representing 'the coercive and punitive force of juridical regulation' to which the 'elite' of the parties spontaneously adhere. In 'their specific internal life', the party elite 'have assimilated as principles of moral conduct those rules which in the State are legal obligations': in the parties 'necessity has already become freedom' (*SPN*, p. 267). But this suggests a 'leap' from one to the other and not a *process* in which necessity and freedom, coercion and consent are involved together throughout. (For a similar point about the 'educative and formative role of the State', see *SPN*, p. 242.) Even in Gramsci's more apparently 'dialectical' passages where the two moments seem almost to fuse, a distinction intended to be merely 'methodological', collapses into one which is 'organic' and a practical, empirical separation is clearly implied. However hard Gramsci may have sought to transcend it, the Crocean spectre remains.

We conclude therefore that Gramsci's analysis of intellectual and moral leadership as a precondition for the exercise of power highlights a problem which dogs the *Prison Notebooks* throughout. In another of the 'celebrated' passages Gramsci refers to the state as the entire complex of activities with which the 'ruling class not only justifies and maintains dominance', but manages to win 'active consent' (*SPN*, p. 244). Again the implication is clear: if in addition to *justifying* domination (a process which already suggests consent), a ruling class wins active support, this can only point to an 'organic' distinction between the antinomies. At times Gramsci's own language reveals the untenability of the mechanical divide which he tried to avoid but which he continued to imply. In his notes on 'intellectuals' Gramsci speaks of the coercive power of the state as necessary for those who do not 'spontaneously' consent to 'the general direction imposed on social life by the dominant fundamental group' (*SPN*, p. 12) and yet it is this very 'imposition' which coercively structures the apparently 'spontaneous' consent which Gramsci separates from the discipline of the state. In other words, if people consent to a direction 'imposed on social life', the coercion does not need to be brought in from 'the outside': it is already *there*. For what else does the word 'imposition' mean?

Gramsci's *attempt* to transcend the arbitrary and mechanical hypostases, the metaphysical abstractions of Crocean liberalism, clearly accords with the spirit of classical Marxism and indeed, in so far as he seeks to tackle the problem of coercion and consent analytically, as two discrete levels, his work represents a potential advance. Yet, his attempt, for all its pioneering significance, *fails*. Where the classics present synthesis without analysis, Gramsci offers analysis without synthesis and so the challenge of the Machiavellian Centaur, how to unite synthetically the analytically separate, still remains. If the state appears to be a paradoxical unity of contradictory opposites, how do we account for its mystified character?

4

THE POLITICAL ECONOMY OF COERCION AND CONSENT

POLITICS AND THE IDENTITY PROBLEM IN MARX AND GRAMSCI

I have argued so far that for classical Marxism, politics stands as a *special* kind of coercion — a coercion able to commend consent. Yet when this paradox is analysed, the synthesis of the 'two levels' simply falls apart and we are left with the irreconcilable 'antitheses' which have plagued liberal political theory for so long. I now want to argue that the reason for this impasse arises from the fact that although the question of coercion and consent is a political problem, it is a political problem which cannot be resolved in purely political terms. Since the paradoxical coercion of the state is rooted in a realm *beyond* the world of politics, it is to these wider class relationships in economy and society that our attention must turn. For Marx, as we shall see in a moment, economic relationships, no less than political relationships, bristle with the presence of coercion and consent.

The question central to this chapter is this, If Marx confronts the problem of coercion in his economic analysis, what relationship does this have to that special coercion we have already identified with the state? This is a matter of great importance for until we can clarify the relationship between politics and the economy, state and civil society, we cannot hope to clarify the relationship between coercion and consent. We have already noted that the thorny question of Marx's 'instrumentalism' can only be tackled in terms of the state as a special instrument of coercion; now we shall see that this specialized instrumentality can itself only be properly understood if we also focus in some depth on another of the errant isms of the classical tradition — the equally unwholesome spectre of a 'reductionism' which apparently treats politics in purely 'epiphenomenal' terms.

The notion that the question of coercion extends beyond politics and the state is not peculiar to Marxism. Central to J.S. Mill's classic *On Liberty* is the existence of 'the moral coercion of public opinion', a 'spiritual domination' (1974, p. 68; p. 73) which 'pacifies' as a result of pressures which are social rather than legal in character. It is hardly surprising therefore, that for Marx, coercion is a central attribute of a class-divided society, that alienated world in which humanity is *dominated* by the forces of its own creation. In the *Manuscripts* of 1844, Marx speaks of human activity as an activity 'under the dominion, the coercion, the yoke of another man' (*MECW* 3, p. 279): a labour which is 'not voluntary, but coerced' (*MECW* 3, p. 274). The capitalist, Marx comments in 1845, may feel at ease and 'self satisfied' in his 'self-estrangement' (*MECW* 4, p. 36) but like the worker, he too is in the grip of forces which enslave him. The very division of society into classes assigns each individual 'a particular, exclusive sphere of activity, which is forced upon him and from which he cannot escape' (*MECW* 5, p. 47). Coercion makes itself felt at every level in class society.

Nor is this argument simply a feature of Marx's early writings. In the *Communist Manifesto*, Marx and Engels speak of workers not only as 'slaves' of the bourgeois class and bourgeois state, but as men and women 'daily and hourly enslaved by the machine, by the overlooker, and above all, by the individual bourgeois manufacturer himself' (*MECW* 6, p. 491). In *Capital*, Marx speaks of the factory code formulated by the capitalist 'like a private legislator' whose autocracy is 'unaccompanied by that division of responsibility, in other matters so much approved of by the bourgeoisie and unaccompanied by the still more approved representative system' (*C* I, p. 424). But if, as Marx says in a colourful passage, the modern capitalist has inherited the power of Asiatic and Egyptian kings, Etruscan theocrats and other autocrats of old, does this not suggest that Marx's *economic* analysis is one which is 'political through and through' (Tucker, 1973, p. 146)? Ellen Meiksins Wood has argued that as a critique of *political* economy, *Capital* should be read as a treatise which reveals the political dimension of the economy that bourgeois economic theory obscures. The relations of production are also relations of politics and law so that the ultimate secret of capitalist production is itself a political one (1981, pp. 67—8). Of course the immense power wielded by the capitalist does not, in Marx's eyes, make him a wholly free agent. Like all the members of a class-divided society, the capitalist, as Marx stressed in his early writings, is 'subsumed' under relations of production which 'stand over him'. The laws of motion, immanent in capitalist production, 'assert themselves as coercive laws of competition' and are brought home to the individual capitalist 'as the directing motives of his operations' (*C* I, p. 316). Even the independent commodity producers 'who acknowledge no other authority but that of competition' (and who are not as yet masters of capital), still suffer 'the coercion exerted by the pressure of their mutual interests' (*C* I, p. 356).

We have thus a problem. Marx's analysis of capitalism is also an analysis of power, domination, repression and alienation. It would seem therefore, that for Marx, the economy is itself a polity, a political system in its own right: in Tucker's words, 'the prime field of power relations between man and man' (1973, p. 149). But if this is so, in what sense can it be said that coercion is a particular property of the *state*? In other words, if coercion appears to be a universal aspect of class-divided societies, how can we distinguish *political* relationships from social relations in general? This is not only a problem for Marx. It creates considerable difficulties for contemporary political science (Dahl, 1976, p. 4) and, as we shall see later, it constitutes a major problem for Antonio Gramsci.

We have already noted Gramsci's comment in the *Prison Notebooks* that 'in actual reality civil society and the State are one and the same' (*SPN*, p. 160): the distinction between them can only be 'methodological' in character. This remark was intended to underline the fact that just as hegemony cannot be divorced from the moment of force, so it cannot be divorced from the 'moment' of economics either (Hoare and Nowell Smith, 1971, p. 207). If 'in actual reality', the coercive and the consensual must interpenetrate, so too must there be unity between base and superstructure (Texier, 1979, p. 49). Hegemony is ethical-political but, writes Gramsci, 'it must also be economic, must necessarily be based on the decisive function exercised by the leading group in the decisive nucleus of economic activity' (*SPN*, p. 161). Hegemony is a necessary form of the 'concrete historical bloc' (*SPN*, p. 56) which in turn stands as 'the complex, contradictory and discordant *ensemble* of the superstructures' as they reflect 'the *ensemble* of the social relations of production' (*SPN*, p. 366). For Gramsci, as for Marx, hegemony is rooted in material reality.

The critique of Croce makes this point clear. Croce's 'arbitrary and mechanical hypostasis of the moment of hegemony' arises not merely because he underplays the role of force in historical conflict, but because he fails to grasp the real meaning of historical materialism. Polemically contrasting the 'structure' as a 'hidden god' and its superstructural 'appearances', Croce misses the *unity* between the two (*SPN*, p. 138; *LP*, p. 189) and thus the fact (and here Gramsci refers to Marx's preface to his *Critique of Political Economy*) that ideological struggle is the consciousness of a conflict rooted in the social relations of production

(*SPN*, p. 138). The Crocean view of politics as mere selfish passion makes it impossible to understand the character of politics as an 'impulse to action' which 'is born on the "permanent and organic" terrain of economic life' (*SPN*, p. 140). Hegemony arises through, as Gramsci puts it, the 'passage from the structure to the sphere of complex superstructures' (*SPN*, p. 181) and the 'organic' intellectual has the role of providing an overall awareness to a 'social group, coming into existence on the original terrain of an essential function in the world of economic production' (*SPN*, p. 5). Even the entrepreneur in industry exercises hegemony as an organizer of workers, the 'confidence' of his investors, customers for his business, etc. (*SPN*, p. 5).

Gramsci followed with particular interest the experiments by Ford in the USA to rationalize production and labour by a skillful 'combination of force (destruction of working-class trade unionism on a territorial basis) and persuasion (high wages, various social benefits, extremely subtle ideological and political propaganda)' (*SPN*, p. 285). Here, said Gramsci, hegemony is born in the factory and requires for its exercise 'only a minute quantity of professional political and ideological intermediaries'. It is true that Gramsci regarded 'Fordism' as a temporary phenomenon linked to a monopoly of new methods and he considered that once these techniques became more widely diffused, high wages, along with 'enormous profits' (*SPN*, pp. 310–11), would probably disappear. But it does not follow from this, as Femia argues, that because 'Fordism' as a mechanism for winning consent was 'geographically and historically doomed', hegemony, for Gramsci, 'could have no firm or lasting basis in the economic structure of capitalism' (1981, p. 31). On the contrary: hegemony, for Gramsci, is expressed through the organs of a 'civil society' which incorporates the 'economic structure of capitalism' and in the passage in which Gramsci 'identifies' civil society and the state, it is not the assertion that 'economic activity belongs to civil society', which he challenges, but the *non sequitur* that 'the State must not intervene to regulate it' (*SPN*, p. 160). Gramsci's view of hegemony 'born in the factory' is of much more general import than Femia would allow (Showstack Sassoon, 1980b, p. 76; Buci-Glucksmann, 1980, p. 89).

All this, however, brings us face to face with an interesting and important problem. Both in Marx, where coercion and consent are synthesized, and in Gramsci, where the two levels are (however problematically) analysed, the question extends beyond politics into the economic realm. Both Marx and Gramsci therefore, confront us with a similar difficulty. For if politics and economics are the 'same', involving a unified expression of coercion and consent, then in what sense can it be said that one is 'basic' and the other 'super-structural'? We have already noted the argument by Gramsci commentators in chapter 1, that his 'broad' view of politics, in unifying base and superstructure (Buci-Glucksmann, 1982, p. 120), transcends the historical materialist 'metaphor' altogether (Showstack Sassoon, 1980a, p. 85). Those who regard this 'Copernican revolution' as a trifle premature and wish to retain the classical Marxist distinction, must never-theless face up to the problem: how is it to be done? How is it possible to avoid either 'reducing' politics to economics or, by extending the scope of the politics to social relationships in general, obliterating its distinctive identity altogether? A closer look is required into just what coercion and consent in the economic realm, hegemony in the factory, actually involves.

COERCION, CONSENT AND THE METAPHYSICS OF THE COMMODITY

For Marx, coercion in the economy is intrinsically linked to 'alienated' labour — labour which is not voluntary but coerced — and the most striking quality of this alienated labour is its *fetishistic* character (Colletti, 1975, p. 37).

A fetishism which mystifies reality since the coercion suffered by the alienated labourer appears, on the face of it, not to be coercion at all. The roots of this paradox lie with the commodity. What workers are obliged to sell, Marx argues, is their labour power, and to understand this particular commodity, it is necessary to understand something about commodities in general. Since we shall say a good deal about the philosophical implications of this analysis in the next chapter, here we will be brief and note only the following. Commodities can only exchange as products of labour when the individual private labour of 'free individuals' has been reduced 'to the standard of homogenous human labour' (*C* I, p. 79) and this process of *abstraction*, essential to equate otherwise different entities, is as real as 'the resolution of all organic bodies into air' (*CCPE*, p. 77). It is the source of the celebrated fetishism of the commodity as a result of which, relations between people in production appear as the relationship between inanimate things. The social dependencies, which are transparent in earlier societies (*C* I, p. 77) now take the form of an equalized exchange between atomized, abstract individuals. Even before Marx introduces the exploited proletarian into his analysis, he has identified a commodity producing (civil) society as one in which the labour time socially necessary for production 'forcibly asserts itself like an overriding law of nature' so that the producers are 'ruled' by their own alienated acts of production (*C* I, p. 75). This coercion is however mystified because, as Marx puts it, the commodity abounds 'in metaphysical subleties and theological niceties': dependence is presented as 'autonomy' since property owners with very different amounts of wealth relate to one another through equalised acts of exchange (*C* I, p. 71). Money as the 'universal commodity' (*C* I, p. 89) compounds these illusions while the exploited labourer, mundane in his misery, endows his employer with the divine quality of being able apparently to conjure up profits out of thin air! The labour power which the worker sells to the capitalist, has the unique (and supremely theological) characteristic of being a source of 'more value than it has itself' (*C* I, p. 193) since the wages a worker receives are necessarily less than the value of his product. The sale of labour power is only possible because the worker is the 'untrammelled owner of his capacity for labour' so that exploiter and exploited have to deal with one another 'on the basis of equal rights'. One is a buyer, the other a seller, but both are equal 'in the eyes of the law' (*C* I, p. 168).

If, as noted above, Marx and Engels's political writings treat the question of coercion and consent only in synthetic terms, here the two halves of the Machiavellian Centaur are subject to acute *analysis*. For now Marx explicitly identifies the act of free consent as essential if commodities are to exchange through the 'coercion of mutual interests' (*C* I, p. 356): interests which the two parties have in *common*. The sale and purchase of labour power, like the sale and purchase of all commodities, is 'a very Eden of the natural rights of man' (*C* I, p. 176) and out of the contract there emerges that illusory element of *generality* we have already encountered in Marx's characterization of the state. The agreement which the contractual partners reach is 'but the form in which they give legal expression to their common will' and hence out of particularistic self-interest, there arises a 'transcendental' community. Each looks only to himself; no one troubles about all the rest and everything works to 'their mutual advantage, for the common weal and in the interest of all' (*C* I, p. 176). We can begin to see why that fusion of coercion and consent which seemed so absurd previously, is amenable to a more rational explanation, for now at least we can see that it has something to do with the 'metaphysical subleties and theological niceties' of the commodity and is an absurdity born of reality itself (*C* I, p. 73; p. 76; Geras, 1971, p. 76). Marx's worker can only be exploited as an 'emancipated slave' and of course, he has to be *legally* free in the sense that 'as a free man he can dispose of his labour power as his own commodity' and *materially* free in the sense that 'he has no other commodity for sale, is short of everything necessary for the realisation of his labour power' (*C* I, p. 176). This second kind of freedom is a condition for the first and, as we shall see, provides the key to an understanding of the peculiar character of the coercion from which he suffers. The producer will only agree, as Marx puts it, to sell his birthright 'for a mess of pottage' (*C* I, p. 271) when he has been divorced from the means of production as a propertyless proletarian. Hence the free labourer is the product of centuries of expropriation, 'written in the annals of mankind in letters of blood and fire' (*C* I, p. 715) and it is only when this process of 'primitive accumulation' has been completed, that coercion can appear as consent.

We have already noted that it is not only in Marx that we find an analysis of coercion within the economy: it is also in Gramsci. How do their respective treatments of the question compare? For Gramsci, the 'principle of coercion, direct or indirect' is involved 'in the ordering of production' (*SPN*, p. 301) since coercion seems essential if the working masses are to be made to 'conform to the needs of the new industry' (*SPN*, p. 306). At the same time, adaption to the new methods of production and work 'cannot take place simply through social compulsion'. This is a prejudice which has arisen, Gramsci comments, because of the endemic unemployment in the period following the First World War. In any 'normal' situation, if the apparatus of coercion is to obtain the desired result, high wages (which are a 'transitory form of remuneration' anyway) are not enough. Coercion has to be 'ingeniously combined with persuasion and consent' (*SPN*, p. 310). Even under fascism, as Gramsci had observed earlier, the capitalists cannot want all forms of organization destroyed. In the factory, 'discipline and the smooth flow of production is only possible if there exists at least a minimum degree of constitutionality, a minimum degree of consent on the part of the workers' (*SPW* II, p. 167). Remuneration is certainly a factor since, in Gramsci's words, 'coercion is combined with consent in the forms specific to this society: money' (Buci-Glucksmann, 1980, p. 319). But other factors must also be involved if a new way of life and new habits are to be adopted. In the case of the USA, Gramsci notes the stress placed on monogamy (so that sexual activity is routinized), puritanical drives (reinforced by the state) to eliminate alcoholism and the general concern about workers' 'morality' (*SPN*, pp. 302–5).

Yet, as fascinating as these comments are, it is not difficult to see that they tackle the problem of coercion and consent in the process of production in quite a different way to the one developed by Marx in *Capital*. For Marx, central to this problem is the 'abstract' labour embodied in the commodity and the source of all its theological niceties, as a result of which, coercion can appear as consent. One is but a mechanism for the other and the distinction between them 'methodological'. For Gramsci, on the other hand, it is clearly 'organic' since, in his analysis, consensual devices *supplement* the use of force: they are not intrinsic to it. It is true that, at one point in the *Prison Notebooks*, Gramsci argues that the development of a new civilization requires a process of coercion to be exercised 'over the whole area of society', with puritan ideologies functioning as 'an external form of persuasion and consent to the intrinsic use of force' (*SPN*, p. 299), but still the relationship between the two seems to be extrinsic, not inherent. Once this new society has been established, this linkage between coercion and consent dissolves, for now, writes Gramsci, the masses have 'either acquired the habits and customs necessary for the new systems of living and working, *or else* they continue to be subject to coercive pressure through the elementary necessities of their existence' (*SPN*, p. 299, stress mine). The dichotomy is all revealing: either the masses consent or they are coerced. For Marx, the opposite holds. Workers consent when they are coerced and because they are coerced. Gramsci, under the influence of Croce, takes consent at face value and hence, inevitably, the 'two levels' stand apart. Marx takes consent in the context of a commodity fetishism whose theological niceties and metaphysical subleties make it possible for the 'coercion of mutual interests' to appear as the mutual consent of contracting partners. What Gramsci overlooks is the nature of capitalism as 'the very Eden of the natural rights of man' and by missing the material roots of these liberal abstractions, he fails to see how the 'arbitrary and mechanical hypostasis of the moment of hegemony' is itself a product of the coercive realities of commodity production.

THE STATE AS THE CONCENTRATED FORCE OF SOCIETY

If, in *Capital*, coercion can be expressed as consent, how is this fetishism to be rationally explained? The answer is now clear. Once the capitalist mode of production is established and the necessity for a 'primitive' expropriation of the producers from the land comes to an end, coercion ceases to be explicitly political and takes on a largely *social* form. Whereas previously the exploited had been compelled to work by law, now the worker, as Marx puts it, 'is compelled by social conditions' (*C* I, p. 271): 'The advance of capitalist production develops a working class which by education, tradition, habit, looks upon the conditions of that mode of production as self-evident laws of Nature. The organisation of the capitalist process of production, once fully developed, breaks down all resistance . . . the dull compulsion of economic relations completes the subjection of the labourer to the capitalist' (*C* I, p. 737). This compulsion is 'dull' because it is implicit; it is unintended and it springs from the conditions of production themselves. Of course, Marx adds, 'direct force, outside economic conditions' is still used, 'but only exceptionally' (*C* I, p. 737). This passage is clearly crucial for it enables us to identify the particular characteristics of the coercion involved in the exchange process. However quasi-political the language Marx may use to describe it, this is a social and economic coercion: it is not, strictly speaking, a *political* coercion at all. On the contrary, the replacement of the kind of 'direct force' inherent in the initial creation of a proletariat, by 'dull compulsion' signals the divorce of the economic from the political. We can now understand why, even for the Marx of 1843, the state appears as 'the *religion* of national life, the heaven of its generality over and against the *earthly existence* of its actuality' (*MECW* 3, p. 31); a state abstracted from society, leaving the 'private spheres' an 'independent existence' (*MECW* 3, p. 32).

With the development of the capitalist mode of production, property, as Marx puts it in the third volume of *Capital*, receives its purely economic form 'by discarding all its former political and social embellishments and associations' (*C* III, p. 618). The coercion involved in the independent 'private spheres' is, therefore, an *economic* coercion and all the more flexible and productive as a result. In the *Grundrisse*, Marx quotes the Methodist clergyman, Joseph Townsend: 'Legal constraint to labour is attended with too much trouble, violence, and noise, creates ill will etc., whereas hunger is not only a peaceable, silent, unremitted pressure, but, as the most natural motive to industry and labour, it calls forth the most powerful exertions' (*G*, p. 845). What makes the 'dull compulsion of economic relations' effective as a means of discipline is that it appears to accord with 'natural law', personal merit and individual responsibility. If Marx at one point in *Capital* describes force as 'an economic power' (*C* I, p. 751), then, as Maguire rightly argues, this comment needs to be understood in the light of a sharp distinction between the coercive character of 'purely economic causes' and the kind of force employed in the genesis of capitalism when a nascent working class was subject to the full rigours of state coercion. Once the economic acquires its autonomy from the political, the direct producer 'is driven rather by force of circumstances than by direct coercion' to provide a surplus 'on his own responsibility' (*C* III, pp. 794–5; Maguire, 1976, p. 326).

We are now in a position to see what the relationship is between Marx's two kinds of coercion, the political and the economic. If capitalist exploitation as a 'hypocritical servitude' perfects slavery through the exercise of a coercion which is implicit and indirect, what has happened to that 'direct force' which had such a prominent role during the 'pre-history' of primitive accumulation? It has become, says Marx, 'concentrated' in the form of the state (*G*, p. 108; Callinicos, 1982, p. 215; Blackburn, 1976, p. 24). The 'religion of national life', the state stands revealed under capitalism as 'the concentrated and organised force of society' (*C* I, p. 751). We have already noted the significance of the state as coercion which is 'organized' — a force generalized in its application, seemingly embodying the interests of society as a whole. Now we can see why it is important to understand also that political coercion is a coercion which is 'concentrated' — a force 'withdrawn', in its overt, direct form, from the economic realm of society and incorporated in those instruments of coercion which are the monopoly of the state. This process of 'concentration' has two aspects: (a) it renders *explicit* the force which is merely implicit in civil society by monopolizing it as the state's particular and separate responsibility, and (b) it encapsulates in *intensified* form the illusory quality of the coercion which commands consent, an illusion inherent in the theological niceties and metaphysical subleties of the exchange process. In other words, the process of concentration makes it possible to understand what *unites* politics and economics without at the same time overlooking their differences. Clearly there is a link between political coercion and that miniaturized expression of it in the 'general will' which emerges from the particular interests mutually recognized in the contract. This link was clearly recognized by the classic theorists of the 'social contract' and it is a link specifically alluded to by Marx.

On the other hand, the difference between the two

coercions is not merely one of degree; it is a difference in *kind* for the spontaneously generated 'universal wills' of the exchange process cannot by themselves (even when lumped together as the 'will of all') serve the 'common interests' of a class and (in its illusory sense), the 'general interests' of society as a whole. For this to occur, a qualitatively different kind of 'universality' is required. The materialistic 'abstractions' of commodity production must be concentrated in the spiritualistic 'generalities' of the state with its rational-legal system, its constitution and its universal declarations of human rights. The representative state, Marx writes, is 'a very specific product of modern bourgeois society which is as inseparable from the latter as is the isolated individual of modern times' (*MECW* 5, p. 200) but this very *specificity* of the state as a product of bourgeois society, can only be grasped when due emphasis is given to the concentrated way in which it expresses the rights and interests of this 'isolated individual'. Political fetishism, in a word Poulantzas much favours, *condenses* economic fetishism (1978, p. 27), because commodity production, particularly when it develops into capitalism, requires the stabilizing framework of a state: the Common Power of a Commonwealth, as Hobbes says, to keep men in awe and 'direct their actions to the Common Benefit' (1968, p. 227) through an apparatus of direct force, sufficient to underpin and sustain the dull compulsion of economic relations. The process of concentration makes coercion explicit and ensures that the theological niceties of the exchange process apply to society as a whole.

It is true that in the 'purest' commodity producing society where class antagonisms are relatively undeveloped, the existence of a 'public' force may, as Engels has noted, be 'very insignificant, practically negligible' (*OFPPS*, p. 230), but as Locke vividly indicated, this 'natural' world, the celebrated 'state of nature' in classical liberal theory, still has its own compulsions. A 'law of nature' governs it which, as Locke says, 'obliges everyone' (1924, p. 119) and gives everyone the right to punish the transgressors of this law (1924, p. 120). With the healthy development of commodity relations to the point that money can be introduced and servants taken for granted (1924, p. 130), 'the consent of men have agreed to a disproportionate and unequal possession of the earth', even 'out of the bounds of society and the compact' (1924, p. 140). What makes the state necessary as a coercion sufficiently concentrated so as to reinforce the dull compulsion of 'natural laws', is the 'partiality and violence of men', the 'inconveniences of the state of Nature which must certainly be great when men may be judges in their own case' (1924, p. 123) and all this is doubtlessly aggravated by the 'great distress' and 'universal ferment' which 'a disproportionate and unequal possession of the earth' is likely to cause (Macpherson, 1962, p. 233). If, as Marx notes, the use of this direct force is 'exceptional', . it is the 'political' exception which proves the economic rule: without it, Locke's theological laws of nature might cease effectively to 'oblige'. Miliband speaks of the dull compulsion of capitalist production as an aspect of the legitimation process which is of 'crucial importance, since it underlies all others' (1969, p. 261). But here it is essential to be clear. This dull compulsion is an economic coercion which only becomes political when it is regularized, generalized, concentrated and rendered explicit. Only thus does it become the *special* coercion of the state.

THE PROBLEM OF PARTICULARITY IN AN AUTONOMOUS POLITICAL SCIENCE

We are now in a position to pull some of the threads together in our assessment of the problem of coercion and consent in Marx and Gramsci. Inevitably this means a return to the errant isms of the classical tradition, for just as the 'special' nature of the state's coercion is overlooked in much of the literature on 'instrumentalism', so its 'concentrated' character is neglected in much of the Western Marxist critique of 'reductionism'. We can now see why the problems raised by the first 'ism' can only be fully resolved when we expose the fallacies of the second, a point which can be illustrated by a brief encounter with the massive 'post-Althusserian' onslaught mounted against classical Marxism in the 1970s by Hindess, Hirst and their like-minded colleagues (see, e.g. Hirst, 1977; Hindess, 1977, 1980; Cutler, Hindess, Hirst, Hussain, 1977). For Hindess, Hirst et al. (hereafter HH), Marx's theory of politics is so fatally flawed by a crippling instrumentalism and reductionism that even the Althusserian revolution is powerless to cure its paralysis. All attempts to reformulate the 'expressive totalities' of Marx the humanist into 'structuralist' totalities of a 'scientific' Marx flounder since any lingering residue of the state's 'superstructural' character or 'instrumental' role damns the entire enterprise as 'economistic'. Either politics is autonomous or it is 'determined': it simply cannot be both: 'The thesis of the irreducibility of politics and ideology entailed in the notions of "determination in the last instance" and "relative autonomy" cannot be sustained. It leads either to irreducibility or economism in disguise or else a denial of the primacy of the economy' (Cutler, Hindess, et al., 1977, p. 172). Hirst lays down a similar gauntlet elsewhere. Either 'economism, or the non-correspondence of political forces and economic classes — this is the choice which faces Marxism' (Hirst, 1977, p. 131).

This is not the place to examine the controversy in depth or explore the substantial literature which it has generated (for an excellent critique, see Harris, 1979), but suffice it to say that the entire HH thesis arises precisely because the problem of particularity in politics is not successfully engaged. We are told that at the heart of the errant isms of classical Marxism lies the absence of any coherent theory of linkage between the political and the economic, for what HH ask, are 'the mechanisms that articulate the political-legal and cultural (i.e. ideological) representation of classes

and class interests on to the economic classes represented?'
(Cutler, Hindess et al., 1977, p. 184; Hirst, 1977, p. 130).
In fact, the 'mechanism' which links politics and economics
is precisely the process of 'organization' and 'concentration'
noted above. Economic relations already involve a curious
kind of coercion, a coercion which commands consent and
politics concentrates and condenses, organizes and univer-
salizes this 'hypocritical servitude' so that individual,
particularistic class interests can be 're-presented' in the
generalized form of an illusory community. In this way, we
can dissolve the dilemma that either politics is 'autonomous'
or it is illicitly 'reducible' as an economic derivative.

The truth is that it is both. Politics *is* derivative because,
as a superstructure, it concentrates the relationships of
society; equally, it *is* 'irreducible' and 'autonomous' because
as a 'concentrate' of society it organizes coercion in a way
which only the state as a 'committee' acting on behalf of a
class, in the name of society, can accomplish. Moreover,
politics must display both attributes because each is
necessary for the existence of the other. The concentrated
nature of state coercion and its special character as an
instrument of class rule can only arise because: (a) politics
has its roots in the coercion of a class-divided society; and
(b) it is tied to those particularistic interests which it seeks
to 'generalize'. Its 'irreducibility' and its derivative nature
go hand in hand, each making the other possible. Unless
Marx assumed the '*general* dependence' of the state upon
economic conditions, then how, as Engels recalls, could he
have dealt almost exclusively with the particular part played
by political struggles and events in the *Eighteenth Brumaire*
(*SC*, p. 402)? The whole analysis of Bonapartism turns, as
we have seen, on a understanding of the state|as a special
instrument of coercion which generalizes the implicit
coercion of economic relationships. Hirst argues that the specificity of 'conjunctural' analyses dissolves into reductionism
and economism when the identity of politics is formulated
in more general terms (1977, p. 126) but this only appears

so if those particular features which make it possible for us to identify the state, its concentrated nature, its organization as an illusory community, are not taken into account. These specifying attributes provide just that coherence to the classical Marxist theory of politics which HH believe cannot be found.

The problem of particularity is, however, not only one which baffles the Althusserians and their epigones. It also plagues many of their critics like those of the 'Capital Logic' school who argue that the emphasis on the autonomy of politics ought to give way to an understanding of the economic and the political as 'forms' of capital itself (Holloway and Picciotto, 1978, p. 14). In this way, the whole question of politics as a superstructure, the *bête noir* of Althusserian Marxists (Poulantzas, 1978, p. 15), can be gainsaid. Politics, like economics, is simply another form of social relations (Meiksins Wood, 1981, p. 68). Yet, if Althusserians present politics as a separate 'level' in a way which problematizes its relationship to society as a whole, the Capital Logicians make a mistake which is the 'identically opposite' in character. By counterposing *Capital* and the *Grundrisse* to Marx's political writings (Holloway and Picciotto, 1978, p. 17), they make it difficult to discover what is 'irreducibly specific' about politics at all (Jessop, 1982, p. 139; Therborn, 1978, p. 30). The argument that the 'reification and autonomisation' of the state is a necessary illusion which springs from the bourgeois mode of production is an important one (Müller and Neusüss, 1978, p. 36) and there can be no doubting the relevance of the analysis of *Capital* to Marx's theory of politics. If, as the Capital Logicians argue, the state is the 'ideal' 'fictitious collective capitalist' (Müller and Neusüss, 1978, p. 36), we need to emphasize not only the state's links with the economy, but also its peculiarly 'ideal', 'fictitious' and 'collective' character. As Engels argues in his letters on historical materialism, politics is a 'form of the class struggle' (*SC*, p. 394) because it has its own 'superstructural' identity.

What endows politics with 'relative independence' and 'a movement of its own' (*SC*, pp. 398–9) is the fact that it stands as an *'internally coherent* expression' of class interests (*SC*, p. 399): an ideological superstructure reflecting economic relations in inverted form. Without conceptualizing the state as a superstructure in a way of which both Althusserians and Capital Logicians disapprove, it is simply not possible to tackle either the specificity of politics or its existence as a derived 'form'. Politics does have a 'derivative' character but this can only be demonstrated because the state as a concentrated and specially organized instrument of coercion has a specific and irreducible identity all of its own.

Well might Engels complain that the critics 'lack dialectics' (*SC*, p. 402). Years earlier, in the context of a discussion on the question of money and power, property and rule, Marx protested against a 'sound common sense' which 'where it succeeds in seeing *differences*, it does not see *unity*, and . . . where it sees *unity*, it does not see *differences*' (*MECW* 6, p. 320). Precisely the problem with so many of the commentators! If politics is autonomous, it cannot be instrumental; if it is ideological, it cannot be coercive; if it has a specific identity, it cannot be dependent upon economic conditions. In fact, as I have tried to argue, the unity of the political and the economic does not contradict their differences: it presupposes them. The instrumentality of the state links it to the interests of a dominant class but in a *special* way. Its coercive character ties it to productive relationships but in a manner which is *concentrated*. Unless it was dependent upon society as a superstructure, politics as the concentrated expression of social relationships, a special instrument of coercion, simply could not exist at all.

We are now in a position to see why 'sound common sense' is not only a problem for the critics, past and present: it is also a problem for Gramsci's autonomous science of politics (*SPN*, p. 136). In the *Prison Notebooks* Gramsci challenges Croce's subjectivist view of politics as 'passion' by arguing that politics 'gives birth to permanent organisations precisely in so far as it identifies itself with economics' (*SPN*, p. 140). But if this is the unity which Croce misses, wherein lies the distinction? Politics, writes Gramsci, transcends the 'permanent and organic' terrain of economic life by bringing into play 'emotions and aspirations' which obey different laws from those of individual profit. But this merely re-expresses the Crocean view of politics as passion and hence the argument goes round in circles. Politics is not just passion in so far as it gives birth to permanently organized class interests which makes it identical to economics. What then makes politics *political*? The fact that as 'an immediate impulse to action' it is passion! If politics is, as Gramsci says, 'born' on the terrain of economic life, the *linkage* between the two remains mysterious.

In a later passage, Gramsci identifies politics with 'conjunctural' movements struggling either to conserve or to overthrow the economic structure of society whose movement is 'organic' (*SPN*, p. 178). But what is the relationship between the two? Organic movements are characterized as 'mechanical'; conjunctural causes as voluntaristic and individual, so that when Gramsci says that 'the dialectical nexus between the two categories of movement' is hard 'to establish precisely' (*SPN*, p. 178), in fact it is impossible. For the contrast between 'passion' and 'permanency', the 'voluntaristic' and the 'mechanical' is an absolute one and even when the definitions of politics and economics change places so that it is *economics* which is the 'egoistical-passional' and politics 'the superior elaboration of the structure into superstructure' (*SPN*, p. 366), the problem remains. How is it possible to move from one abstractly conceived opposite to another? For Gramsci, politics is either the same as economics or it is totally different: what he fails to explain is how it can (and indeed must) be both *at the same time*. Autonomous as the *special* instrument of class coercion; derivative as a concentrated expression of *economic* force.

Gramsci's failure to establish effectively an autonomous

political science is reflected in his failure to draw consistently the boundaries between state and civil society. Civil society is sometimes outside the state (*SPN*, p. 170; p. 238) and sometimes inside it (*SPN*, p. 160; p. 261; p. 244); at times civil society is identified with the economy (*SPN*, p. 160) and at times 'between the economic structure and the State' (*SPN*, p. 208). This 'oscillation' and 'conceptual slippage', as Anderson calls it (1976–7, p. 40; p. 49), arises not only because Gramsci is unclear as to the unity and difference between politics and economics, but because he fails to distinguish properly between Marx's two levels of coercion and consent. The coercion which commands consent with the exchange of commodities and the coercion which commands consent as it is re-expressed in the state as the institution which concentrates the contradictory relationships of civil society. Unless both the unity and the differences between these two levels is taken into account, no consistent and coherent view of an autonomous science of politics is possible.

It is true that Gramsci is conscious of what he calls a 'social compulsion' (*SPN*, p. 310) where the mass of the population is 'subject to coercive pressure through the elementary necessities of their existence' (*SPN*, p. 299). Yet he nowhere distinguishes this social coercion from the coercion of the state and, as noted earlier, he analyses this force in 'organic' separation from the moment of consent. In fact, only by sharply distinguishing between the two kinds of coercion and consent, can we see why this organic contrast can appear so plausible and why it is, nevertheless, so misleading. If we look for the moment only at the 'direct force' of the state as it coerces the recalcitrant individual, it seems impossible to say with Rousseau that one is being forced to be free. Without invoking the idealist mystification of a higher 'rational will', the notion that a murderer can consent to die or that 'liberty' can be enscribed on the doors of prisons simply appears as a grotesque paradox If the 'will' of the state enslaves the will of the individual, to speak of the latter's 'wilful' consent seems self-destructively absurd. On the other hand, trace the 'paradox of self-government' back to its economic roots and replace explicit, political force with implicit (unintended) social coercion and the absurdity lessens. The *'establishment of the political state'*, as Marx puts it, 'and the dissolution of civil society into independent *individuals' (MECW* 3, p. 167) leaves these individuals in an apparently autonomous realm where (a) their acts of free consent are only possible because (b) they are subject, not to political force, but the 'coercion of circumstances'. Of course, even to say that an individual consents to *social* coercion still seems somewhat absurd and in the next chapter we will attempt further clarification. But at least it is an absurdity which Marx has helped to make rather more intelligible by tracing it to an alienated form of production in which people's social action takes 'the form of the action of objects, which rule the producers instead of being ruled by them' (*C* I, p. 75).

What happens however when this contradictory relationship between coercion and consent is concentrated into the organs of the state? As individuals consent to their own social coercion, the development of commodity production into capitalism sees the deepening of class divisions and the generation of a 'partiality and violence' which, as Locke notes, is highly 'inconvenient'. An explicit political coercion is necessary to reinforce the dull compulsion of economic relations and since individuals can only continue to consent to social coercion when this coercion and consent is reinforced by the 'concentrated' agencies and 'generalized' declarations of the law, it is easy to see how a problem which is only moderately mystifying at the social level, now reappears in a starkly paradoxical form. In concentrating the contradictions of civil society in its public force, the state also serves to mystify them further. Not for nothing is politics, as Marx comments, 'the scholasticism of national life' (*MECW* 3, p. 31): relationships which are problematic in civil society are 'condensed' to the point of outright absurdity. Since the state reinforces the theological niceties and metaphysical subtleties of commodity production, it now appears that the individual as citizen must consent to the direct force of his own explicit coercion, the chastising activities of his own 'higher' will.

Gramsci's own difficulties should now be plain. His Crocean background predisposed him towards an 'organic' separation between coercion and consent, as exemplified not only, as we have seen, in his initial response to the Russian Revolution but also in his analysis of the Factory Council as the consensual counterpart to the coercive trade union (*SPW* I, p. 100; p. 110; p. 189; Hoffman, 1978a, p. 98). In the *Prison Notebooks* he seeks to assimilate this Crocean heritage critically, linking consent to force and bringing hegemony into the factory so as to emphasize what he called 'the principle of coercion, direct or indirect, in the ordering of production' (*SPN*, p. 301). But Gramsci needed to carry his analysis further and without, for example, teasing out the distinction between coercion direct and indirect and the linkage between politics and political economy, it proved impossible to establish the kind of autonomous science of politics he desired or an analysis of the coercion/consent problem which was 'methodological' rather than 'organic'. Certainly Gramsci was familiar with *Capital*, but there is nothing to suggest in his *Notebooks* that he regarded Marx's analysis of commodity and capitalist production as having any particular significance for a theory of politics. It may be unfair to argue, as Femia does, that 'for the purely economic theories of Marx and his later disciples, Gramsci showed neither sustained interest nor profound understanding' (1981, p. 62) but it is true that Gramsci did not see anything in *Capital* which could help to resolve the problem of coercion and consent. Yet, as we have seen, this is a question which is both political and economic. We shall now see why it is also a question which is philosophical in character.

5

ABSTRACTION, WILL AND NECESSITY: THE PHILOSOPHICAL UNDERPINNINGS

CONSENT AND THE REFLECTIONIST THEORY OF ABSTRACTION

I have stressed in previous chapters the importance of *analysing* the problem of coercion and consent and have argued that this analysis can only be dialectical rather than mechanical, when the roots of the problem are traced to the metaphysical subtleties and theological niceties of commodity production. We can now *begin* to see how the absurd might be possible, but all is by no means clear. For what can 'consent' really mean in the context of a 'coercion of mutual interests'? Is the freedom of will implied in the concept of consent actually compatible with a coercive domination of people by their own social circumstances? Hobhouse has argued that 'true consent is free consent, and the full freedom of consent implies equality on the part of both parties to the bargain' (1964, p. 50), but if workers are helpless in the face of their employer, then, in Hobhouse's words, where is the 'effective liberty in such an arrangement' (1964, p. 47)? In an alienated society can anyone be said to *consent*? To pursue these questions further, we must first say something about the 'dialectic method' Marx employs in his analysis in *Capital*.

In analysing relationships in the economy, Marx tells us,

the 'force of abstraction' is necessary to understand the 'commodity-form' or 'value-form' of the product of labour (*C* I, p. 8). For products to exchange and take the form of commodities, the labour which makes them, everyday 'concrete' labour, has to be stripped of its specific qualities and, as we have seen, rendered 'abstract'. This process of abstraction is essential if products, as far removed from one another as boot polish and crystal palaces, are to 'exchange', change places. It is a process which is perfectly real but it is also a process which is somewhat curious. For what makes a product a *commodity* is the fact that as the embodiment of 'homogenous' human labour 'in the abstract', it has an 'ideal form'. Hence, as Marx puts it, 'the value of commodities is the very opposite of the coarse materiality of their substance, not an atom of matter enters into its composition' (*C* I, p. 47).

This process of abstraction mystifies as a result the whole character of commodity production. Since the producers do not come into contact with each other until they exchange their products, a 'definite social relation between men', Marx argues, 'assumes in their eyes, the fantastic form of a relation between things' (*C* I, p. 72). The relations connecting the labour of one individual with that of the rest are *concealed* by the fact that producers only come into direct contact when they exchange 'things'. In other words, 'this Fetishism of commodities has its origin . . . in the peculiar social character of the labour that produces them' (*C* I, p. 72). If this fetishism which 'reifies' social relationships is to be properly understood, then the *method* of abstraction which Marx employs in his analysis must be seen as nothing more than a mental reflection of that *actual* process of abstraction taking place in the real world of commodity exchange. 'With me', comments Marx, 'the ideal is nothing else than the material world reflected by the human mind, and translated into forms of thought' (*C* I, p. 19). For Hegel, as an idealist, the dialectic is 'standing on its head' (*C* I, p. 20) and this too is precisely the problem with the commodity. As an embodiment of abstract labour, a product 'is changed into something transcendent. It not only stands with its feet on the ground, but in relation to all other commodities, it stands on its head' (*C* I, p. 71) and like Hegel's transcendental dialectic, it must be turned right side up again! Contrary to Geras's view (1971, p. 75), the commodity as a 'fantasic form' is therefore also an *illusion* but it is an illusory form of *reality* for its abstract nature conceals the fact that, like all human products, it has its origins in social labour. Hence a reflectionist theory of abstraction is crucial for without it, the commodity would appear simply to be 'a thing' and not, as a deeper analysis of its 'illusory reality' suggests, a product abstracted from the social relations of production. The 'vulgar' economists' way *'of looking at things'*, Marx tells Engels, 'arises . . . because it is only the immediate phenomenal *form* of these relations that is reflected in their brains and not their *inner connection*' (*SC*, p. 179).

This question of abstraction and reflection has an important bearing on the problem of consent. Objects can only relate to one another as commodities, Marx comments, if their guardians relate to one another as 'persons whose will resides in those objects' and who behave in such a way that each does not appropriate the object of the other and part with his own 'except by means of an act done by mutual consent' (*C* I, p. 84). This consent is at once a 'juridical relation' as the 'relation between two wills' and 'the reflex of the real economic relation between the two' (*C* I, p. 84) and hence a double process of creating 'illusions' is at work. It appears to the 'guardians' that they are free individuals, exchanging their products according to a 'natural right' which arises prior to their social contact. Mutually recognizing in each other 'the rights of private proprietors' (*C* I, p. 84), they naturally view the world through the prism of liberal illusions, a world where 'there alone rule Freedom, Equality, Property and Bentham' (*C* I, p. 176). But these illusions are not, of course, pure fantasies — they reflect the fantasic form of commodity exchange. The mystical quality of their autonomous, yet 'mutual' consent reflects the mystical quality of a social production which appears as the 'material relations between persons and the social relations between things' (*C* I, p. 73). Since the 'will' of commodity producers 'resides in their object', the 'consent' to its exchange necessarily takes an asocial, abstract form. Just as the commodity as an embodiment of abstract labour appears to 'transcend' the social production necessary for its creation, so the act of consent as a 'relation between two wills' appears to transcend all the pressures and constraints which arise from social relationships.

This illusion of an unrestrained 'will', free from the 'eternal nature-imposed necessity' (*C* I, pp. 42–3) of production reaches grotesque proportions, as we have seen, when the worker can only sell his labour power because he retains his *rights* of ownership over it (*C* I, p. 168). The contract proves 'in black and white' that he has disposed of himself freely but, with the bargain concluded, he discovers that 'the time for which he is free to sell his labour power is the time for which he is forced to sell it' (*C* I, p. 302). His very 'freedom' leaves him peculiarly vulnerable to those coercive circumstances which confront all the agents of capitalist production as 'overwhelming natural laws that irresistibly enforce their will over them' (*C* III, p. 831). Our paradox appears at its roots. On the one hand, consent is overwhelmed by a seemingly 'natural' coercion: on the other hand, it is idealistically abstracted from it. Hence we can see that the 'arbitrary and mechanical hypostasis of the moment of hegemony' (Anderson, 1976–7, p. 47), about which Gramsci so rightly complains, is no simple mental aberration on the part of Croce. On the contrary, it arises from what might be called the 'hypostasization' process of commodity production, the appearance of relations as things, so that consent is 'organically' separated from coercion, the individual from society and the product from its producer in that 'enchanted, perverted, topsy-turvy world, in which Monsieur le Capital and Madame la

Terre do their ghost-walking as social characters and at the same time directly as mere things' (*C* III, p. 830). It is an arbitrary and mechanical hypostasis which cannot be understood without Marx's reflectionist theory of abstraction.

Colletti has shown how the Marxists of the Second International frequently regarded Marx's view of 'abstraction' as nothing more than a process of *mental* generalization and hence, in Bernstein's words, saw the value-form of the commodity as a 'mere thought construct' (Colletti, 1972, p. 80), linked to Marxism's penchant for 'excessive abstraction' and 'theoretical phraseology' (Colletti, 1972, p. 49). As far as Bernstein is concerned, Marx's theory of value is basically the same as Adam Smith's (1961, p. 33) and Marx's stricture of classical political economy — that 'it never once asked the question' why human labour takes on the form of the value of things (*C* I, p. 80; Colletti, 1972, p. 77) — is simply ignored. Marx's notion of value as 'a philosophical atom endowed with a soul' is a 'scholastic-theological product' which hinders his theory more than it helps it (Bernstein, 1961, p. 38; Colletti, 1972, p. 82) and is an abstraction brought about through defective logic rather than through the 'scholastic-theological' processes of material reality.

In rejecting the abstraction and reflection of Marx's dialectical method, Bernstein, like many of the Marxists of his time, embraced a 'vulgar' empiricist standpoint of the world as a series of disconnected 'things' whose relationships are imposed 'from above' by hypotheses and 'mental generalizations' (Gay, 1962, p. 145). Sticking stoically to 'the soil of empirically ascertainable facts', Bernstein not only accepted what Marx had called 'the estranged outward appearances of economic relations' (*C* III, p. 817): he also endorsed the naive and fetishistic view of morality and consent which went with them. Ironically echoing the themes of Marx's *Jewish Question*, Bernstein was to speak of democracy as the 'suppression of class government' (1961, p. 144), the 'indication of a social condition where political privilege belongs to no one class as opposed to the whole community' (1981, p. 142). Here is Marx's 'perfected state', enthusiastically acclaimed on its own terms! With this 'empiricist' endorsement of political idealism, the coercion/consent paradox returns with a vengeance. Democracy substitutes for the class war (1961, p. 164) and yet alongside this abstract consent, we see the retention of state coercion in *permanent* form: 'The so-called coercive associations, the state and the communities, will retain their great tasks in any future I can foresee' (Gay, 1962, p. 246). Just why democracy should make its members 'partners' in the community and yet still require an apparatus of institutionalized coercion, remains as mysterious for Bernstein as it was for that liberal tradition to which his socialism is 'legitimate heir'.

We have already noted that Gramsci was himself familiar with Marx's *Capital* but like the Marxists of an earlier generation, he saw no particular relevance for an understanding of politics in its philosophical methods and concepts. In a revealing passage, he comments that 'the philosophy of praxis was born in the form of aphorisms and practical criteria for the purely accidental reason that its founder dedicated his intellectual forces to other problems, particularly economic (which he treated in systematic form)' (*SPN*, p. 426). Yet, to see Marx's turn to economics as a turn away from philosophy, is to miss the point that it was precisely in the sphere of political economy that, even with Smith and Ricardo, 'vulgar' empiricist thinking had begun to be challenged (Ilyenkov, 1977, p. 91) for this is the arena in which the problems of 'ideality' and 'values' can be tackled at their material roots (Hoffman, 1980, p. 127). Lenin underlined the philosophical importance of *Capital* by asserting somewhat flamboyantly that without having studied 'the *whole* of Hegel's *Logic*' (*LCW* 38, p. 180; Pilling, 1980, p. 7) nobody can understand Marx. Although Gramsci could defend *Capital* against Croce (*SPN*, p. 401), the question of Marx's method nowhere appears as a major bone of contention and, as Nemeth comments, at least in this case 'Gramsci failed to penetrate beneath the surface of the economic writings' (1980, p. 46; p. 65). The English editors of the *Prison Notebooks* comment on the fact that 'Gramsci tends in general to underplay the element of "abstraction" inherent in Marx's method, attributing it to simple "pedagogic" necessities' (Hoare and Nowell Smith, 1971, p. 368) and this, as we have seen, was precisely the problem with the Marxists of the Second International. Without an understanding of how the abstraction inherent in Marx's method reflected the abstract character of commodity production, it proved impossible to grasp the question of *fetishism*, the central category of Marx's political economy (Pilling, 1980, p. 8). In Gramsci therefore, the difficulty we confront is this: how can one penetrate Croce's mechanical hypostasis of the moment of hegemony without at the same time making a philosophical break with the world of 'estranged appearances'?

Gramsci's failure really to assimilate Marx's reflectionist theory of abstraction arises from the tendency in his philosophical writings to identify *vulgar* materialism with materialism *tout court*. To take an instructive example: in rejecting what he (wrongly) regards as a purely vulgar materialist conception of the 'thing in itself' and 'the external objectivity of the real', Gramsci argues that in 'the *Holy Family* it is said that the whole reality is in phenomena and that beyond these phenomena there is nothing, and this is certainly correct' (*SPN*, p. 368). Although the editors declare themselves unable to trace such a statement in the text (Hoare and Nowell Smith, 1971, p. 368), it is at least possible that Gramsci had in mind Marx and Engels's amusing critique of the method of 'speculative construction'. If, says Marx, from real apples, pears, strawberries and almonds, I form the general idea 'Fruit' and then imagine that my abstract idea 'Fruit' is an entity existing outside of me, and that the 'empirical' fruits are themselves mere 'forms' of this 'higher' abstracted substance, truly I am speaking 'in the *language of speculative* philosophy' (*MECW* 4, pp. 57—8). Now the implications of this argument are not as Gramsci might have supposed, that the whole of reality is 'in phenomena', for if it *were* true that beyond phenomena 'there is nothing', how would it be possible to distinguish the *concept* of Fruit as the 'unreal *creation of the mind*' from the 'real *natural objects*' which this concept reflects? 'Outward appearances' would blur into 'inner connections' and it would be impossible to 'compare' the 'semblances' of fruit with their 'natural reality'. Marx does not, of course, challenge the legitimacy of abstracting a concept of Fruit from its empirical particulars (*MECW* 4, p. 57; p. 60), but what he does reject is the use of these entirely legitimate abstractions as if they were the creator and not the *reflection* of an empirical world (Arthur, 1979).

Gramsci's 'phenomenalism' leads him to embrace what he calls an 'absolute historicism' or 'absolute humanism', a standpoint which makes the external world dependent on human cognition (McLennan, 1981, p. 23; *SPN*, p. 445). Hence ironies abound. While Gramsci condemns materialism as mystical and religious (*SPN*, pp. 444—5), his own 'absolute historicism' leads to a 'speculative *mystical identity* of *being* and *thinking*' which also takes the form, as Marx and Engels puts it in the *Holy Family*, of an 'equally mystical identity of *practice* and *theory*' (*MECW* 4, p. 193) — a 'practice *in abstracto*' (*MECW* 4, p. 40). Gramsci was to argue that the Crocean heritage could only be critically assimilated through a 'concept of the unity of theory and practice' (Fiori, 1970, p. 106) but this unity can only be meaningfully sustained in terms of a *distinction* between ideas and the 'external objectivity of the real', the material world 'reflected by the human mind and translated into forms of thought' (*C* I, p. 19). If, as Gramsci puts it, creativity teaches that 'reality does not exist on its own, in and for itself, but only in an historical relationship with the men who modify it, etc.' (*SPN*, p. 346), then it is hardly surprising that the 'objective' and the 'subjective' should become indistinguishable (*SPN*, p. 445). A 'philosophy of praxis' which is unable to account for the '*difference* between *being* and *thinking*, between *consciousness* and *life*' (*MECW* 4, p. 53), simply collapses into a 'mystical identity', a practice *in abstracto*. In other words, Gramsci's rejection of what he calls 'common sense criticism' (*SPN*, p. 444) led him to embrace its idealist opposite.

No one demonstrates more vividly than Gramsci the centrality of philosophical argument to the coercion and consent problem. The concept of hegemony, he declared, represents a great philosophical advance 'as well as a politico-practical one' (*SPN*, p. 333) and in a striking elaboration of the same point, he comments that 'the theoretical-practical principle of hegemony has also epistemological significance, and it is here that Illich [Lenin's] greatest theoretical contribution to the philosophy of praxis should be sought' (*SPN*, p. 365). Yet Lenin's epistemology, whether we think of *Materialism and Empirio-Criticism* (1907) or his *Philosophical Notebooks* (1914), centres on a materialist theory of reflection (Hoffman, 1975, pp. 74–81) and this is the very philosophical standpoint which Gramsci appears to reject. His own epistemology, as we have seen, involves an 'absolute historicism' quite at variance with the philosophical underpinnings of classical Marxism. What relation does it have to his conception of hegemony? Linking hegemony with historicism is Gramsci's philosophy of praxis for if hegemony encapsulates the formation of a 'national-popular collective will' (*SPN*, p. 133), the philosophy of praxis explores the 'relationship between human will (superstructure) and economic structure' (*SPN*, p. 403): the conceptual basis for the 'theoretical-practical principle'.

WILL AND THE PROCESS OF PRODUCTION

For Marx 'the principle of politics is the *will*' (*MECW* 3, p. 199) and so it was for Gramsci. As we have noted in chapter 3, Gramsci was particularly preoccupied with the importance of political leadership and he shared Lenin's antipathy towards 'economism' and 'spontaneity'. In the *Prison Notebooks* Gramsci is concerned not only with the political aspects but with what he sees as the philosophical expression of these 'Menshevik' misdemeanours — the problem of determinism and fatalism. While the 'ideological aroma' of fatalism is, Gramsci argued, understandable in a 'subaltern class' resisting a will external to itself, it becomes a cause of passivity and 'idealistic self-sufficiency' in a leadership seeking to exercise hegemony over society as a whole (*SPN*, pp. 336–7). This problem can take different forms. It can appear as an 'economism' which presents 'organic' movements (i.e. within the economic structure) as though they were conjuctural (i.e. immediate) or it can take the form of an 'ideologism' which presents these immediate causes as though they were the only effective ones (*SPN*, p. 178). To Rosa Luxemburg's 'spontaneist prejudice' (*SPN*, p. 233), there corresponds, in other words, Bernstein's idealistic socialism 'as a piece of the beyond' (Gay, 1962, p. 158). Kautsky's *Ethics and the Materialist Conception of History* (1906) provides a good example of how a fatalistic 'necessity' is tied to an abstract conception of freedom (1918, p. 60) and as Colletti has demonstrated in his critique of Second International Marxism, 'economism' and 'ideologism' can amicably coexist within the same body of theory, 'internally consistent within this opposition' (1972, pp. 74–5).

If then Gramsci was clearly right to be concerned about the problem of a 'subaltern' Marxism without any place for a conception of politics as organized 'will', how successful was he in breaking through the vicious circle of a 'fatalistic voluntarism'? Here his philosophical relationship to Marx is revealing. The crucial point, as Gramsci sees it, is to 'put the "will" (which in the last analysis equals practical or political activity) at the base of philosophy' (*SPN*, p. 345). For Marx however, the problem appears strikingly different: it is not the 'will' but the importance of objective circumstances which need to be defended against those, as he puts it in 1843, who are 'all too easily tempted ... to explain everything by the *will* of the persons concerned' (*MECW* 1, p. 337; *SC*, p. 399). Whether this notable difference of emphasis between Marx and Gramsci had more substantial theoretical consequences is a matter to which I now want to turn.

As early as 1837 Marx informs his father that he intends to establish that 'the nature of the mind is just as necessary, concrete and firmly based as the nature of the body' (*MECW* 1, p. 18) and it is doubtless this same critical scepticism which leads Marx in 1842 to ridicule the deputy who justifies the privileges of forest owners in terms of their 'free will' (*MECW* 1, p. 244). In his *Critique of Hegel's Philosophy of Law*, he attacks Hegel's 'logical, pantheistic mysticism' (*MECW* 3, p. 31) for the way, for example, it converts the attributes of a constitutional monarch into 'the absolute self-determination of the will' (*MECW* 3, p. 25). Nor is it of course only the 'idealism of the state' which perverts empirical facts into metaphysical axioms (*MECW* 3, p. 25); it is also the 'materialism of civil society' whose abstract individuals, with their self-willing wills, declare war on society as isolated monads (*MECW* 3, p. 162; p. 167). Thus, when Marx in 1844 does come to speak of the principle of politics as will, he stresses the illusory character of its '*omnipotence*', its '*natural* and spiritual *limits*' and the dangers of a political mentality unable to discover the material roots of social problems (*MECW* 3, p. 199; for a fuller discussion, Hoffman, 1978b, pp. 24–32).

Gramsci, it should be noted, was by no means oblivious to the existence of 'limits' on the 'omnipotent' will and in arguing that the 'will' must be placed at the base of philosophy, adds: 'But it must be a rational, not an arbitrary, will, which is realised in so far as it corresponds to objective historical necessities' (*SPN*, p. 345). The question however which Marx wants to pose, even in 1844, goes beyond this. It is not just a problem of how the will *corresponds* to objective historical necessities, but of how the will *arises out of* these historical necessities. Since Hegel's 'absolute idea' demonstrates in all its empty formalism that 'only *nature* is something' (*MECW* 3, p. 343), humanity must be part of this 'something', its physical and spiritual life 'linked to nature', given the fact that 'history itself is a *real* part of *natural history* — of nature developing into man' (*MECW* 3, pp. 303—4). But if this is so, then the question of 'correspondence' must yield to the more profound question of 'origins': how does the human will, with its spirituality, freedom and indeed capacity to consent emerge from this coercive world of natural necessities?

In an important dissenting note on Lukacs, Gramsci appears to endorse Marx's argument above. Human history should also be conceived as the history of nature, he comments, and any presupposition of a 'dualism between nature and man' would be wrong (*SPN*, p. 448). But how are we to visualize this unity between 'nature and man'? Gramsci introduces elsewhere in the *Notebooks* the crucial question of production. 'Man', he writes, does not enter into relations with the natural world 'just by being himself part of the natural world', but 'actively, by means of work and technique. Further: these relations are not mechanical. They are active and conscious' (*SPN*, p. 352). The young Marx agrees: 'free, conscious activity is man's species character'; 'the productive life is the life of the species' (*MECW* 3, p. 276). Yet what is revealing is that although Gramsci acknowledges this link between humanity and nature through production, he gives it no particular emphasis. The most satisfactory answer to the question 'what is man?' is the one that asserts that 'human nature' is the 'complex of social relations' (*SPN*, p. 355). Out of a concern to reject crude biological or vulgar materialist accounts of the human identity ('man is what he eats'), Gramsci appears to give pride of place to the existence of human consciousness. He interprets Marx's sixth thesis on Feuerbach ('man . . . is the ensemble of the

social relations') to mean that the 'nature of man is "history" '
and he adds that 'in this sense, given history as equal to
spirit', 'the nature of man is spirit if one gives to history
precisely this significance of "becoming" ' (*SPN*, pp. 355–
6).

The contrast between this answer and the answer which
Marx and Engels give in 1845 to the same question is indeed
striking, for Marx and Engels specifically *challenge* the
adequacy of distinguishing humans from animals 'by
consciousness, by religion or anything else you like' (*MECW*
5, p. 31). Humans themselves 'begin to distinguish themselves
from animals as soon as they begin to *produce* their means
of subsistence' and this assertion (*MECW* 5, p. 31) has
philosophical implications of a far reaching kind. Gramsci
does not, we repeat, ignore this link with nature through
production and even in his more abstract 'definitions' it is
clearly implied. Humanity is not just 'spirit', it is 'spirit'
which 'becomes': humanity is 'concrete will', 'the effective
application of the abstract will or vital impulse to the concrete
means which realise such a will' (*SPN*, p. 360). Nevertheless
in Gramsci, humanity's defining attribute is spirit and will,
in Marx it is production.

Why do Marx and Engels regard production as so important?
Because, if we may briefly recall the themes of *The German
Ideology*, production provides the *basis* for humanity's
'complex of social relations'. People must be in a position
to live in order to be able to 'make history' and this life
involves 'before everything else' eating, drinking, housing,
clothing, etc. Producing the means to satisfy human needs
is the 'first historical act' and it is 'an historical act, a
fundamental condition of all history, which today, as
thousands of years ago, must daily and hourly be fulfilled
merely in order to sustain human life' (*MECW* 5, pp. 41–
2). Undoubtedly, the most philosophically pregnant word
in all this is 'must'. Whereas for Gramsci, some social
relations 'are necessary, others are voluntary' (*SPN*, p. 353),
for Marx all social relationships are underpinned by the

human necessity to produce. This difference dramatically affects the analysis of will and consciousness. Whereas for Gramsci, 'man is concrete will' — will *plus* circumstances, for Marx, will is a *response* to circumstances and hence because humans *have* to produce, they 'work under definite material limits, presuppositions and conditions independent of their will' (*MECW* 5, p. 36). Humanity's nature as 'spirit' means that for Gramsci social relations 'correspond to the greater or lesser degree of understanding that each man has of them' (*SPN*, p. 352). For Marx on the other hand, these social relations must be analysed not 'as they may appear' in 'people's imagination, but as they *actually* are' (*MECW* 5, p. 35). Since relationships are 'entered into' independent of the will, they exist independently of the way in which people happen to understand them.

Gramsci, as we have noted above, was deeply concerned that his philosophy of praxis should have no place for the kind of 'determinism' which induced economism and passivity. He considered it crucial therefore to avoid any residue of mechanical materialism with its reduction of human activity to the instinctive behaviour of animals. This 'reductionism' had been a common feature of much Second International Marxism where human freedom could, on occasion, be characterized as a 'subjective, inevitable feeling' which humans shared with the animals (Kautsky, 1918, p. 61). This was indeed a *vulgar* materialism and it goes hand in hand with a 'technological' reading of historical materialism of the kind Gramsci saw in Bukharin and which, he argued, had originated in Italy with Loria's 'historical economism'. Forces of production are reduced to mere 'technical instruments' and physical tools and it appears, as Colletti notes, that because production is a 'material' process, it can be 'emptied of any effective *socio-historical* content, representing, on the contrary, an antecedent sphere, prior to any human mediation' (1972, p. 65; for a meticulous analysis of the problem, see Cohen, 1978, chapters 2–4).

If Gramsci was certainly right to be wary of a vulgar

materialist view of production and the baroque conviction that the more one goes back to 'material' objects, the more orthodox one must be (*SPN*, p. 461), how are we to justify Marx's insistence, throughout all his writings, that people, in the social production of their existence, 'inevitably enter into definite relations, which are independent of their will' (*CCPE*, p. 20). For this creates an intriguing problem. If humanity is an ensemble of social relations, then how are such relationships possible without 'will', spirituality and consciousness? Indeed, it would seem to be just these attributes which make human production so distinct. As Marx puts it in 1844, while the animal produces only under the dominion of 'immediate physical need', 'man produces even when he is free from physical need and only truly produces in freedom therefrom' (*MECW* 3, p. 276). Indeed, in an important and often quoted passage in *Capital*, the question of will seems central to the productive process. The conscious nature of human production is underlined — 'the architect raises his structure in imagination before he erects it in reality' (*C* I, p. 178) — so that, as Colletti notes, the human, as a product of 'material causation', is at the same time the beginning of a new causal process, in which the point of departure is the *idea* (1972, p. 66). At the end of the labour process we get a result that had already existed in the imagination of the labourer at the commencement (*C* I, p. 178) but it is not just the will of the individual which is involved. The worker, Marx continues, 'not only effects a change of form on the material on which he works, but he also realises as a purpose of his own that gives the law to his modus operandi, and to which he must subordinate his will' (*C* I, p. 178). If his will is 'subordinate', it is still governed by a 'purpose of his own' and this appears to suggest that a subjective will yields to an 'objective will' i.e. that collectivity of relationships which give the 'law' to the worker's *modus operandi*. Is this not Gramsci's point: that 'man is concrete will'? If production is only possible through 'an act of imagination', does this not substantiate

Hegel's assertion that human inventions 'belong to Spirit' (1956, p. 241), particularly as it is not so much the using of tools but the *making* of them which accounts for the key discontinuity between humans and apes (Woolfson, 1982, p. 39; p. 42)?

We appear to come to a philosophical impasse with serious implications for resolving the problem of coercion and consent. If, as Marx says, the production process takes place independent of the will, then human activity appears to be the same as the instinctive 'production' of animals. If, on the other hand, as Marx also says, production takes place *through* the will, it seems that spirituality is its distinguishing attribute and the only limit to the 'individual will' is the 'objective will' of social production. The accent, in other words, should be laid on the *historical* rather than on the materialism (*SPN*, p. 465). But if this *is* so, then a chasm yawns between the 'rational will' and the historical necessities to which it must correspond. There are in Croce's words, no 'ultimate causes' (*SPN*, p. 460), merely an 'organic' divide between the 'coercion' of circumstances and the 'consenting' will, and Marx's assertion that conscious, active producers enter into social relationships independently of their will, appears as an impossible conundrum.

NATURE, FREEDOM AND NECESSITY

We now need to see why it is that Marx considers human production as a material process. This 'materiality' arises for three reasons:

(a)   humans have physical needs which provide 'the first premise of all human existence' (*MECW* 5, p. 41);

(b)   the fact that people are producers is 'a step conditioned by their physical organisation' (*MECW* 5, p. 31);

(c)   In order to produce, people have to enter social relations independent of their will.

I shall say a few words about each in turn.

In *The German Ideology* Marx and Engels speak of the satisfaction of needs as 'the first historical act' but they also refer to the 'creation of new needs' as 'the first historical act' (*MECW* 5, p. 41). Both statements appear possible because, for Marx, human needs are natural needs which have become 'humanized' i.e. altered by the activity of people. Consumption, as much as production, involves and therefore is transformed by social relationships and, as Marx says of 'consumption' in the *Grundrisse*, 'as urgency, as need', it is 'itself an intrinsic moment of productive activity' (*G*, p. 92). This 'urgency' or 'need' to which humans must respond is a natural necessity which is continually being socialized. Eating, drinking, procreating, etc. may in an alienated society appear to be purely animal functions; in fact, argues Marx, they are 'genuinely human' (*MECW* 3, p. 275). The individual produces and consumes 'as a whole man' (*MECW* 3, p. 299) and, as Marx puts it in an extremely significant sentence, the '*senses* have therefore become directly in their practice *theoreticians*' (*MECW* 3, p. 300). When therefore Marx comments, as noted above, that the human produces even when free from physical need and 'only truly produces in freedom therefrom' (*MECW* 3, p. 278), this should not be taken to mean that people produce 'in freedom' from *all* needs, but from those 'unmediated' animal needs which, as producers, they continually 'transcend' through socialization.

This brings us to the second of the material aspects of the production process mentioned above, 'the physical organisation of individuals' and 'their consequent relation to the rest of nature' (*MECW* 5, p. 31). For like 'physical' needs, people's 'physical' organization should not be construed theologically as, in Green's phrase, 'the wild beast in man' (1941, p. 217) for this physical organization has itself been humanized in the course of the history of 'nature developing into man' (*MECW* 3, p. 304). It is not difficult to see why Marx and Engels should have greeted the publication of the *Origin of the Species* with such enthusiasm for they saw in Darwin's arguments, support for 'the class struggle in history from the point of view of natural science' (*SC*, p. 115), indeed, 'the natural historical foundation of our outlook' (*W* 30, p. 418). By examining the 'history of Nature's Technology', as Marx puts it in *Capital*, Darwin has stimulated interest in 'the history of the productive organs of man' (*C* I, p. 372) and it is clear that this refers not just to human tools but to human *faculties*. Indeed, it was just such a 'history' that Engels sought to sketch briefly in his *Dialectics of Nature* in an essay which has been recently acclaimed as 'a brilliant scientific anticipation of what is now thought, by some writers at least, to be the likely pattern of early human evolution' (Woolfson, 1982, p. 3). What Engels argued was that the hand and the brain with 'attendant senses' are not merely an organ of labour, but within the evolutionary process of a 'nature developing into man' (*MECW* 3, p. 304), are also a *product* of labour (*DN*, pp. 176–7). If this is right, then we have to assume that the 'natural bases' from which Marx and Engels say historical writing must start, and which are modified 'in the course of history through the action of men', include not only climatic, geological, oro-hydrographical conditions, etc., but 'the actual physical nature of man' (*MECW* 5, p. 31).

We come to the third and from our point of view, the most crucial aspect of Marx's materialist analysis of production: the analysis of the 'economic formation of society as a process of natural history' (*C* I, p. 10) which involves people independent of their will. For what follows from the two aspects noted above, is that for Marx, the concept of nature is a concept of *natural history*. This is not the 'one-sided' materialism of Hobbes and the thinkers of the French Enlightenment which Marx characterizes as an 'abstract materialism' but the kind of materialism which, 'surrounded by a sensuous poetic glamour', is able to 'attract man's whole entity by winning smiles'. It is a materialism which has a place for 'man' for in rejecting the 'abstract materialism of the geometrician' (*MECW* 4, p. 128), it embraces a concept of matter, not just in 'motion', but in development: a concept which, as Engels later puts it, comprehends all 'processes occurring in the universe, from mere change of place right up to thinking' (*DN*, p. 70). The 'natural' is therefore conceived by Marx as a 'necessarily disappearing necessity' (Meszaros, 1970, p. 242) and if humans are unique as conscious producers, this is because they are unique as 'natural beings'. The discontinuities which divide humans from animals arise precisely through the process of 'nature developing into man'. The fact, as Gramsci puts it, that humanity is in a state of 'becoming' (*SPN*, p. 356) makes it possible to answer the question which the 'old materialism' never put to itself (*MESW*, p. 623) — how the human will emerges natural-historically as a force for self-creation.

The apparently impossible conundrum can now be explained. If, on the one hand, people 'can work only as Nature does, that is, by changing the form of matter' (*C* I, p. 43), on the other hand by making use of the mechanical, physical and chemical properties of some substances to make other substances subservient to their aims (*C* I, p. 179), the actual way in which they 'change the form of matter' is clearly unique. People produce through the will in conditions which are independent of the will and therefore even as they increasingly transform their environment, this 'human world' is but a fragment of those wider processes of natural history, infinite in their complexity, evolutionary gradations and changing forms, out of which humanity itself evolved. To say, as Hegel does, that the 'universal idea' exists 'as the substantial totality of things' (1956, p. 36), only makes sense if we assume that consciousness is itself a universal attribute of all matter-in-motion and not, as Engels puts it, the 'highest product of organic matter' (*DN*, p. 23) in which all other material development has (to recall the analysis of state and society) been 'concentrated'. Consciousness can never be anything else than 'conscious being' (*MECW* 5, p. 36) and this 'being' ties humanity to nature in a way which is wholly distinct. As natural beings, people have to produce and hence have no choice (*SC*, p. 30); but because they have to *produce*, they can only do so through a will and freedom which acknowledge these 'eternal nature-imposed' necessities. It is because people produce in conditions which are independent of their will, that they have a 'will' through which to produce. Without the wider 'compulsions' of natural-history, there would be no human freedom at all.

We are now in a position to work our way out of the impasse noted earlier and the best way to overcome a problem is to understand how it has arisen. Marx's 1844 *Manuscripts* are justly famous for their analysis of alienation, the process by which human products become alien, hostile and independent objects (*MECW* 3, p. 278); human needs appear as though they were animal (*MECW* 3, p. 275); social activities are valued only as *things* and 'subjectivity and objectivity, spirituality and materialism, activity and suffering' take on an 'antithetical character' (*MECW* 3, p. 302). In short, the world in which vulgar materialists with their reductionist necessities confront abstract idealists with their metaphysical will! It is clear that these are not simply philosophical problems. When Rousseau writes that 'in the power of willing', 'nothing is to be found but acts which are purely spiritual and wholly inexplicable by the laws of mechanism' (1913, p. 54), he takes precisely for granted what Marx and Engels wish to *challenge*, namely, the division of mental and material labour, the class divided society in which production and consumption 'devolve on different individuals' (*MECW* 5, p. 45). It is as a result of the division of labour that human consciousness appears other-worldly, flattering itself that it really represents something without representing something real, and the natural appears inhuman. A 'fleshless' will counterparts a 'misanthropic' matter (*MECW* 4, p. 128). Since the labour which is planned is not carried out by those who plan it, all merit for the swift advance of civilization is 'ascribed to the mind'

(*DN*, p. 180) and the social institution which embodies most comprehensively the 'Divine Idea as it exists on earth', the unity of the universal and the subjective will (Hegel, 1956, p. 39), is, of course, the *state*.

To become practical, the philosophical will must become political. When the state constitutes, as Hegel puts it, 'a community of existence', 'the contradiction between Liberty and Necessity vanishes' (1956, p. 39) — as the expression of a 'universal will', all lesser wills are beholden to it; all particularistic conflicts find their reconciliation through its universal mediations. Here is the solution to our 'paradox of self-government' in its most brilliantly *fictional* form as the 'camera obscura' of perfectly real, but wholly alienated, life processes (*MECW* 5, p. 36). Here is the explanation to 'the illusion that the law is based on the will, and indeed on the will divorced from its real basis — on *free* will' (*MECW* 5, p. 90). If hegemony is a collective political will, it cannot arise *in opposition to* natural-historical necessities, for the labour process in which this hegemony is rooted, is at once compelling, yet liberating. If this is not the naturalistic necessity of the mythical Centaur and the theologians' 'spiritless' flesh, it is a humanized, socialized necessity nevertheless and the coercive character of social relationships stands as an enduring and inescapable premiss of all human history. The fact that humans produce through acts of will which tranform the world, clearly points to their *freedom*: but this very capacity to produce, form relationships and indeed consent is itself only explicable because people are part of a 'law-governed' natural history. Engels was to argue that at every step we are reminded of the fact that we by no means rule nature like a conqueror, 'like someone standing outside nature'. On the contrary 'all our mastery of it consists in the fact that we have the advantage over all other creatures of being able to learn its laws and apply them correctly' (*DN*, p. 183). Without *recognizing* the fact that humans are compelled even by their own unique social relationships, no freedom or consent would be possible.

This act of 'recognition' involves *both* a passive response to determining circumstances *and* an active counter-response which proceeds to transform them. Unless both moments are grasped, then no dialectical view of the will and determinism is possible. Engels comments in *Anti-Dühring* that 'Hegel was the first to state correctly the relation between freedom and necessity. To him, freedom is the appreciation of necessity. "Necessity is *blind* only in so far as it is not understood" ' (*AD*, p. 157) but here we need to be careful. If the general formula is correct — to be free, we must recognize necessity — the act of 'appreciation' and the character of this 'necessity' cannot itself be interpreted in purely Hegelian terms. For if nature is 'blind' in the sense that it is merely *mechanistic*, a chaotic set of forces, as Hegel supposed, going round in circles 'repeating the same thing' (Schmidt, 1971, p. 210), then the 'freedom' which 'appreciates' it, becomes a mystical, otherworldly 'self-willing will'. In other words, if freedom is simply the 'recognition' of a necessity 'external' to it, then the old antithesis of a 'fatalistic' compulsion and a 'spontaneist' consent is recreated and the notion of a 'creative recognition' disintegrates into the juxtaposition of a 'pure passivity' and the 'pure activity' which it necessarily presupposes. The dialectical character of the 'formula' disappears. As Bogomolov has commented, 'freedom is not the subjection of man to the necessity of nature and society, but the ability (depending, naturally, upon the knowledge and objective powers man has at his disposal) to transform nature on the basis of recognising this necessity' (1983, p. xviii).

If freedom is taken to mean 'subjection', it ceases to be freedom; if recognition is interpreted simply as *creation*, then it is pulverized into a mystical subjectivity. Marx speaks of the worker making 'use of the mechanical, physical, and chemical properties of some substances in order to make other substances subservient to his aims' (*C* I, p. 179) and this implies: (a) recognizing what these necessary properties *are* in order (b) to transform them into something else.

If we describe this, in Gramsci's words, as a 'necessity' turning into 'freedom' (*SPN*, p. 242), a necessity which serves 'man', it still remains a 'necessarily disappearing necessity' for humans can only work 'as Nature does' by 'changing the form of matter' (*C* I, p. 43). The human creation is itself a compelling necessity which has to be recognized.

This is precisely the point missed in the *Prison Note-books*. In the numerous passages in which Gramsci refers to the relationship of freedom and necessity (e.g. *SPN*, p. 367; p. 370; p. 407; p. 242), the linkage is mechanical and abstract, and the reason is this. Despite his critical note on the young Lukacs (*SPN*, p. 448), Gramsci appears sceptical about a dialectical categorization of natural processes (*SPN*, p. 469) and inverts Marx's epistemological analysis of production by arguing that we never really *know* the natural world, we merely transform it. Hence electricity is an abstract historical 'nothingness' before its human discovery (*SPN*, p. 467). Marx's point is just the opposite: in order to use nature, we have to know what it *is*. Only by recognizing electricity as a natural-historical necessity in its own right, can it then become a qualitatively transformed natural-historical necessity to serve humanity!

Since Gramsci's conception of nature tends to be abstract and mechanistic, it is not surprising that the same 'abstract naturalism' permeates his analysis of the economy as the structure of society. Ricardo's notion of a 'determined market' is taken as Marx's model of 'necessity and regularity' (*SPN*, p. 411), despite the fact that Marx, unlike Ricardo, stresses the changing *form* of natural laws (*SC*, p. 196) while Machiavelli's concept of *Fortuna* is identified with the Marxist view of historical necessity (*SPN*, p. 249; p. 413) even though the Florentine clearly regarded 'our free will' as divine in its origins (Machiavelli, 1970, p. 123). One of the reasons Gramsci gives in his argument against making predictions is the fact that 'reality is a product of the application of the human will to the society of things'

(*SPN*, p. 171) and hence 'laws' are to be appraised through statistical methods rather than through abstraction (*SPN*, p. 412). The 'will' confronts these mechanical regularities as a force from the outside. For all Gramsci's (justified) hostility to vulgar materialism, he transcends it only by putting in its place a 'vulgar' idealism — the *alter ego* of a mechanical unity of opposites. In seeking to avoid all forms of 'monism', Gramsci merely dissolves objective reality into the 'impure' acts of a spiritualized history (*SPN*, p. 372) and hence overlooks the wider processes of natural-history which render explicable the 'identity of contraries in the concrete historical act' (*SPN*, p. 372) as the differentiated moments of a dialectical universe. Humanity is a humanized nature, the will a necessary dimension of social production and free activity the conscious recognition of what has to be done. Without the wider 'monism', the 'identity of contraries' organically divide and the young Marx's 'riddle of history' (*MECW* 3, p. 297) remains unresolved.

In an important sentence in the *Notebooks*, Gramsci speaks of the passage from the purely economic to the 'ethico-political', from structure to superstructure as the passage from 'objective to subjective' and from 'necessity to freedom' (*SPN*, pp. 366–7). Structure, Gramsci adds, 'ceases to be an external force which crushes man, assimilates him to himself and makes him passive; and is transformed into a means of freedom, an instrument to create a new ethico-political form and a source of new initiatives' (*SPN*, p. 367). Although Hoare and Nowell Smith argue in a footnote to this passage that 'Gramsci's treatment of the notion of the passage from the realm of necessity to the realm of freedom differs slightly from that of Marx' (1971, p. 367), in fact the difference is quite substantial. For Marx, the structure exists as an external force 'which crushes man' only in the alienated world of fetishised *appearances*: in essence, and this is a truth which capitalism's 'constant revolutionising' of production dramatically underpins (*MECW* 6, p. 487), the basis demonstrates just what human activity 'can bring about', a synthesis of freedom and necessity which compels creativity through social production.

If Gramsci accepts the 'collective will' of political hegemony uncritically, it is because he also takes the absurd appearances of alienated production at face value. One mechanical hypostasis transcends the other and Gramsci goes 'so far as to affirm' that in a 'unified' (i.e. communist society) 'many idealist conceptions, or at least certain aspects of them which are utopian during the reign of necessity, could become "truth" after the passage' (*SPN*, p. 407). The conception of necessity is superseded by the conception of freedom (*SPN*, p. 382) as the vulgar materialist 'base' yields to the idealist dreams of the superstructure. It is not simply, as Hoare and Nowell Smith suggest, that Marx in contrast is 'more cautious'. His philosophical assumptions are different, for his theory centres not on the passage from nature to history, matter to spirit, quantity to quality, necessity to freedom as though each antinomy simply 'replaced' the other. Marx's conception is that of a process of natural history which is a dynamic necessarily disappearing necessity in all its phases. At a point in the development of this natural history, nature develops 'into man' (*MECW* 3, p. 304) and a socialized necessity emerges in which people 'change the form of matter' consciously, through acts of will and expressions of consent while, at the same time, working 'only as Nature does' (*C* I, p. 43). If in Marx's famous prediction a 'true realm of freedom', the development of human energy as 'an end in itself' can become possible, this higher freedom can only blossom with the 'realm of necessity as its basis' (*C* III, p. 820). Here, in a dramatically humanized form, is that same dialectic of 'necessity into freedom' which is inherent in the production process *from the start* just as this dialectic is itself a humanization of the natural-historical evolution which precedes and presupposes it. The problem of coercion and consent has to be underpinned by a firm grasp of the dialectical development of continuity through change, if we are to avoid the antagonistic antinomies and paralysing paradoxes which have troubled political theory for so long.

CONSENT AS THE DIALECTICAL NEGATION OF COERCION

It might be argued that the analogy implied in the argument so far, between consent on the one hand, and freedom on the other, is a misleading one. Freedom, after all, pin-points the 'moment' of activity, of will, of self-determination; consent, by way of contrast, suggests an element of passivity, a *willingness*, an agreement to accept the initiatives of another. Yet, although the emphasis of the two terms does differ, each contains the 'moment' of the other: consent implies a recognition which is *voluntary* while freedom is only viable as a concept when it is linked to an understanding of what has to be done. Hence it seems to me perfectly acceptable that in classical liberalism, in Gramsci and indeed, in the Marxist tradition as a whole, consent and freedom should be treated as homologous terms. Freedom is not simply 'pure activity' for it involves an acceptance of restraint: likewise, consent is not 'pure passivity'. What I want to argue is that while consent arises through the 'coercion' of natural-historical circumstances, it stands, at the same time, as the 'negation' of the coercion of which it is an organic part. For this reason, the analogy with freedom can only help. If to be free involves a recognition of necessity, to consent involves a recognition of coercion and just as freedom cannot be simply extinguished by necessity, so consent, if the concept is to have a *distinct* meaning, cannot merely be collapsed into coercion. Freedom, as we have already noted, transforms the necessity which it recognizes and, in the same way, consent, although the relatively passive moment of a relationship with another, is never simply a fatalistic acceptance of what 'is'. To consent is also to transform, for in 'consenting', the individual enters into a relationship and by participating in such a relationship, social reality becomes something *other* than what it would have been, had the act of consent not occurred.

People therefore not only can be 'forced to be free', they must, for consent can only arise as a response to coercive social necessity. But because this response involves the formation of a social *relationship*, the act which accepts the coercion also alters it so that even the most passive forms of consent which deeply trouble theorists like Rousseau, negate to some degree the very coercion which occasions them. Even slavery, as Rousseau recognizes, is a relationship and if, as he says, those 'who think themselves the masters of others are indeed greater slaves than they' (1968, p. 46), then a *mutual recognition* is involved and hence, to some albeit relatively minor degree, consent and coercion change places. It seems absurd to say that the murderer consents to die because this 'active recognition' extinguishes the relationship between coerced and coercer, but once we accept that people consent to the coercion of circumstances, we can also understand how they can be said to consent to the concentrated coercion of the state. For even Rousseau's macabre example of liberty inscribed on the doors of the prison (1968, p. 153) points to the irreducible element of consent inherent in all (coercive) social relationships, for unless A recognizes B's ability to coerce him, this coercion cannot be sustained in relational terms. Unless the prisoner consents, however minimally, he either ceases to be a prisoner because he escapes or he ceases to be a prisoner because, in some way or other, he is rendered senseless and ceases to be an active human being at all. Of course, this consent is mostly passive and hence, since the component of freedom as the active moment of consent is minimal, it can be said that there is not 'much' consent. But that is not the point. The point is that even the most draconian forms of coercion, if they are to exist in the form of social relationships, require 'some' consent and this can be legitimately identified as consent because even within the context of a prison, accepting coercion means altering coercion and making social necessity something other than what it would have been.

This is why, as Ball has shown, the 'agency model' of classical liberalism is incapable of really understanding the nature of coercion. For liberalism dissolves human beings into 'distinct, contiguous, contingently related entities' (1978, p. 100) and presents the properties and characteristics of individuals *qua* individuals as fixed and unchanging (p. 102). By way of contrast, the 'structural' model which Marxism favours, analyses individuals through the social roles they play so that the identity of each is formed through the medium of the other. The exercise of coercion in this model presupposes relationships, whereas the classical liberal notion of people as 'billiard-ball entities' denies them. Hence, as a bizarre consequence, since a slave only forms an identity in relation to a master, he cannot in classical liberal eyes, actually suffer coercion (1978, p. 108)!

Understanding coercion as a relationship is not only essential to understand coercion; it is also essential therefore to understand consent. The concept of coercion enables us, as we have seen, to link socialized necessities to the wider natural historical 'compulsions' from which they have arisen. Consent no longer has to contend with the problem of an 'immaculate conception' and hence the question of the 'organic' separation which bedevils Gramsci's analysis can at last be consistently dealt with. Consent can be defined as the conscious recognition of the coercion of relationships — a mechanism without which coercion could not be sustained and through which coercion is itself transformed. If consent is clearly part of coercion, it has nevertheless its own distinct identity. By making it possible to identify consent meaningfully, we also make it possible to distinguish its different degrees. In Gramsci, this problem simply leads to paradox for the more that Gramsci acknowledges that consent can be 'passive', the more absurd it becomes to argue that this consent is exercised outside of the apparatus of state coercive power (*SPN*, p. 12). Gramsci, as Femia recalls, analyses consent along a spectrum in which 'integral hegemony' gives way to 'decadent hegemony' only to become the 'minimal hegemony' that is 'merely an aspect of the function of domination' (Femia, 1981, p. 48). As the distinction ceases to be 'organic', consent ceases to have its own identity and hence, although the problem of how we might differentiate degrees of consent is an important one, it cannot be tackled unless, as it were, we *start* with coercion and *then* establish the existence of consent as a 'moment' within its wider processes.

Once this is done, and we acknowledge that all forms of consent involve the active recognition of coercion, we can usefully distinguish the 'willing slave' from the rebellious subaltern. The consent of the willing slave must be deemed minor and relatively insignificant, since the extent to which he alters the coercive relationship he accepts, is itself minor and insignificant. The 'rebellious subaltern', on the other hand, is also obliged to accept the social relationships which coerce him, but his consent has a dramatic, emancipatory impact on society, since he recognizes the realities of his oppression, only to transform them radically! The 'more' people consent to the relationships which compel them, the more they are able to change them into something else. But even the act of revolutionary 'will' is no 'pure' act of consent, since unless, as Marx said reprovingly of his 'idealist' critics in the Communist League, the revolution is seen 'as the product of realities' (*MECW* 10, p. 626), abstract acts of will inevitably generate, through their futility as gestures, a quietistic pessimism.

The argument therefore that consent must be analysed as the dialectical negation of coercion, a recognition of that coercion which it thereby transforms, makes it possible to take up the challenge of the Machiavellian Centaur, the problem which Gramsci raised but was unable to solve. The two levels are clearly distinct since consent is the recognition of the coercion which compels it — what might be called the passive face of freedom. On the other hand, the distinction is purely methodological, since without that willingness to enter into social relationships which are 'independent of the will', no social coercion would be possible. Even masters require recognition from their slaves. This analysis of consent as the dialectical negation of the coercion from which it arises, holds for social coercion in all its forms, political and non-political alike. It is only through the mechanical hypostasis of commodity production with its theological niceties and metaphysical subtleties that things appear otherwise, for in fact, an 'organic' separation between Gramsci's 'two levels' would require the destruction of the entire ensemble of social relations to bring it about.

6

POLITICAL STRATEGY AND THE 'DEMOCRATIC ROAD'

PROLETARIAN CONSENT AND THE PROBLEM OF FETISHISM

We have already noted the relevance of Marx's analysis of commodity fetishism to the question of coercion and consent in political theory, for the state, as we have seen, not only concentrates the 'dull compulsion' of social relations into direct force, but it also generalizes the consensual illusions inherent in alienated production so that the particular interests of an exploiting class can appear as an expression of society's interests as a whole. The democratic state 'perfects' these illusions and its representative nature is, in Marx's eyes, as 'inseparable from bourgeois society' as the 'isolated individual of modern times' (*MECW* 5, p. 200). To the 'universal' citizen, there corresponds the reified atoms of civil society.

It would appear therefore that in the 'Eden of natural rights' with its emancipated slavery and 'perfected state' a veritable harmony of alienated bliss has been secured. The worker consents to his own exploitation, looking upon 'the mode of production as self-evident laws of nature' (*C* I, p. 737), while the citizen consents to the representative state which, through its 'democratic' laws, compels him to be free. Enoch Powell as a militant logician of the right, vigorously expresses the relationship between the market with its individualistic logic and the representative state which gathers up all the autonomous acts of individuals and 're-presents' them as a 'general will', when he argues that 'the free enterprise economy is the true counterpart of democracy: it is the only system which gives everyone a say. Everyone who goes into a shop and chooses one article instead of another is casting a vote in the economic ballot box . . . in this great and continuous general election of the free economy nobody, not even the poorest, is disenfranchised. We are all voting all the time' (Powell, 1969, p. 33; Hoffman, 1983, p. 80). This argument presents us with a problem. For if, as it appears, the worker's act of consent simply binds him all the more securely to his economic and political masters, wherein lies its potential for freedom?

In the previous chapter we argued that while consent is a product of social coercion, it also transforms the coercion which produces it; yet in the situation noted above, no such 'negative dialectic' appears to work since emancipation seems merely to have consolidated slavery. Marx, as is well known, described the vote as a 'means of deception' (*MESW*, p. 660) and Engels in a comment in 1844 referred scathingly to 'democratic equality' as a 'chimera', insisting that 'the fight of the poor against the rich cannot be fought out on a basis of democracy or indeed of politics as a whole' (*MECW* 3, p. 513). Miliband recalls through the words of Rokkan that while the secret ballot helped to reduce the bribery of the economically dependent by their superiors, the provisions for secrecy could also 'cut off the voter from his *peers*' and in this way reduce pressures towards 'conformity and solidarity within the working class' (1969, p. 194).

The need to be wary of democratic illusions is a constant theme of Marx and Engels's writings. If the *Neue Rheinische Zeitung* was the 'organ of democracy', their editors' 'considered it essential to keep an especially close watch on the democrats' (*MECW* 7, p. 365) and Engels speaks of the danger posed to the working class by 'that democratic influence which led them into an endless series of blunders and misfortunes during 1848 and 1849' (*MECW* 11, p. 38). The parliamentary left in Germany, whose leaders were mostly from the petty bourgeoisie, seemed peculiarly prone to the 'incurable malady' of *'parliamentary cretinism'* — the disorder which 'penetrates its unfortunate victims with the solemn conviction' that the entire world, past and present, is determined by the majority of votes as expressed in 'that particular representative body' (*MECW* 11, p. 79; see also, p. 161). What else is Bonapartism in France but a political system in which the logic of representation reflects the peasant individualism of a nation 'formed by a simple addition of homologous magnitudes, much as potatoes in a sack form a sack of potatoes' (*MECW* 11, p. 187)?

If the illusion of 'politics as will' seems the 'natural expression' of petty bourgeois interests, it is clear that this 'peculiar malady' affects workers as well. Under the regime of Louis Napoleon, there can be no denying, Engels tells Marx, the effect which 'the establishment of the secret ballot has had on the bourgeoisie, the petty bourgeoisie and, *au bout du compte, upon many proletarians as well*' (*MECW* 38, p. 512) for workers are in no way immune from, in Engels's words, 'the old, vulgar, democratic logic of the kind disseminated whenever the revolutionary party suffers defeat' (*MECW* 38, p. 511). Prolonging this vulgar, democratic logic are the 'bourgeoisifying' effects of prosperity and the prospect of 'la gloire de l'empire' (*MECW* 39, p. 196) and Marx and Engels pay particular attention to the role which colonialism plays in generating abstract political illusions. If in the case of Britain, workers can 'cheerfully consume their share' of their country's monopoly of the world market and the colonies, they will think 'the same as the bourgeois think' (*SC*, pp. 330–1), while Engels tells Marx on his return from a trip to Ireland, 'one can already notice here that the so-called liberty of English citizens is based on the oppression of the colonies' (*SC*,

p. 86). Colonial rule over Ireland deepens working class divisions and leads the British worker to regard himself 'as a member of the *ruling* nation' (*SC*, p. 222). The worker who consents to the system of colonialism, thereby strengthens the 'domination *over himself*' (*SC*, p. 222) and contributes to that 'political nullity' (*SC*, p. 344) which makes him no more than an appendix to the politics of liberalism.

It seems curious in the light of the statement above that Carol Johnson should argue that Marx's analysis of workers' movements in his political writings is unrelated to his theory of commodity fetishism and that the latter poses serious problems for the former (1980, p. 89). In fact, as we have seen, the 'hypocritical servitude' of capitalism provides the basis for the hypocritical politics of democracy and the worker, through his consent, seems to be snared in both. The bourgeois republic is precisely the system 'in which free competition rules supreme in all spheres of life' (*MECW* 11, p. 334) and what makes the 'democratic swindle' the 'best machinery in the world by which to establish a despotism upon a firm and comely basis' (Schonfield, 1971, p. 368), is the fact that its political institutions concentrate the fetishism and illusions of a capitalist commodity producing society.

What does pose a serious problem for our analysis is this. If the citizen-worker consents, as in the Powellite utopia, in a way which can only consolidate the instruments of his own coercion, then, contrary to our argument above, consent appears devoid of any dynamic capacity to transform the coercion which has produced it. It ceases to exist as a negation of coercion and functions instead simply as its passive instrument. Our earlier line of argument is brought to a dead end.

To tackle this problem, we need to return to Marx's analysis of fetishism in *Capital*, for if this is a theory of the *raison d'être* of mystifications, it is also a theory, as Geras rightly notes (1971, p. 83), of demystification as well. The natural laws of capitalist production are not fatalistic laws of a mechanistic kind: they are natural-historical laws and as such, carry within each of their 'moments', the seeds of their own supersession. It is crucial for our analysis of coercion and consent that we should understand why. When Marx refers to the liberal abstractions of Freedom and Equality which provide the 'Free-trader Vulgaris' with the standard by which he judges a society based on capital and wages (*C* I, p. 176), he refers specifically to things as they seem in the sphere of exchange. The worker who descends into the 'hidden abode of production' however, learns otherwise. Having consented to sell his labour power freely, he discovers, of course, that the contract is based on force and hence, as Marx puts it, he comes 'out of the process of production other than he entered' (*C* I, p. 301). What has changed? The worker learns through his own experience that 'beneath' an equalizing process of exchange lies radical inequalities in the possession of power. If commodity production, notes Marx, is 'to be judged according to its own economic laws, we must consider each act of exchange by itself, apart from any connexion with the act of exchange preceding it and that following it' (*C* I, p. 586). The worker, by virtue of the fact that he is continuously engaged in a process of production which radically disadvantages him, cannot avoid seeing the social relationships which underpin his exploitation. Given the tendency of capitalist production (commented on by Marx elsewhere) to depress the value of the worker's labour power to its ultimate limit, the worker is compelled if only to ensure his survival even as a seller of his labour power, to unite with his fellow workers and struggle collectively in the first instance, for 'a fair day's wage' (*MESW*, pp. 228–9). In other words, in consenting to exploitation, the worker cannot fail to see increasingly his contractual exchange with the capitalist as a social relationship involving power and class. To survive even as a commodity, he has to *unite* and hence in 'recognizing' the realities of his situation, he comes to apply 'standards entirely foreign to commodity production' (*C* I, p. 586). Trade unionism therefore for Marx, at once rationalizes capitalist relations of production and *points beyond them*. The engagement of workers in collective struggle necessarily disrupts the fetishism of the exchange process: (a) because individual sales and purchases now stand revealed as a relationship between social collectivities and; (b) because the 'ever expanding union' centralizes local struggles and begins to concentrate economic protests into a *political* movement. The alienated autonomy of the state from society, central to commodity fetishism, is challenged.

This is why Marx considered the victory of the British workers in 1847 in securing the passage of the Ten Hours bill as a development of the greatest importance. This reform, he declares, has made 'the English factory workers' the 'theorists' of the modern working class generally: 'the first to throw down the gauntlet to the theory of capital' (*C* I, p. 299). This was, he told members of the First International, 'the victory of a principle'; 'the first time that in broad daylight the political economy of the middle class succumbed to the political economy of the working class' (*FI*, p. 79). Here indeed is the explicit recognition of 'standards entirely foreign to commodity production', for what is the political economy of the working class if it is not 'social production controlled by social foresight' (*FI*, p. 79)? If this 'political economy' is foreign to commodity production, it is a political economy nevertheless which is generated by the contradictory logic of capitalist production, for exploitation necessarily involves relations of production whose *social* character contradicts the fetishised individualism of the exchange process. Hence we can see why the worker's consent to his own coercion is not as passive as it first appears. In order to survive even as a commodity, the worker must organize and as he does so, competition gives way to association, local struggles are centralized, economic movements become political, disparate individuals are united into a conscious *class* and with the formation of a revolutionary party, the system as a whole is placed on trial. The development of capitalism itself, as the *Manifesto* puts it, 'cuts from under its feet the very foundation on which the bourgeoisie produces and appropriates products' (*MECW* 6, p. 496).

Johnson's argument that Marx's 'optimistic perspectives concerning the development of proletarian revolutionary consciousness' stand in contradiction to his theory of commodity fetishism (1980, p. 94) arises because of a tendency to see only *mystification* in the capital-labour contract and not that contradictory relationship between the social and the individual which pushes capitalist exploitation 'beyond itself'. In accepting his contract, the worker's act of consent brings him face to face with the social character of the coercion which 'forces him to be free' and this is a recognition of necessity which obliges him, even to survive as a commodity, to apply 'standards entirely foreign to commodity production'. The fact that proletarian politics arises as 'a natural process from the workers' everyday struggle under capitalism' (Johnson, 1980, p. 81) does not conflict with Marx's analysis of commodity fetishism: on the contrary, it is a reflection of its dialectical, natural-*historical* character.

If, as I have argued, proletarian consent has a critical quality which points beyond the mystified relations of which it is part, how does this enable the worker as citizen to break free from the 'vulgar logic' of political democracy? Marx does not, of course, only see the vote as a 'means of deception' but also as an instrument of 'emancipation' (*MESW*, p. 660). This should not be taken to mean that the suffrage has two 'organically' separate aspects, for a dialectical view of the coercion/consent problem shows precisely why the 'deceptive' and the 'emancipatory' are so closely interrelated. When Engels attacks democratic equality as a 'chimera', he also speaks of democracy as 'the last purely political remedy which has still to be tried and from which a new element is bound to develop at once': the democracy towards which 'England is moving is a *social* democracy' (*MECW* 3, p. 513). The reason for this is that for the worker, the vote has an essentially social significance. Political rights are 'knife and fork questions' (*MECW* 4, p. 519) and therefore, unlike the bourgeois who votes in order to preserve an existing state of affairs where economic and social security has *already* been obtained, the worker votes as an individual whose 'individuality' can only acquire serious meaning through *social reform*. What is the point of voting as the member of a class which 'has nothing of its own to secure and fortify' (*MECW* 6, p. 495), unless in the words of the Reverend Stephens, it brings 'a good house, good food and drink, prosperity, and short working hours' (*MECW* 4, p. 519)? Unlike the bourgeois, the worker is far from being 'at ease' in an alienation with 'its semblance of a human existence' (*MECW* 4, p. 36) and hence when he consents politically, he expresses and exposes the gulf which exists between legal freedom and social slavery. 'A new element', as Engels says, 'is bound to develop at once', even if the development of this social into a socialist consciousness is a protracted process. The contradictory character of proletarian consent is established nevertheless.

On this, Marx's analysis of the events in France, 1848–52, is particularly instructive. Although the Paris proletariat initially revel in the 'magnanimous intoxication of fraternity' (*MECW* 10, p. 58) which the suffrage brings, working class support for their bourgeois allies forces the new Provisional Government to announce '*a republic with social institutions*' (*MECW* 10, p. 66). In order to remove these concessions, the June insurrection is provoked and the workers crushed but a 'fundamental contradiction' remains. The classes, whose 'social slavery the constitution is to perpetuate', still enjoy the vote (*MECW* 10, p. 79) and what else is the suffrage but a bourgeois politics which transcends the bourgeois order? As Marx puts it in a remarkable passage, 'By ever and anon putting an end to the existing state power and creating it anew out of itself, does not universal suffrage put an end to all stability, does it not every moment question all the power that be . . . does it not threaten to elevate anarchy itself to the position of authority?' (*MECW* 10, p. 131). By inviting workers to consent to their coercion, the suffrage compels them to look beyond it; hence to overcome the contradiction between the social *content* of the vote and its individualized form, the French bourgeoisie abolish universal suffrage altogether!

It is true that Bonaparte restores the vote and appears to an exhausted and defeated proletariat as 'the patriarchal benefactor of all classes' (*MECW* 11, p. 195), but even here, it is necessary to initiate a public works programme for popular employment in order to sustain the demagogic appearances of what Guizot calls *'le triomphe complet et definitif du socialisme'* (*MECW* 11, p. 184): socialism with an imperial face! Even if the 'immediate and palpable result' of universal suffrage brings Bonapartism, the 'overthrow of the parliamentary republic contains within itself the germ of the triumph of proletarian revolution' (*MECW* 11, p. 184) and with the formation of a social republic through the Paris Commune in 1871, the emancipatory potential of universal suffrage becomes fully apparent. For long periods, the contradictory character of the vote as a consent which challenges the coercion which produces it, lies 'dormant', seemingly smothered by a routinized normality, but even the deception is deceptive, for in periods of crisis, the capacity of universal suffrage to 'unchain the class struggle' (*MECW* 10, p. 65) becomes dramatically apparent. The suffrage is a 'school of development' (*MECW* 10, p. 137) which makes it possible for the proletariat to penetrate increasingly the fetishism of emancipated slavery and the perfected state and implant within the heart of the capitalist system a logic which is social and ultimately, socialist in character.

Johnson misses the dialectical character of this proletarian consent when she argues, quoting Fernbach, that Marx fails to 'leave a theoretical space for the possibility of a workers' movement that is organized politically as a class and yet solely struggles for reforms within the capitalist system' (1980, p. 59). For while it is true that reforms may reinforce illusions of community and brotherhood, the political organization of a workers' movement expresses a collectivist logic entirely 'foreign to the standards of commodity production'. It not only extends the principle of 'social production controlled by social foresight' (*FI*, p. 79), but by posing the need to bring products under the control of their producers, it also challenges the very notion of the state as an illusory community. Hence, as Engels puts it, the 'new element' which develops through proletarian politics is *'a principle transcending everything of a political nature'* (*MECW* 3, p. 513). All this is naturally only embryonic under capitalism, but if reforms generate 'reformism', they do so in the form of a consent to developments which intensify the contradictory logic of a system of 'privatized' social relationships. If it were true that the workers' movement struggles for 'reforms solely within the capitalist system', how are we to explain the 'rise of the social market economy' (Gamble, 1979) in the late 1970s as an anti-Keynesian *revanchism* which seeks to cleanse 'welfare' capitalism of all its logical impurities? The working class franchise is both negative as well as positive, deceptive as well as emancipatory. Fraudulent, because consent is itself a product of coercion, yet meaningful, because through multiple acts of economic and political consent, the workers increasingly penetrate the fetishistic appearances of capitalism and come to grasp its concentrated and 'circumstantial' coercion as an historically transitory reality.

PROLETARIAN COERCION AND THE 'DUAL PERSPECTIVE'

Although proletarian consent arises, as we have seen, as a response to social and political coercion, this response is necessarily an organized one. Expressed initially through trade unionism as workers defend their immediate interests (even as labour powering commodities), it involves an 'ever-expanding union' (*MECW* 6, p. 493) which becomes political when the particular interests of particular workers are presented as *social* principles and projected in a 'general form' (*SC*, p. 255). As the proletariat is 'concentrated in greater masses' and feels its strength more, so specific grievances are 'concentrated' into political demands and the proletarians are organized into 'a class, and consequently into a political party' (*MECW* 6, pp. 492–3). This requires, as noted in earlier chapters, a struggle for hegemony, a leadership which brings 'to the front the common interests of the entire proletariat' (*MECW* 6, p. 497), the search for allies and, as the passage of the Ten Hours bill revealed, an ability to profit from divisions among the propertied classes themselves. Clearly then, this pursuit of hegemony involves consent — a recognition of coercive realities — but it also involves something more. If the worker is compelled to consent, then since, as argued above, this consent is never purely passive, he is also compelled to resist, and what else is the projection of one will to counter another, but a *coercion to transform coercion*? If consent is the 'passive face of freedom', a *counter*-coercion is the 'active face' of the consensual response. Consent cannot be a dialectical negation of coercion, unless it mounts at the same time a 'counter-coercion' of its own. Even within the act of the respondent who consents to the pressures from without, there can be no 'organic' divide, for a dialectical view of the problem demands that 'the educator must himself be educated' (*MECW* 5, p. 7). The implicit force involved in the individual's resistance to social circumstances and the coercion of law becomes the increasingly explicit force of political organization as these piecemeal acts of resistance are gathered up nationally, generalized ideologically and directed at the state. Hegemony stands, in other words, as a process of: (a) developing mass support in order (b) to organize counter-coercion.

We are now in a position to see what is so problematic about the strategic inferences which Gramsci was to draw from his analysis of the 'two levels'. Gramsci argued that in Europe after 1870, the development of democracy, mass political parties and the 'great economic trade unions' created trench-like fortifications of ruling class interests (*SPN*, p. 243) and this meant therefore that a 'war of maneouvre' with its sudden, sharp 'lightning' attacks designed to overwhelm an enemy rapidly, had increasingly to become a 'war of position' with its slow, methodical, trench warfare and for which 'an unprecedented concentration of hegemony is necessary' (*SPN*, p. 243). If, in the East, where 'civil society' is weak and the state is 'everything' a war of manoeuvre still applies, in the West, with its 'proper relation between State and civil society' (*SPN*, p. 238), a war of position is the only form possible (*SPN*, p. 237). This analysis, as Anderson has pointed out, 'disconcertingly' echoes the argument by Kautsky in 1910 that while a 'strategy of overthrow' (Gramsci's war of manoeuvre) had predominated from 1789 to 1870, following the fall of the Paris Commune it had been superseded by a 'strategy of attrition' (Gramsci's war of position). Kautsky cited in defence of this argument Engels's famous preface to the *Class Struggles in France* where, he said, Engels had discarded 'the old revolutionary strategy' (Anderson, 1976–7, p. 63). Since Engels's introduction has an important bearing on the coercion/consent problem in the formation of political strategy, Kautsky's claim merits a moment's attention.

Certainly he was not the only one to read Engels's introduction in this way. Bernstein referred to the introduction as evidence that Engels had become 'thoroughly convinced' that 'the tactics based on the presumption of a catastrophe have had their day' (1961, p. xxviii) while Hunt has recently argued that the introduction 'constitutes a major departure from the conception of socialist revolution advanced by Marx in *Class Struggles* and also, even more significantly, in *The Civil War in France*' (1983, p. 96). Engels himself says that 'the mode of struggle of 1848 is today obsolete in every respect' and that history 'has proved us, and all who thought like us, wrong' (*MESW*, pp. 655—6). Yet what precisely was it that Engels was repudiating? Hunt complains that in important respects, Engels fails to follow through the implications of his own analysis and 'retains a different version of the "insurrectionist" perspective' (1983, p. 97). But this 'failure' arises because Engels's self-criticisms are essentially of a tactical kind. While he finds old style, street fighting with barricades largely obsolete (*MESW*, p. 661), he expresses an enthusiastic preference for 'open attack' (*MESW*, p. 663). Engels advises his fellow socialists to increase their electoral support and avoid being provoked into playing 'the part of cannon fodder' but this merely means that they should keep their 'daily increasing shock force' intact until 'the decisive day' (*MESW*, p. 665). Although Bernstein claims that Engels had abandoned the tactics of the 'catastrophe', in fact when his introduction was first published in the SPD's *Neue Zeit*, it had to be censored. References to the 'decisive day' and the need for 'open attack' were omitted as was the comment that should the government act unconstitutionally, Social Democracy will also be free to do as it pleases (*MESW*, p. 667; for the omissions, footnotes pp. 662—7).

If it were true, then, as Moore has argued, that the *Introduction* represents a break with the *Communist Manifesto* and its 'Blanquist call for minority revolution' (1963, p. 18; Johnstone, 1983, p. 311), why is it that Engels explicitly affirms a strategic continuity with the past? The *Manifesto*, he writes in 1895, 'had already proclaimed the winning of universal suffrage, of democracy, as one of the first and most important tasks of the militant proletariat' (*MESW*, pp. 659—60). Granted, the emphasis in 1848 is very different. But if stress is placed in the *Manifesto* on the 'strategy of overthrow' or the 'war of maneouvre', attention is also given to a 'strategy of attrition' or 'war of position'. Revolution is depicted as a process and winning the battle for democracy involves a series of interconnected measures, economically insufficient and untenable in themselves, which in turn necessitate 'further inroads upon the old social order' (*MECW* 6, p. 504). A transitional programme was devised as an instrument to consolidate hegemony, so much so that Wagner and Strauss have even argued that the 'insufficient' and 'untenable' measures were intended to secure goodwill and co-operation from industrial sectors of the bourgeoisie (1969, p. 479)!

What was illusory in 1848 was not the strategy of the *Manifesto* but the belief that it could be implemented given the 'unripeness of proletarian aspirations' at the time (*MESW*, p. 657). The 1888 edition of the *Manifesto* declared that the proletarian movement must be 'the independent movement of the immense majority' which is 'self-conscious' and Engels doubtless added this latter phrase in the revised version (*MECW* 6, p. 495) in order to give a renewed emphasis to the majoritarian perspectives which he and Marx had presented some 40 years before. The war of position does not contradict the war of manoeuvre: it makes it all the more effective. The two moments necessarily interpenetrate and to say that the *Introduction* is 'ambiguous' (Miliband, 1978, p. 160) rather misses the point that, for Engels, the electoral advance is part of a process which culminates in a revolutionary upsurge on the 'decisive day'. The fact, as Mandel rightly notes, that Engels 'in no way ruled out recourse to insurrection' should not be taken to mean, as Mandel wrongly supposes, that Engels rules out 'a peaceful, legalist, gradualist, electoralist road to socialism' (1978, p. 180). On the contrary, both 'moments', the insurrectionary and the gradualist are involved. In the *Manifesto* the 'forcible overthrow of all existing social conditions' (*MECW* 6, p. 519) is preceded by a protracted process of development in which the phases of the civil war are 'more or less veiled' (*MECW* 6, p. 495): likewise in the *Introduction* the 'natural process' of 'tranquil' electoral advances necessarily culminate in the confrontation of a 'decisive day' (*MESW*, p. 665). If the emphasis differs, the logic is the same, for proletarian use of the suffrage does not imply the repudiation of coercion in favour of consent. Electoral struggle is itself an instrument for creating 'a daily increasing shock force' ultimately capable of implementing 'socially coercive force' in a 'general form'. It is the coercive character of the political process in all its phases as a coercion able to command consent, which makes it possible to see the underlying unity between the positions of 1848 and those advanced almost 50 years later.

What was for Engels tactical, was for Kautsky *strategic*. For Kautsky, electoral struggle was a 'natural process' which obviated the need for a 'decisive day' since proletarian respect for democracy 'as a strategy' could only impress upon the bourgeoisie the futility and immorality of violently resisting the 'slide' to socialism (Salvadori, 1979, p. 41; p. 130). Questions of a 'frontal clash' can be 'tranquilly left to the future' for, as Salvadori comments, Kautsky 'erected — and this was to remain a central feature of his writing — a sort of no-man's land between strategy and tactics that could never be crossed in practice' (1979, p. 80; p. 69; p. 90). Kautsky's misreading of Engels reflects the mechanistic tenor of his writings as a whole and the radical divorce he presented between the 'strategies' of 'overthrow' and 'attrition' derived in particular from a failure to grasp the coercive and consensual moments of politics in synthetic terms.

Although Gramsci, as Femia has noted (1981, p. 205), rejected the obvious face of 'vulgar democracy' with its 'parliamentarist illusions', there can be little doubt that he showed some sympathy for the basic drift of Kautsky's analysis. In the period after 1870, he argues, the 'Forty-Eightist formula of the "Permanent Revolution" is expanded and transcended ... by the formula of "civil hegemony" ' (*SPN*, p. 243) and yet there is an important ambiguity here which needs to be cleared up. Both in 1848 and in 1917 it could well be argued that we encounter *two* rival concepts of 'permanent revolution' and that only in the case of *one* of these concepts would it be true to say that 'civil hegemony' was seriously lacking. Gramsci, we will try to show, tended to confuse them.

According to Richard Hunt, the slogan of the 'permanent revolution' can only be attributed to classical Marxism with 'the most severe reservations' (1974, p. 246). Yet even if we accept Hunt's argument that the *slogan* was used by Marx as an attempt to reconcile deep fissures within the Committee of Communist League, Marx's view of the permanent revolution is quite distinct from that of Blanqui and his Communist League supporters. The slogan parallels, as Hunt notes, the reference in the *Manifesto* to the bourgeois revolution in Germany as 'the prelude to an immediately following proletarian revolution' (*MECW* 6, p. 519; Hunt, 1974, pp. 187–9) and it served to emphasize for Marx and Engels, a general point of political theory. Revolution was to be conceived of as a *process* in which a bourgeois revolution was the first step towards a socialist one. Hence, although the *Manifesto* speaks of a proletarian revolution which 'immediately follows', no particular timescale is implied as to just how long this process which must begin immediately, will take to complete. The March Address to the League in 1850 raises the 'battle cry' of 'The Revolution in Permanence' but also contends that the German workers, for example, will not be able 'to attain power and achieve their own class interests without completely going through a lengthy revolutionary development' (*MECW* 10, pp. 286–7). What makes the revolution 'permanent' is that it is a process through *stages* and it is surely revealing therefore that however much Marx's Blanquist opponents may have cherished the slogan before 1850, after the *March Address* they dropped it and resorted openly, as Hunt notes, to 'a single one-step revolutionary strategy involving immediate seizure of power' (1974, p. 246). As far as Marx and Engels were concerned, the 'Forty-Eightist formula' of the permanent revolution, as they interpreted it, was a majoritarian strategy based on the need to secure proletarian hegemony.

But what of the even more famous controversy over

Lenin's relationship with Trotsky in 1917? It has been widely held among commentators that in the spring of 1917, Lenin jettisoned the analysis he had developed in 1905 and came to embrace Trotsky's theory of the permanent revolution (see e.g. Harding, 1977, p. 198; Howe, 1978, p. 38; Liebman, 1975, p. 188; Geras, 1975, pp. 26–8). Even the young Gramsci considered it 'well known' that in November 1917, Lenin and the majority of his party 'had gone over to Trotsky's view' (*SPW* II, p. 192). In fact, as with Marx and the Blanquists of 1848, things are not so simple.

In September of 1905, Lenin had written that 'from the democratic revolution we shall at once, and precisely in accordance with the measure of our strength . . . begin to pass to the socialist revolution. We stand for uninterrupted revolution. We shall not stop half-way' (*LCW* 9, pp. 236–7). Yet according to Knei-Paz, this was an atypically 'impulsive reaction to the events of 1905' and Lenin returned thereafter to 'the orthodox view that Russia must first go through a bourgeois revolution before there could be talk of a socialist one' (1978, p. 170). In fact, Lenin's reference to 'uninterrupted revolution' was in essential accord with the 'orthodox' view that the democratic revolution must come *first*, the revolution can only be permanent because it occurs through *stages* and the socialist 'dictatorship of the proletariat' must be *preceded* by a 'democratic dictatorship of proletariat and peasantry'. This was Lenin's view in 1905 and it was his view in 1917. Although he accepted that the February revolution was incomplete in the sense that many of the 'tasks' normally associated with the democratic revolution had not been carried out, he still insisted that the 'Bolshevik slogans and ideas *on the whole* have been confirmed by history' (*LCW* 24, p. 44). If 'the basic sign' of a revolution is 'the passing of state power from one *class* to another', then 'to this extent' the bourgeois-democratic revolution in Russia 'is *completed*' (*LCW* 24, p. 44). As far as Lenin was concerned, Trotsky's conceptual *bête noir* 'the revolutionary-democratic dictatorship of the proletariat and peasantry' had *already* become a reality. It is true, as Geras notes, that Lenin could also say later that the Bolshevik revolution had 'carried the *bourgeois* revolution to its conclusion' (*LCW* 28, p. 301; p. 314) and that the second revolution 'solves the problems of the first' (*LCW* 33, p. 54; Geras, 1975, p. 39), but however 'Trotskyist' these formulations sound, their logic is quite different. One revolution precedes the other, even if *all* its tasks are not complete and the transition from the first stage to the second is only possible when the ground has been prepared and the movement occurs 'in accordance with the measure of our strength' (*LCW* 9, p. 237). Hence Lenin in 1917 explicitly rejects the Trotsky-Parvus slogan of 'No Tsar, but a *workers'* government' (*LCW* 24, p. 48) since the 'rule of the proletariat' requires a 'period of *transition*' from the rule of the bourgeoisie in order to ensure that it can emerge as 'the direct, immediate and unquestionable rule of the *majority*' (*LCW* 28, p. 49).

For all its apparent similarities, Trotsky's theory of permanent revolution is quite different from that of Lenin's (*LCW* 15, p. 371; *LCW* 16, p. 379; *LCW* 21, p. 418; see also Johnstone, 1968, pp. 8–16; Basmanov, 1972, pp. 18–25). Trotsky, as we have already noted in chapter 3, rejected the notion of the democratic revolution as a separate *stage*, declared the concept of the 'democratic-dictatorship' to be a 'metaphysical construct' (1971, p. 332) and saw no dividing line between minimum and maximum programmes (Geras, 1975, p. 26). A different concept of strategy stemmed from a different conception of politics. If in Lenin as in the classical Marxist tradition generally, politics involved a coercion which commands consent, in Trotsky, a spontaneist view of proletarian 'self-activity' (Knei-Paz, 1978, p. 190) coexisted with a mechanistic view of 'brute force' (1971, p. 399). Coercion was necessary because of the *absence* of consent and thus Trotsky believed, as Knei-Paz puts it, 'collectivist measures, supported by state power, would be a substitute for national consensus': 'Without consensus, without agreement about the future, a dictatorship — of the workers, the only force prepared and capable of carrying out modernization — becomes essential and inevitable' (Knei-Paz, 1978, p. 163). Since the democratic revolution can only take place as 'a *consequence*' of the proletarian revolution (Geras, 1975, p. 39), here is a version of the permanent revolution which echoes the Blanquist formulas of 1848 (Hunt, 1974, p. 220) in seriously understating the importance of hegemony.

Gramsci was certainly critical of Trotsky's views but the contrast he drew between the two concepts of permanent revolution is far from clear. 'In the case of Trotsky', he writes, 'you had the Jacobin temperament without an adequate political content', while in the case of Lenin, you had 'a Jacobin temperament and content derived from the new historical relations, and not from a literary and intellectualistic label' (*SPN*, p. 85). But in what sense can it be said that they were both *Jacobins*? The term is ambiguous in Gramsci, implying on the one hand, 'audacious, dauntless' leadership (*SPN*, p. 84), while on the other, a formula of permanent revolution in which the war of movement is 'the whole' of the war and therefore lacks the element of 'position' (*SPN*, p. 243). Thus, as we noted above, Gramsci characterizes the October revolution as 'the war of manoeuvre applied victoriously', while the 'war of position' is the 'only form possible in the West' (*SPN*, p. 237). Hegemony is a strategy which transcends the Forty-Eightist formula of the permanent revolution (*SPN*, p. 243).

Gramsci linked his emphasis on the war of position with the Comintern's formula of the 'United Front' and argued that Lenin himself had understood that 'a change was necessary' (*SPN*, p. 237). Indeed Lenin in his critique of 'Left-wing Communism' *had* stressed the importance of educating the people for socialism in the countries of Western Europe where 'the backward masses of the workers and — to an even greater degree — of the small peasants are much more imbued with bourgeois democratic and parliamentary prejudices than they were in Russia' (*LCW* 31, p. 65). In Russia, where these 'prejudices' were not so deeply rooted, starting the revolution, Lenin commented earlier, had been 'as easy as lifting a feather' (*LCW* 27, p. 99). But did this imply that where the state was 'everything' and civil society 'primordial and gelatinous' (*SPN*, p. 238), the struggle for hegemony was irrelevant? If this was Gramsci's position as some of his commentators suggest (Femia, 1981, p. 54; Showstack Sassoon, 1980b, p. 198), it was certainly not Lenin's. The attack on 'Left-wing Communism' was essentially an argument for the international *relevance* of the Russian Revolution (*LCW* 31, p. 22) and in particular, for an understanding of those 'thorough, circumspect and long preparations' without which 'we could not have achieved victory in October 1917, or have consolidated that victory' (*LCW* 31, p. 31). How then was it possible that Gramsci, who had praised Lenin for carrying out 'the theorisation and realisation of hegemony' (*SPN*, p. 357) and had alluded to the element of this hegemony within the *Bolshevik* version of permanent revolution (*SPN*, p. 85), could at the same time present the Russian Revolution as a war without 'position'? Gramsci's passages on the distinction between East and West all suffer, as Anderson has commented, 'from the same flaw'; their 'ultimate logic is always to tend to revert to the simple schema of an opposition between 'hegemony' (consent) in the West and 'dictatorship' (coercion) in the East: parliamentarism versus Tsarism' (1976–7, p. 52). The distinction which should be 'methodological' is, as always, 'organic' and, as Anderson adds, the 'mere counterposition of the "war of position" to the "war of manoeuvre" in Marxist strategy in the end becomes an opposition between reformism and adventurism' (1976–7, p. 77): the 'reformism' of Kautsky's 'strategy of attrition' set against the 'adventurism' so often implied in Rosa Luxemburg's spirited defence of a strategy of 'overthrow' (Anderson, 1976–7, p. 65).

Once we grasp the nature of politics as an organized

movement which concentrates the coercion of social relations, we can see why the two moments of the 'dual perspective' interpenetrate at every level. Since consent is a response to coercion, the passive moment of politics involves a recognition of realities, the winning of support from the masses. The fact that Gramsci sometimes links his notion of 'passive revolution' to a war of position (*SPN*, pp. 108–11) bears this out. It is the sober moment of preparation. Yet consent also involves as a *response* to coercion, a counter-coercion of its own and hence the element of position passes into the element of manoeuvre. Indeed, Gramsci himself puts the point well when he says, speaking of Cavour as the exponent of passive revolution/war of position and Mazzini of popular initiative/war of manoeuvre: 'are not both of them indispensable to precisely the same extent?' (*SPN*, p. 108). Yet, Gramsci could only have sustained the dialectical unity of his two strategic moments, avoiding the 'organic' divide of an East/West contrast, if he had, at the same time, resolved the problem of coercion and consent. Manoeuvre, without position, is the untenable abstraction of a pure coercion; a war of position 'on its own' implies the mechanical hypostasis of the moment of consent.

EUROCOMMUNISM, LENIN AND THE CONCEPT OF THE MAJORITY

In chapter 1, we encountered the rise in the middle of the 1970s of a new trend in communism — a *Euro*communism — whose proponents present a new political strategy and indeed a new theory of politics as the solution to the 'crisis of Marxism'. A 'simple choice' between two roads to socialism confronts Marxists (Balibar, 1977a, p. 146): if the old Marxism tended to favour dictatorship and coercion (thus laying the basis for 'the crisis'), the new Marxism looks towards a strategy and a socialism rooted in democracy and consent.

As we also noted in the first chapter, this conception of the 'democratic' road to a 'democratic' socialism is seen by Eurocommunist writers as fundamentally 'Gramscian' in origin and inspiration. Gramsci's 'text' on the 'structural differences' between Tsarist Russia and Western Europe is considered 'seminal' to Eurocommunist thought and, it is argued, capitalism's ability to survive economic depression, political crisis and world war has 'rendered the frontal assault, "war of manoeuvre", insurrectionary model inappropriate' (Bridges, 1978, p. 125). In elaborating their party's case for the 'democratic road to socialism', leading French communists place particular stress on Gramsci's concept of hegemony (Fabre, Hincker and Sève, 1977, p. 71) while Carrillo's *'Eurocommunism' and the State* projects a strategy which is rooted in 'Gramsci's idea of the organic intellectual' (1977, p. 44). Whether the Eurocommunism is of a 'leftwing' or 'rightwing' variety (Jessop, 1982, p. 14), Gramsci's influence appears pivotal (Hobsbawm and Napolitano, 1977, pp. 46–7; Azcarate, 1978, p. 16; Buci-Glucksmann, 1980, p. ix; Simon, 1982, p. 124; Gibbon, 1983, pp. 328–35).

Yet we are now in a position to see why the relationship between Gramsci and Eurocommunism is rather more complex than is so often assumed. Whereas Gramsci sought to integrate the 'war of manoeuvre' with the 'war of position' (Femia, 1981, pp. 205–6), Eurocommunist theoreticians tend to treat them as *separate* strategic options; while Gramsci attempted to unite hegemony with force, in Eurocommunism a mechanically 'hypostasized' consent serves as the identifying attribute of a separate road to socialism. If the 'democratic road' is Gramsci's 'war of position', it is Gramsci's conception shorn of its ambiguities, uncertainties and above all, its profoundly dialectical aspirations. The 'organic' divide between political and civil society, coercion and consent which Gramsci struggled so hard to avoid, now becomes explicit.

Praise for Gramsci is accompanied by a sharp critique

of Lenin (Mercer, 1980, p. 126; Hunt, 1980, p. 7). If, for Carrillo, the classical Marxist heritage on the question of democracy is generally unsatisfactory, Lenin's views on the subject are seen as particularly unhelpful (1977, p. 14; p. 88), and, as far as Hunt is concerned, a 'recognition of the contradictory character of bourgeois democracy' is absent in Lenin (1980, p. 13). It is sometimes said that the 'younger' Lenin regarded democracy as emancipatory, while the Lenin post-1917 emphasizes only its fraudulent, deceptive character (see e.g. Liebman, 1975, p. 163). Yet as early as 1894 Lenin had stressed that 'political liberty will primarily serve the interests of the bourgeoisie' (*LCW* 1, p. 294) and as late as 1919, after the acrimonious exchanges with Kautsky had begun, Lenin could still emphasize that only through the democratic republic and universal suffrage, can the proletariat 'achieve its present unity and solidarity' in the struggle against capital (*LCW* 29, p. 486). Indeed, it might well be argued that it is precisely because Lenin *did* recognize the contradictory character of 'bourgeois democracy' as a polity whose pretensions are not to be taken at face value, that his writings are regarded by contemporary Eurocommunism with suspicion and unease.

Woddis, however, has sought to present the 'two levels' of Gramsci's Machiavellian Centaur as a view of political power which was shared by Lenin. He cites Lenin's reference to the fact that 'the bourgeoisie maintains itself in power *not* only by force but also by virtue of the lack of class-consciousness and organisation, the routinism and down-trodden state of the masses' (*LCW* 24, p. 46–7; Woddis, 1977, p. 17). Lenin, says Woddis, makes the same point a few months later (September 1917) when he contrasts the two methods used by bourgeois and landowner governments to keep 'the people in subjection'. The first is the method of violence, the Russian Tsars' reliance on the hangman, while the second, 'best developed by the British and French bourgeoisie', is 'the method of deception, flattery, fine phrases, promises by the million, petty sops and concessions of the unessential . . .' (*LCW* 24, pp. 63–4). But Lenin's distinction here is not as Woddis suggests, a distinction between coercion and consent (1977, p. 29) of a Gramscian kind, but a distinction between the concentrated force of the state (the 'hangman') and the dull compulsion of economic relations ('routinism', 'flattery', etc.). Lenin appears to be under no illusion about the coercive character of the method of deception and refers a few years later to the importance of *Capital* to an understanding of democracy. Marx, he declares, had ridiculed freedom, equality and the will of the majority as phrases used by the owners of capital 'to oppress the masses of the working people' (*LCW* 29, p. 352). Lenin's 'method of deception' differs from Gramsci's moment of consent because as an instrument of bourgeois hegemony, it is characterized in a way which is pejorative rather than moralistic in tone and unambiguously implies the generation of consent through social and political coercion.

According to Woddis, however, since Lenin considered that there were 'two rather different methods of bourgeois rule', then it is not illogical to argue that 'there could be generally speaking, two different methods of ending that rule' (1977, p. 29). But here we need to be careful. For this is only true if the 'two different methods' are regarded as two tactical moments within a *single* political strategy which combines coercion in all its forms. It is quite *illogical* to present one of these 'moments' as the basis of a strategy which is democratic and the other, the basis of a strategy which is dictatorial and coercive in character. Yet this is the direction in which Woddis's analysis proceeds. He presents the classical Marxist strategy of 'smashing the state' (which is undeniably coercive in its implications) as a minoritarian strategy for taking power and hence irrelevant to the conditions of advanced capitalist countries. He quotes Lenin as saying in 1919 that the proletariat must first overthrow the bourgeoisie and then use its state power 'for the purpose of winning the sympathy of the majority of the working people' (*LCW* 30, p. 263). The proletariat, 'even when it constitutes a minority of the population', is capable of winning to its side 'numerous allies from a mass of semi-proletarians and petty bourgeoisie who never declare in advance in favour of the rule of the proletariat': only through 'their subsequent experience' do these allies 'become convinced that the proletarian dictatorship is inevitable, proper and legitimate' (*LCW* 30, p. 274). But what are the implications of this analysis? For Woddis, 'the argument is clear enough. Under conditions of capitalism it is not possible to win a majority for socialism' (1977, p. 31). The Bolsheviks triumphed with the support of a minority in a way which would be inconceivable in the liberal capitalist countries of the West.

We have however a problem. In the same article from which Woddis draws his citations (1977, pp. 30–1), Lenin ridicules 'the talk' about the Bolsheviks having only a 'minority' of the proletariat behind them (*LCW* 30, p. 256). In his earlier polemic with Kautsky, he refers to the 'ridiculous fable that the Bolsheviks only have a backing of a minority of the population' (*LCW* 28, p. 296). Woddis himself is puzzled to find Lenin saying in July 1924 at the Third Congress of the Communist International that to win and retain power, not only is 'the majority of the working class' essential, but 'also the majority of the working and exploited rural population' (*LCW* 32, p. 476). Quoting these words (1977, pp. 32–3) Woddis adds: this 'meant, in practice, an absolute majority of the population'. Yet, significantly, this is precisely what Lenin does not say. He prefaces his reference to the winning and retaining of power with the words, 'an absolute majority is not always essential' (*LCW* 32, p. 476). In fact, a crucial point of theory is involved here. An absolute majority is not always essential for Lenin because the concept of a majority is not an 'absolutist' one. Although Woddis complains in a later chapter of his book (1977, p. 204) that the concept of a 'relative majority' is unclear, this is the very concept which Lenin appears to have in mind. The masses are transformed into a majority, he writes, not simply a majority of the workers alone 'but the majority of all the exploited' when 'the revolution has been sufficiently prepared' (*LCW* 32, p. 476). Under what conditions can it be said that the revolution is sufficiently prepared? When, as Lenin puts it elsewhere, it can be brought 'to a victorious conclusion' (*LCW* 31, p. 476)! This is why an 'absolute' majority (the 51 per cent vote) is not always essential and indeed, arguably in some circumstances, it may not even be enough. What hegemony requires is the kind of majority which makes it possible to carry through a revolution successfully.

Woddis is therefore wrong to suppose that Lenin's speech in July 1924 represents 'a fundamental modification of his former views' (1977, p. 33). A majoritarian logic is evident in all Lenin's strategic assessments. Hence we find Lenin arguing in July 1917 that at that point in time victory was impossible because 'we still did not have a majority among the workers and soldiers of Petrograd and Moscow' (*LCW* 24, p. 23). Only in mid-September in the wake of the Kornilov revolt and the resignation of the Socialist-Revolutionary Chernov from the government, does Lenin declare that 'we have a following of the majority of the people' (*LCW* 26, p. 24). But what kind of majority? Lenin's own statistics show that the Bolsheviks only secured an electoral or 'arithmetic' majority in the All-Russian Soviets in *October* and in the Constituent Assembly elections in November 1917 his party only obtained one quarter of the votes (*LCW* 28, p. 271; *LCW* 30, p. 256). It is clear that the majority to which Lenin refers cannot be understood in 'absolutist' terms. It is a concept which is 'relative' in the sense that it relates to the realities of power: it is a political concept rather than an abstract arithmetical one. Of course, in assessing whether such a majority exists, arithmetic has its part to play and it was undoubtedly the sharp increase in the Bolshevik vote in the Petrograd and Moscow local elections in August and September of 1917 which helped to convince Lenin that a political majority had now been secured (Zaradov, 1975, p. 20).

It is therefore incorrect to argue, as Carrillo does, that the October revolution was one in which 'the armed masses had destroyed a crumbling State without making use of universal suffrage' (1977, p. 71). As far as Lenin was concerned, winning electoral majorities in areas of great strategic importance, like the army, navy, the Soviets and the largest industrial centres, proved crucial in preparing for the vital break (Zaradov, 1979, p. 39). The political majority does not exclude arithmetical considerations: it transcends them. In the article in which Woddis finds a minoritarian strategy, Lenin writes: 'the proletariat cannot achieve victory if it does not win the majority of the population to its side. But to limit that winning to polling a majority of votes in an election *under the rule of the bourgeoisie*, or to make it the condition for it, is crass stupidity, or else sheer deception of the workers' (*LCW* 30, p. 265). A fetishistic deception? The concept of the majority for Lenin cannot be understood in terms of electoral consent because it denotes a political relationship which expresses the capacity of the proletariat and its allies to bring the revolution to a 'victorious conclusion' (*LCW* 31, p. 476). Clearly consent is involved, for a movement can only be said to have won a majority when it is able to impose its will on society *as a whole*. But this consensual hegemony is always fused with the moment of force. What makes the majority of a party and movement *political* is the fact that it has the strength to 'enforce its interests' in 'a form possessing general, socially coercive force' (*SC*, p. 255). If this majoritarian logic appears 'unclear' or unacceptable to Eurocommunist critics of Lenin (Willetts, 1981, pp. 11–12), this is because they have themselves moved away from the classical Marxist view of politics as a coercion which commands consent. Universal suffrage, in Engels's famous comment, is 'the guage of the maturity of the working class'; 'it cannot and never will be anything else in the modern state' (*OFPPS*, p. 232). To present the suffrage, as Kautsky does (1964, p. 47), as 'a powerful source of moral authority', protected by but yet separate from the use of force, can only mystify the realities of the political process. It involves abstracting the 'political will' from all those coercive circumstances from which it arises and to which it must respond (*LCW* 26, p. 196).

Lenin's concept of the majority as a *political* idea cannot be understood if the moment of consent is emphasized at the expense of coercion. The converse of course also holds. Reduce the concept of the majority to 'pure' force and it dissolves altogether and this point can be well exemplified if we contrast Lenin's analysis of the dissolution of the Constituent Assembly with that of Trotsky. For Trotsky, as we have already noted, rejected Lenin's theory of socialism *through* democracy and in 1919, although he defends the dissolution of the Constituent Assembly, he presents Bolshevik strategy in the very way Kautsky did, as the triumph of dictatorship over democracy. The 'attainment of a majority in a democratic parliament by the party of the proletariat is not an absolute impossibility' (1961, p. 42), Trotsky writes, but in the circumstances of the Russian Revolution, there were only two forces: 'the revolutionary proletariat, led by the Communists, and the counter-revolutionary democracy, headed by the generals and the admirals' (1961, p. 43).

It appears that for Trotsky, democracy *itself* is but a metaphysical mask for political mystification (1961, p. 40) and needs to be thrown aside and *replaced* by 'the mechanism of the proletariat, at the moment when the latter is strong enough to carry out such a task' (1961, p. 41). Since such a task achieves meaning 'not in statically reflecting a majority, but in dynamically creating it' (1961, p. 65), the relatively passive moment of consent, the element of *position*, is simply brushed aside and yields to an abstractly conceived element of *manoeuvre*, a spontaneist conception of force which is mystically attributed to the direct will of a class (Knei-Paz, 1978, p. 250). For Trotsky, therefore, the Constituent Assembly reveals the 'opportunist majority' of a 'counter-revolutionary democracy' (1961, p. 43): for Lenin, on the other hand, the Constituent Assembly was not, in any meaningful political sense, majoritarian or democratic at all. As he argued in 1918, the Constituent Assembly could have been 'a correct expression of the people's will' only if the parties drawing up the electoral lists had been 'truly representative of the mood, the wishes, the interests and the will of the groups of the population electing them' (*LCW* 26, p. 485). What made the Constituent Assembly counter-revolutionary was not that it was 'democratic' but rather that it *perverted* democracy since the electoral lists were drawn up in early October before the Socialist-Revolutionaries had divided into a pro and anti-revolutionary wing and the voting took place (November 1917) after the revolution had occurred. Thus, even from the 'formal standpoint of the lists and the election', no one, argued Lenin, 'can refute our assertion that the Constituent Assembly was unable to give a correct expression to the people's will' (*LCW* 26, p. 487).

The concept of the popular will only becomes 'a philosophic mask for political mystification' when it is abstracted from the ensemble of circumstances in which it is expressed. When Kautsky complains that 'the Soviet Government rules by the will of the minority, since it avoids testing its supremacy by universal suffrage', Trotsky replies that such a blow misses its mark since the democracy of the revolutionary dictatorship 'goes a little deeper down than parliamentarism' (1961, p. 45). But this appears to suggest not that universal suffrage is a 'gauge of political maturity', 'an index reached by the various classes in their understanding of their problems' (*LCW* 30, p. 271), but that, as a static reflection of a majority, it is a 'mystification' which can be dispensed with altogether! An abstractly conceived moment of coercion must replace an abstractly conceived moment of consent. Socialism does not arise through democracy but democracy develops as a by-product of the dictatorship of the proletariat. Trotsky's theory of permanent revolution is, as Gramsci said, 'literary' and 'abstract' (*SPN*, pp. 84–5) and it expresses itself in a concept of the majority which inverts, rather than transcends, the 'old base logic of the democrats'. 'Reformism' and 'adventurism', as we have noted earlier, might ferociously confront one another as a unity of one-sided opposites: in practice, they share the same political premisses.

THE COUP IN CHILE AND THE 'DEMOCRATIC ROAD'

On 11 September 1973 the Popular Unity Government of Salvador Allende was overthrown by military force and it is doubtful, as Woddis has commented, whether any coup of recent years has provoked such discussion and controversy 'in the international revolutionary movement' and among commentators on Marxism (1977, p. 154). A vast literature has sprung up and it is impossible here to do more than to allude to a small portion of it. My brief is simply to focus on the Chilean experience as it sheds a critical light on the concept of the 'democratic road' and the problem of coercion and consent in Marxist political theory. This is why the response of those who were soon to declare them-selves 'Eurocommunist' is of particular interest because there can be little doubt that the events in Chile, 1970–3, played a key part in stimulating those 'reflections' which later crystallized into Eurocommunist conceptions of the 'democratic road'. We will also try to show how this abstract conception of 'consent' was echoed on the extreme left by an equally abstract analysis of the question of coercion.

Shortly after the coup, Enrico Berlinguer, General Secretary of the Communist Party of Italy, wrote a series of articles in which he argued that careful reflection on the political tragedy in Chile is indispensable for a deeper assessment of the strategy and tactics of the working class movement. What makes this tragedy of particular relevance, Berlinguer contends, is the fact that, for all the differences between Chile and Italy — institutional, social and economic — the Chilean Communists and Socialists, like their Italian counterparts, had 'set out to pursue a democratic road to Socialism' (1974, p. 42). But what are the defining characteristics of this 'democratic road'? On this, there is a degree of ambiguity. Certainly, says Berlinguer, this is not the 'smooth and painless' road envisaged by the social democrats and he makes the point, to which we shall return, that as the popular forces in Chile began to take control of the fundamental levers of power, 'anti-democratic reaction' became all the more violent and fierce (1974, p. 43). Italian experience also bears out the fact that taking up 'the flag of the defence of democracy and the democratic method' inevitably results in 'bitter struggles', 'acute clashes' and 'more or less deep ruptures or threatened ruptures'. Hence, comments Berlinguer, we have 'always considered it mistaken to see the democratic road simply as a parliamentary road' (1974, p. 44).

Yet this is precisely how some Eurocommunists *did* project their strategy from the mid-1970s (see e.g. Carrillo, 1977, p. 111; p. 133) and as a way of resolving those ambiguities inherent in Berlinguer's analysis of 1973. For while Berlinguer argues that strategy cannot be reduced to a schematic choice 'between a peaceful and non-peaceful road' (1974, p. 44), he also makes it clear that the Italian 'road' is democratic because of its *constitutional* nature: 'the working class movement's decision to maintain its struggle on the terrain of democratic legality' (1974, p. 45). This can only imply that the strategy of 'Socialism in democracy and peace' (in Togliatti's phrase) rests upon the equation of democracy = legality = peace. The democratic road is the 'parliamentary road' and by implication, as was later stated at an international communist conference, 'the other ways to socialism are undemocratic' (*World Marxist*

Review, 1979, p. 50). Is this a democratic road based purely on 'consent'? Apparently not, since, argues Berlinguer, 'the democratic road needs both force and consensus in all its phases' (1974, p. 46). But this argument is deceptive, for Berlinguer concedes that an armed, liberation movement would also require 'the support and consensus of the vast majority of the population' and this is true of political struggle generally because even Fascism 'cannot win with reactionary violence alone' (1974, p. 46). But if *all* movements combine force and consent, what is the defining attribute of the 'democratic road'? The fact that it is legal and constitutional i.e. the fact that it avoids violence and is based on consent! There is an unmistakeable echo of Kautsky's argument noted above (1964, p. 47), that while force may be necessary to *defend* democracy from attack, this coercion is 'organically' distinct from the consensual process of politics based on the law. The concept of the 'democratic road' makes it impossible to sustain Gramsci's celebrated dichotomy in purely 'methodological' terms.

It is significant therefore that Chilean communist assessments of the Popular Unity movement made after the coup, are generally critical of the 'democratic road' as a way of conceptualizing strategy. In so far as this conception did gain currency during the Popular Unity period, it is considered 'a mistake' for it meant, as Teitelboim comments, that 'during the growing revolutionary process in Chile, the forms of struggle were considered as important as its goals' (1977, p. 34). 'In the light of our experience', argues Insunza, the concepts of the 'peaceful' and 'armed' road must be 'stripped of all ambiguity' and 'we must realise that they belong not to the sphere of strategy but to that of tactics, which changes according to circumstances' (1977, p. 77). To characterize a peaceful 'tactic' as a democratic 'strategy' can only mean that *one* form of struggle is thereby absolutized and what happened in Chile under Popular Unity rule, therefore, as Teitelboim recalls, was that 'many regarded preparations for an eventual change of path . . . as absolutely unacceptable' (1977, pp. 34—5): 'when the concrete situation changed, the masses found their hands tied' (1977, p. 34). Indeed, it is revealing that there was a tendency, during the Popular Unity period, to refer to the peaceful form of struggle as 'the natural channel' (Insunza, 1977, p. 77) for this phrase not only evokes that curious blend of fatalism and voluntarism we find in Kautsky (see e.g. 1964, p. 13), but is central to Carrillo's arguments in *'Eurocommunism' and the State*. With the advance of working class struggle and the achievement of socialism, the 'overcoming of social differences' will 'follow a natural process and will not be the result of coercive measures' (1977, p. 80). The process is natural, democratic, hegemonic, because it *avoids* coercion.

The experience in Chile demonstrates precisely the problems with this 'naturalistically' conceived democratic road. For between 1970 and 1973, as support for Popular Unity (hereafter PU) 'naturally' increased, so too did the *reaction* to these advances. In the municipal elections of 1971, the vote for PU reached 50.8 per cent and in 1973 it received 44 per cent of the vote in the National Assembly elections, a 7 per cent advance on the 1970 Presidential vote for Allende. Yet, as Woddis rightly points out, 'it was precisely because Popular Unity, despite the grave difficulties confronting it, was still assured of popular support at the polls, that the counter-revolutionary forces became more desperate and intensified their violence in order to overthrow the Government' (1977, p. 190; see also Miliband, 1973c, pp. 454—5). These are, of course, precisely the kind of circumstances which require a 'change of path', particularly as the conservative majority in parliament was determined to make it as difficult as possible to tackle the problem of subversion and reactionary violence 'legally'. Indeed, ironically the peaceful form of struggle can only succeed if it interpenetrates, at the same time, with other forms of struggle, for what was needed, Sobolev argues, was 'the creation of a social, political, economic and ideological mechanism', powerful enough to 'compel the exploiter classes to bow to the people's will', that would 'force them to accept the inevitability of the socialist road of development effected in a peaceful form' (1974, p. 34). In other words, a capacity and readiness to employ *all* forms of struggle is essential to the success of any *one* of them.

It is worth noting in this context that although the Russian Revolution did take the form of an armed uprising, Lenin insisted that everything should be done to 'ensure a peaceful development of the revolution' and it was only the failure to secure agreement from the Mensheviks and Socialist-Revolutionaries that made the insurrectionary 'form' inevitable (*LCW* 26, p. 60; pp. 67–8; Gollan, 1964, p. 204). No one form of the struggle should be absolutized and Lenin was to declare in an argument with Bukharin, that 'Marx did not commit himself, or the future leaders of the socialist revolution, to matters of form, to ways and means of bringing about the revolution. He understood perfectly well that a vast number of new problems would arise, that the whole situation would change . . . *radically* and *often* in the course of revolution' (*LCW* 26, p. 343). The fluid movement from one form to another, the capacity to employ all forms of struggle in order to ensure the success of any one of them, is premissed on an understanding of politics as a *coercive* process. For Teitelboim, the experience of the 1000 days of PU rule emphasizes the importance of restoring to our conception of revolution 'its highly dialectical nature' (1977, p. 34) and this break with the conception of the 'democratic road' is only possible when we grasp the fact that, in Insunza's words, a revolution 'always entails force and social coercion', even where it 'does not always assume armed forms' (1977, p. 77).

This coercion, as the events in Chile show, not only has to be a coercion which commands support, but the kind of coercion which *sustains* it. Without Allende's Presidential vote of 36.3 per cent, the first phase of the revolutionary process could not have begun and to have got this far required the defeat of the attempted coup of 1969 by the counter-coercion of a general strike and divisions within the military officers' ranks. Between 4 September and 3 November 1973 an epic struggle was waged to ensure that Allende, having received 36 per cent of the vote, would then be selected by the Congress and Senate as President, despite the fact that the opposition parties had most of the votes. By winning Christian Democratic support for Allende as President and for one of the key planks in the PU's programme, the nationalization of copper, the victory of 1970 demonstrated the capacity of the popular movement to secure 'a triumph of the majority' (Castillo, 1974a, p. 28). For such a majority to be sustained and developed, its political character must first be recognized and it is revealing that because Woddis argues that PU did not have a majority (1977, p. 205), he is unwilling to accept the necessity for the kind of 'all-embracing mass organisations' which Sobolev sees as essential if a passive, electoral majority is to become an active, 'solidly organised' one (Sobolev, 1974, p. 35). Although Sobolev merely says that such mass organizations must have the capacity 'to break the reaction's resistance' (1974, p. 35), Woddis assumes that since they would clearly be coercive, they would have to be *armed* and this, he protests, would have 'provoked army action much earlier' (1977, p. 205). By characterizing the Chilean movement as 'a strategy based on a constitutional, non-insurrectionary road' (1977, p. 206), Woddis appears, therefore, to have no room in his analysis for the existence of those mass, coercive organizations which are crucial if a political majority is to be sustained.

For Teitelboim, a political majority, to a greater extent than 'an arithmetical (or mechanical) majority', must be expressive of the *'existence of a representative social bloc of the greater part of the population'* (1977, p. 33). PU had, I would argue, such a majority in 1970 and part of 1971 but to sustain it, it needed to defeat its enemies, not only on the right, but also on the extreme left. Berlinguer stresses the importance of 'drawing the social and political forces in the centre in to consistently democratic positions' (1974, p. 48), but how is this to be done? In Chile, ultra left groups 'rejected all compromise and alliances' (Castillo, 1974a, p. 29). Taking the view that there could be no democratic stage of the revolution aimed specifically against the monopoly sectors of the bourgeoisie (who were seen by PU as dependent on imperialism), these groups provoked clashes with small and middle entrepreneurs, instigated the seizure of factories and real estate of no real importance and helped therefore to push the intermediate strata into the arms of the extreme right (Castillo, 1974a, p. 29). This naturally ruptured the already fragile understanding between PU and the Christian Democrats and made it more difficult to cement an alliance with the constitutionally minded section of the armed forces. Leftist conceptions of voluntarism and spontaneity obstructed the introduction of measures to strengthen the economy and boost productivity and concessions to 'unbridled "economism" ' (Millas, 1975, p. 34) helped to facilitate the 'economic subversion' from the right (Fazio, 1976, p. 30). Roxborough, O'Brien and Roddick in their study of Chile advance the argument that 'a revolutionary seizure of power' was required *against* the government of Popular Unity as 'an act of will, an act of courage' through the spontaneous intervention of the most conscious elements of the working class (1977, pp. 268–9). Yet, in the eyes of Chilean communists, it was precisely this kind of thinking, prominent among the supporters of the far-left MIR, that helped to destroy PU's political majority and create the conditions for a successful counter-revolutionary coup.

The existence of this 'unconstitutional' leftism, like its far-right counterpart, creates serious problems for the Eurocommunist conception of the democratic road. Woddis refers to the need to 'mobilize' the support of the working class and other popular forces 'for activity to counter the extra-parliamentary support for reaction' (1977, p. 206).

But how is this to be done in the absence of those coercive mass organizations to which Sobolev alludes and which, in Woddis's eyes, conflict with the strategy of the 'constitutional and non-insurrectionary road' (1977, p. 206)? For Berlinguer, the 'new "model" of Socialism' (1974, p. 47) can only be realized through a strategy which avoids 'a confrontation and head-on clash' between two parties, each with a popular base (1974, p. 48), but in so far as this is a 'confrontation' which can be minimized, it implies a capacity by the popular movement to exercise a coercion which transcends the limits of 'democratic legality' i.e. the parliamentary constitution. What is required, argues Teitelboim, is 'total political struggle aimed at disuniting the central forces of the conspiracy from top to bottom and in every respect — economically and psychologically, publicly and otherwise, but above all militarily' (1977, p. 37). What Teitelboim characterizes as the 'weakness and untenability' of 'our attitude to the armed forces' expressed itself as a tendency to exaggerate their 'neutrality'. It is an attitude which inevitably arises when the peaceful road is absolutized and the coercive pressures upon the armed forces to become 'executioners and stranglers of the popular movement' (1977, p. 38) do not receive the attention and emphasis they deserve.

The defeat of PU was primarily a *political* defeat — 'the isolation of the working class from its allies' (Castillo, 1974a, p. 30) — and its failure to exert sufficient mass coercion to maintain and extend the political majority acquired in 1970 lies at the root of the problem. If, as Castillo says, 'violence is part of every path to power by the working class and the people', no one form of the struggle must be privileged, for 'violence need not mean recourse to arms' (1974b, p. 32). The tendency by Chinese communists in the 1960s to argue that the coercive character of revolution can only imply, in Mao Tse-tung's words, 'the seizure of power by armed force' (Gollan, 1964, p. 199) involved just such an absolutization of one form of struggle. Mao's famous dictum — 'Political power grows out of the barrel of a gun' (Schram, 1963, p. 209) — is problematic for this reason. Coercion arises, as we have seen, from social relationships, not from 'things' and this coercion can only be effective if the working class 'wins over the greater part of society' (Castillo, 1974b, p. 32).

This is the point which Miliband misses in his own assessment of the Chilean events. While he rightly rejects simplistic exhortations to 'revolutionary terror' (1973c, p. 473) and the fatalistic resignation of the proponents of the democratic road (1973c, p. 471), he underestimates the extent to which an 'organised, mobilization of popular forces' can only be effective as a coercion which commands consent. By saying nothing about the *negative* role played by the far-left in moving Christian Democracy to the right, Miliband implies a somewhat spontaneist view of political mobilization and by ridiculing PU's stress on winning over the intermediate strata — 'Better not to start at all' (1973c, p. 457) — he neglects the all-important unity of mass coercion with mass consent. As Insunza recalls, it was both the 'repudiation of the need for any dictatorship', on the one hand, and the leftist attempts to establish a 'proletarian dictatorship' immediately, on the other, which weakened PU's campaign to transform society and the state (1977, p. 83).

The experience of the PU government in Chile serves, therefore, to underline the dialectical character of the distinction between coercion and consent in Marxist political theory. If the Eurocommunist conception of the democratic road abstracts consent from coercion, the advocates of 'revolutionary terror' abstract coercion from consent and in Mandel's critique of the 'peaceful road to socialism', the two abstractions coexist. Political alliances are brushed aside in favour of transforming defensive struggles into 'pre-revolutionary and revolutionary explosions' (1978, p. 186) and to this spontaneist conception of coercion, there corresponds a spontaneist view of consent, for precisely how Mandel proposes to guarantee 'complete respect for political, ideological and cultural pluralism' (1978, p. 171) in a situation of intensifying revolutionary and counter-revolutionary coercion is something which he never explains. The passivism of the democratic road is simply inverted when it is replaced by the 'activism' of the revolutionary 'explosion'. The mysticism of the abstract 'will' remains.

7

COERCION, CONSENT AND THE
STATE UNDER SOCIALISM

PROLETARIAN DICTATORSHIP AND THE 'VARIETY OF FORMS'

We have already noted that for Marx and Engels, the proletariat can only resist the capitalist 'coercion of circumstances'
through trade union organization. In so far as the bourgeois
state concentrates this coercion of circumstances into the
direct force of politics and the law, so the counter-coercion
of the proletariat has to be concentrated into the organization of a party, able to challenge this state, win the 'battle for
democracy' and raise the proletariat to the position of 'ruling
class' (*MECW* 6, p. 504). The need for a proletarian state to
replace a capitalist one — historically, of course, a burning
point of contention between Marx and the anarchists (Maximoff, 1953, p. 286) — arises from the way in which classical
Marxism conceptualizes the political process. The coercion of
the old order yields to the coercion of the new, and given the
fact that 'a revolution is certainly the most authoritarian
thing there is' (*MELAAS*, p. 103), it is hardly surprising that
even where this new coercion is primarily social in character,
it is likely to require at least some reinforcement from the
state.

It is true that, as we have already seen, proletarian politics
is a self-annulling politics since it embodies a principle transcending everything of a political nature (*MECW* 3, p. 513).
But why should this be? The *Manifesto* explains. Since the

proletarians have 'nothing of their own to secure and fortify', they have to 'become masters of the productive forces of society' by abolishing the 'previous mode of appropriation' (*MECW* 6, p. 495). How is this to be done? Against the 'coercion of circumstances' which dominates people, they pit the organization of a coercion which dominates circumstances. Whereas bourgeois politics perpetuates the divide between the 'materialism of civil society' and 'the idealism of the state' (*MECW* 3, p. 166), proletarian politics seeks to transcend this 'dualism' by making the illusory community into a reality. It is revealing, therefore, that whereas the conception of 'concentration' under capitalism denotes a process of snatching activity away from society, in the development of socialism 'concentration' implies a process which is exactly the reverse. As the proletariat becomes 'concentrated' in greater masses, writes Marx and Engels, it feels its strength more (*MECW* 6, p. 492), and hence although it is true that this process of concentration does involve the centralization of the 'instruments of production in the hands of the State, i.e. of the proletariat organized as the ruling class' (*MECW* 6, p. 504), this is a politics to end all politics. Once 'all production has been concentrated in the hands of a vast association of the whole nation', this signals an end to class distinctions and the 'public power will lose its political character' (*MECW* 6, p. 505). But, and this is the crucial point, this power over production must first be public before it can lose its political character: until it has been concentrated *through the medium of the state*, it cannot become the social property of the 'whole nation'. The state must, as Engels puts it elsewhere, take 'possession of the means of production in the name of society', before it can be expected to 'wither away' (*AD*, p. 385).

Harding has however argued that the 'model' of the proletarian state in the *Communist Manifesto* is in sharp contrast to Marx's conception of the Paris Commune which had actually ceased to be a state 'in the normal Marxian definition of that term' (1981, p. 89). Whereas the emphasis in the

Manifesto model is centralist, with initiative in both the political and the economic spheres proceeding 'from the top downwards' (1981, p. 86), in the Commune model, the functions of the state have been returned to society and a much more decentralized and variegated style of planning is indicated. What we have therefore are 'two widely differing models' (1981, p. 91) which reflect an 'unresolved dualism in the Marxist theory of the state' (1981, p. 92). The one thing especially which was proved by the Commune, Marx and Engels were to comment in 1872, was that 'the working class cannot simply lay hold of the ready-made State machinery and wield it for its own purposes' (*MESW*, pp. 31–2), and this meant, argues Harding, 'dramatically re-defining their whole political strategy' (1981, p. 87).

One can certainly accept a difference of emphasis between the *Manifesto* and the Commune model of working class power. After all, it could be argued that the *Manifesto* was written particularly with Germany in mind, where in 1848 'there are still so many remnants of the Middle Ages to be abolished . . . so much local and provincial obstinacy to be broken' (*MECW* 10, p. 285), whereas the context of the Paris Commune is that of a France with its 'centralised State power' originating from the days of the Absolute Monarchy, followed by the gigantic broom of the French Revolution which has swept away all manner of localized 'medieval rubbish' and culminating in the Bonapartist perfection of Executive rule (*PC*, pp. 68–71). It is also of some historical interest to note that in 1848, Marx and Engels's allies were ultra-centralist followers of Blanqui; in 1871, the minority of the Commune who did belong to the First International were adherents of Proudhon's strongly anti-statist school of socialism (*PC*, p. 30). If then, we can see why a difference of emphasis might arise between 1848 and 1871, is this a difference of *substance*, reflecting 'two widely differing models' and an 'unresolved dualism in the Marxist theory of the state'?

In fact, neither in the *Manifesto* nor in the *Civil War in*

France is there serious evidence for the 'widely differing models' to which Harding alludes. After all, in the *Manifesto* the organization of workers into a class arises out of the centralization of 'numerous local struggles' (*MECW* 6, p. 493) through a movement characterized as the 'independent movement of the immense majority' (*MECW* 6, p. 495). How can it be said that in this model initiative only proceeds from the top downwards, when it is the distinctive feature of the *Manifesto*'s communism that it is able only to 'express, in general terms, actual relations springing from an existing class struggle, from a historical movement going on under our very eyes' (*MECW* 6, p. 498)? Politics concentrates what is diffused and dispersed.

As for the Paris Commune, while the context and emphasis is different, Marx is still analysing a *state*-form which has the task of concentrating coercion and centralizing power. Hence Marx explicitly rejects the 'Girondin' view which mistakenly portrays the Commune as an attempt to break up 'that unity of great nations which, if originally brought about by political force, has now become a powerful coefficient of social production' (*PC*, p. 73). As with the *Manifesto*, if social production is to be concentrated in the unity of the nation, political centralization must be taken for granted. Of course, since 'united co-operative societies are to regulate national production upon a common plan' (*PC*, p. 76), this is a centralization expressed through local autonomy and 'the self-government of the producers' (*PC*, p. 72) and Marx argues that to pit 'local municipal liberty' against the 'now superseded, State power' would simply mean 'as in England', the 'completion' of a central state by corrupt local authorities (*PC*, p. 74). Both political abstractions must be transcended by dissolving the concentrated power of the state into the organization of planned social production. Centralism and leadership become all the more effective as a result and Marx takes it as self-evident that regulating 'national production upon a common plan' requires that the 'unity of the nation' is not to be 'broken' but 'organized' and made into a reality

(*PC*, p. 73). The rural producers are to be brought under the 'intellectual lead' of the central towns of their district (*PC*, p. 74); the Paris Commune is to serve as the model for 'all the great industrial centres of France' and the political form of even the smallest country hamlet is to be the same as that of the largest centre (*PC*, p. 72). Does this not imply the highest degree of centalization expressed through the greatest possible municipal liberty? This is not to be confused with what Marx and Engels refer to in 1850 as 'democratic talk' which would 'cripple the central government' (*MECW* 10, p. 285) and produce, as Engels later noted, not provincial self-government but 'narrow-minded' 'communal self-seeking' (*MECW* 10, p. 286).

The Commune was, of course, for Marx 'a thoroughly expansive political form' (*PC*, p. 75). Marx's reference to 'the now, superseded State power' (*PC*, p. 74) meant not, as Harding supposes, that 'the state ceased to exist' (1981, p. 89) but that it was *ceasing* to exist. That Marx's comment denotes a process and not a simple rupture, is made clear by his characterization of the Commune as 'the political rule of the producer' (*PC*, p. 75). Clearly this was, as Engels told Bebel, 'no longer a state in the proper sense of the word' (*SC*, p. 275). Since its function was to concentrate resources in the hands of the nation — to regulate national production upon a common plan — it would have to restore government to the people as a 'truly national Government' (*PC*, p. 79), bringing 'plain working men' into the hitherto privileged world of their 'natural superiors' (*PC*, p. 76). But despite this, there can be no doubt that for Marx, the Commune was a *state* ceasing to be a state and as 'the political form at last discovered under which to work out the economical emancipation of Labour' (*PC*, p. 75), it still had an explicitly *political* role to play. If the Commune aimed to expropriate the expropriators and serve as a lever for uprooting the 'economical foundations upon which rests the existence of class' (*PC*, p. 75), then how would this be possible unless the process of concentrating resources in the hands of the nation was underpinned by the concentrated coercion of the state?

In his first draft of the *Civil War in France*, Marx un-ambiguously equates the Commune as a 'political form' with the Commune as a form of the state: 'As the state machinery and parliamentarianism are not the real life of the ruling classes, but only the organised general organs of their domination, the political guarantees and forms and expres-sions of the old order of things, so the Commune is not the social movement of the working class and, therefore, of a general regeneration of mankind, but the organised means of action' (*PC*, p. 156). Because it does not 'represent a peculiar interest', it is not a 'normal' state: on the contrary, it re-presents the class striving to abolish all classes. But it still remains an instrument of class rule. Hence the Commune does not do away with class struggles but rather 'affords the rational medium in which that class struggle can run through its different phases in the most rational and humane way' (*PC*, p. 156). It is, to reiterate, *not* the social movement of the working class but the organized general organ of its class dominion.

Marx and Engels, as the *Civil War in France* and their subsequent correspondence make clear, were not uncritical of the Commune. What they criticized however was not the fact that it was a state ceasing to be a state, but that it sought to dissolve itself into society too quickly and was thus *in-sufficiently* political in character. Marx not only says that the Commune would have 'shamefully betrayed its trust' by affecting to 'keep up all the decencies and appearances of liberalism as in a time of peace' (*PC*, p. 81), but he makes it clear that he thinks that this is precisely the direction in which the Commune erred. The 'magnanimity of the armed working men' in allowing the old government to retreat to Versailles, is described by Marx as an 'indulgence' (*PC*, p. 63) and he later told Kugelmann that 'conscientious scruples' prevented the Communards from taking swift reprisals against the former Governor and the National Guard (*PC*, p. 284). As for the Central Committee, it 'surrendered its power too soon to make way for the Commune. Again, from a too "honourable" scrupulosity' (*PC*, p. 284). Nevertheless, given the fact that for Marx and Engels the Commune was *less* of a state than it should have been (*PC*, p. 292), it would not have even lasted a day, Engels contended, had it not made use of the 'authority of the armed people' (*MELAAS*, p. 103): had it not expressed itself as the organized activity of a *state*.

Harding cites Engels's famous remark in 1891 directed against the 'Social-Democratic philistine' — 'Look at the Paris Commune. That was the Dictatorship of the Proletariat' (1981, p. 91; *PC*, p. 34) — and insists: 'Marx himself never asserted that they were the same, he *never* identified the commune as the dictatorship of the proletariat' (1981, p. 91). But this is almost certainly incorrect. In September 1871 Marx is reported to have stated that 'the Commune was the conquest of the political power of the working classes', adding that before the Commune could remove the basis of class rule and oppression, 'a proletarian *dictature* would become necessary' (*PC*, p. 266). Even if Marx had not actually used the 'words' in the context of the Commune, his whole analysis of the 'political rule of the producer' in the *Civil War in France* clearly implied that the Commune was the 'most rational and humane' form of the 'proletarian *dictature*'. *Pace* Claudin, the Commune was for Marx 'the positive form of the Republic' (*PC*, p. 71; Claudin, 1977, p. 72).

Harding's claim, therefore, that there is an 'unresolved dualism in the Marxist theory of the state' (1981, p. 92) brings us back to our old friend the 'organic' divide. Either politics involves coercion 'from above' (the *Manifesto* model) or consent 'from below' (the model of the Commune): centralism and dictatorship versus participation and democracy. In fact, what *resolves* the problem of dualism in Marxist political theory is the way the 'two levels' dialectically intertwine. While the proletarian state is uniquely transitional as an 'expansive political form', dispersing its concentrated coercion back into society itself through the mechanisms of accountability, universal suffrage, mass participation and the regulation of national production upon a common plan (*PC*, pp. 73–6), it still remains until its final moment of self-extinction, the special instrument of coercion which reinforces the coercion of society itself.

Once we grasp the dictatorship of the proletariat as a transitional form of the *state*, it then becomes possible, as with our earlier analysis of the state under capitalism, to begin to interrelate its varying forms. According to Harding, the 'unresolved dualism in the Marxist theory of the state' with its 'widely differing political models', was to be 'replicated and thrown into high relief by the actual practice of Soviet government in the first year of its existence' (1981, p. 92), and we shall now see why resolving the problem of the Commune model is crucial to an understanding of developments in the new Russia after October 1917. The first edition of Lenin's *State and Revolution* was written in August 1917 in a situation in which Lenin was preoccupied with the problem of imperialism and, as he puts it, 'the monstrous oppression of the working people by the state' (*LCW* 25, p. 383). Chapter 3 of his pamphlet is devoted to a sympathetic summary of Marx's *Civil War in France* and reaffirms the importance of the Commune model of the proletarian state as a state without a standing army, without a police opposed to the people, without an officialdom placed above the people (see also *LCW* 24, p. 49). The Commune theme, so prominent in Lenin's political thought between March and October 1917, is however, as Meszaros has noted, premissed on the assumption that the Bolsheviks can hold state power because 'behind us stand the immeasurably larger, more developed, more organised world forces of the proletariat . . . temporarily held down by the war' (*LCW* 26, p. 127; Meszaros, 1979, p. 113). Russia's backwardness could be rapidly overcome and the need for a 'political cloak' in the socialist order speedily dispensed with, given the fact that the immense wealth and experience of the advanced capitalist world would be placed at Bolshevik disposal.

It is significant that although Kautsky's reference to the Paris Commune as a government in which 'all shades of the Socialist movement took part' (1964, p. 1) was not quite accurate (*LCW* 28, pp. 239–40), Lenin even after the revolution, had by no means ruled out the possibility of a non-Bolshevik socialist government. While he insists that 'there must be no government in Russia other than the *Soviet Government*', 'the transfer of government from one Soviet party to another', he adds, 'is guaranteed without any revolution, simply by a decision of the Soviets, simply by new elections of deputies to the Soviets' (*LCW* 26, p. 303). Yet by the end of 1918, the Bolsheviks remained the only fully legal party in the country and the Socialist-Revolutionaries (SRs), the Mensheviks and the Anarchists had been eliminated from the Soviets. In Janaury 1918, the Constituent Assembly had been dissolved and with the decision taken by the Mensheviks and the Right SRs to support foreign intervention to topple the new regime, their papers were closed down and their representatives excluded from all political bodies (Johnstone, 1970, p. 285). By the middle of the year, the Left SRs had been subjected to measures of repression, following their involvement in armed uprisings against the Bolshevik government, and Rosa Luxemburg protested that 'with the repression of political life in the land as a whole, life in the soviets must also become more and more crippled. Without general elections, without unrestricted freedom of press and assembly, without a free struggle of opinion, life dies out in every public institution' (Claudin, 1977, p. 74).

Clearly the political landscape had dramatically changed and it is therefore revealing that when Lenin published the second edition of his *State and Revolution* in December 1918, he added a new section to one of his chapters, which concluded with the following words: 'Bourgeois states are most varied in form, but their essence is the same: all these states, whatever their form, in the final analysis are inevitably the *dictatorship of the bourgeoisie*. The transition from capitalism to communism is certainly bound to yield a tremendous abundance and variety of political forms, but the essence will inevitably be the same: *the dictatorship of the proletariat*' (*LCW* 25, p. 413). Marx had already noted the 'motly diversity of form' among bourgeois states (*MESW*, p. 331): well might Lenin reflect at the end of 1918 how the same was becoming true of the proletarian state as well! The Constitution of July in that year had disenfranchised the bourgeoisie but this, Lenin insisted, was not 'a necessary and indispensable feature of the dictatorship of the proletariat' (*LCW* 28, p. 271) and like the other measures of repression and exclusion during this period and indeed up until 1922, it was not, as Johnstone has shown in detail, regarded by Lenin as a question of principle, but the product of exceptional circumstances which had emerged unforeseen in the course of the struggle (Johnstone, 1970, p. 284). But what did the civil war, tighter political controls, one man management in the factories, a growing concern with recruiting specialists and draconian security measures mean for the dictatorship of the proletariat?

Rosa Luxemburg was in no doubt about the consequences of a trend to authoritarianism. 'Public life', she declared, 'gradually falls asleep, a few dozen party leaders of inexhaustible energy and boundless experience direct and rule' and with the working class reduced to a state of passivity, what results is 'a dictatorship, to be sure, not the dictatorship of the proletariat, however, but only the dictatorship of a handful of politicians, that is a dictatorship in the bourgeois sense, in the sense of the rule of the Jacobins' (Claudin, 1977, p. 74). Kautsky's response was much the same: this was no longer 'in any sense the dictatorship of the proletariat, but a dictatorship of one part of the proletariat over the other' (1964, p. 46). Certainly, the form of political rule had altered and, as Nove comments, 'the bitter experience of government under conditions of civil war' had taught Lenin and his comrades some unforgettable lessons (1975, p. 23). But what of the dictatorship of the proletariat in its 'essence'? It is hardly surprising that after 1917, the main themes of

State and Revolution recede further and further from Lenin's thought and positive references to the Paris Commune disappear from his speeches and writings (Meszaros, 1979, p. 114), but are we to assume from this that the dictatorship of the proletariat *itself* had changed into something else?

Meszaros contends that Lenin failed to 'envisage the possibility of an objective contradiction between the dictatorship of the proletariat and the proletariat itself' (1979, p. 113). Yet it has to be said that while the Soviet system had undoubtedly become more 'aloof' from society in the civil war period, the existence of an 'objective contradiction' between the proletariat and its dictatorship is inherent even in the Commune form itself. All forms of the dictatorship of the proletariat, since they are forms of a *state*, exist as a *generalized* expression of class rule. Even the Paris Commune was not the 'social movement of the working class' but the 'organized means of action' (*PC*, p. 156), functioning on its behalf. Of course, in the Commune form, the identity of the state as an 'officialdom above the people' is hardly in evidence, since this is a form of the state in which the proletariat rules most directly, the 'most rational and humane way' (*PC*, p. 156) the class struggle can be conducted. But even here, as I have argued above, the state still exists as a special instrument of concentrated coercion and is thus relatively autonomous from society at large. To say, as Meszaros does, that Lenin bypassed the problem of the relationship of the working class to its own political rule because he referred to the existence of a separate 'proletarian state power' (*LCW* 30, p. 108; Meszaros, 1979, p. 114) would seem to imply that a proletarian state can be something *other* than the 'organised means of action' above and outside of the social movement of the working class.

Lenin was acutely conscious of the fact that, given Russian backwardness and isolation, Soviet rule had come to involve 'the dictatorship of the proletariat in its harshest form' (*LCW* 28, p. 207). Since, as he put it in 1919, 'other countries will travel by a different, more humane road'

(*LCW* 29, p. 271; Johnstone, 1970, p. 352), it is clear that the Russian 'model' had not followed the Commune form. Such are the organizational, cultural and educational problems facing the new Soviet republic that, Lenin comments elsewhere, 'the Soviets, which by virtue of their programme are organs of government *by the working people*, are in fact organs of the government *for the working people* by the advanced section of the proletariat, but not by the working people as a whole' (*LCW* 29, p. 183). Was this not an admission that proletarian dictatorship had 'degenerated' into government by 'a handful of politicians', a dictatorship over and not *of* the proletariat?

The Luxemburg/Kautsky critique can only be sustained if we mechanically separate out the two aspects of politics which make even the dictatorship of the proletariat a form of the state. The dictatorial from the participatory; the instrumental from the ideological; the consensual moment from the moment of force. For Rosa Luxemburg, only a 'spontaneist' form of proletarian politics can be *the* dictatorship of the proletariat: for |Kautsky, in so far as the term is acceptable at all, it stands only as a somewhat 'parliamentarized' version of the Paris Commune, resting upon the higher moral authority of the vote (1964, p. 47). Consent is abstracted from coercion and, in its mechanically hypostasized form, is declared to be the conceptual soul of the true proletarian state. It is only when we link together the 'two levels' (and all the differing expressions which Gramsci's antinomy can take), that it becomes possible to understand how, as with the bourgeois state, the dictatorship of the proletariat yields an abundant 'variety of forms'. All of them, from the most exceptional to the most direct, involve an 'objective contradiction' between the proletariat and its political rule, for all of them involve a generalized concentration of coercion over and above the coercion of society itself. Naturally, as we shall see, the differences between one proletarian state and another are important, but these differences themselves cannot be grasped unless we get to grips with the reality of working class politics in all its forms. This point is so central to the problem of coercion and consent in Marxist political theory, that it requires further elaboration.

THE STATE WITH A BUREAUCRATIC TWIST TO IT ...

The Hungarian communist Georg Lukacs was to comment in 1919 on 'the most oppressive phenomena of proletarian power' as it arises in the context of scarce goods, high prices and a slackening of labour discipline. Help comes, he declares in two ways: 'Either the individuals who constitute the proletariat *realize* that they can help themselves only by bringing about a voluntary strengthening of labour discipline ... or, if they are incapable of this, ... they create a legal system through which the proletariat *compels* its own individual members, the proletarians, to act in a way which corresponds to their class interests: *the proletariat turns its dictatorship against itself*' (Meszaros, 1979, p. 116). Clearly, Lukacs here poses the false antithesis of either a consent without coercion or a coercion without consent. Yet, if we dialectically interrelate the two aspects, what does this imply? Lenin in his second edition of *State and Revolution* argued that in the transition to communism 'the state must inevitably be a state that is democratic *in a new way* (for the proletariat and propertyless in general) and dictatorial *in a new way* (against the bourgeoisie)' (*LCW* 25, p. 412). But can this state also, as Lukacs asserts, be dictatorial against the proletariat itself?

It is ironically Kautsky who helps to provide the basis for an answer. Dictatorship 'as a form of government', he asserts, is something quite different from the dictatorship of a class, since, as he puts it, 'a class can only rule, not govern' (1964, p. 45). Lenin responds to this argument with great irritation, saying that it is 'altogether wrong' to contend that a *class* cannot govern: such an absurdity could only have been uttered by a 'cretin' who sees nothing but bourgeois parliaments and 'ruling parties'. Any European country will provide Kautsky with examples of government by a ruling class (*LCW* 28, p. 241). But Lenin passes over Kautsky's point too hastily. While it is certainly true that the government of a ruling class is also dictatorial since it functions as an instrument of coercion, nevertheless the distinction between 'governing' and 'ruling' is a useful one, for it underlines the classical Marxist contention that the state 'represents' the particular interests of a ruling class in general form. It has a real, if relative autonomy, and hence there is necessarily a *gulf* between the two. Of course, the power of the ruling class is still ultimately decisive for although, as Kautsky says elsewhere (with reference to the capitalists), a dominant class 'rules but does not govern', nevertheless, 'it contents itself with ruling the government' (Miliband, 1969, p. 55). But to what extent is this also true of the proletariat under socialism?

The dictatorship of the proletariat, as we have seen, is not a state in 'the strict sense of the term' since it seeks to dissolve its concentrated force into the 'concentrated' associations of the community and the mechanism upon which it relies to carry through this self-annulling process, is that of mass *participation*. But two things have to be said about the participatory character of the transitional proletarian state. The first is that it involves (as with the Paris Commune) increasingly accessible representation to workers and peasants through the election of a wide range of officials who are subject to the right of recall, and the provision of buildings, printing presses, etc. which are placed at the disposal of the 'average rank and file worker' (*LCW* 28, p. 243). Participation involves, in a word, *democracy* as workers and poor peasants 'for the first time in centuries' set about 'building the new, socialist edifice with their own hands' (*LCW* 27, pp. 516–17): collectively planning their lives. But the second thing which has to be said about this 'participatory democracy' is that if it involves mass consent, it also involves mass coercion. Lenin was to tell the Hungarian workers that 'the essence of proletarian dictatorship is not in force alone, or even mainly in force' (*LCW* 29, p. 388), but if 'its chief feature' is not the 'direct force' of the state, it is nevertheless the *social* coercion embodied in 'organisation and discipline'. This social coercion is necessary, not only to break the resistance of capitalists and 'bourgeois intellectuals' who resist consciously, but to organize and discipline 'the vast mass of the working people, including the peasants, who are shackled very much by petty-bourgeois habits and traditions' and who often resist unconsciously (*LCW* 29, p. 389).

But although social coercion is the primary characteristic of the transitional state as it dissolves into society, it is not enough. If cultural and ideological factors are important, 'proletarian affinity to the mentality of every working man', proletarian prestige 'with the disunited, less developed working people in the countryside', these factors have to be placed alongside 'the rule of one class', 'its centralised power' (*LCW* 29, p. 389). Social coercion has to be underpinned by and mediated through the concentrated coercion of the state. 'We must organise everything, take everything into our own hands', declares Lenin, and this requires that we 'keep a check on the kulaks and profiteers at every step, declare implacable war on them and never allow them to breathe freely, controlling their every move' (*LCW* 27, pp. 517–19). It is impossible to divide the social discipline organically from the political coercion which reinforces it. Even although Lenin implies that direct force exists mainly for those who consciously resist i.e. the 'class enemy', it has to be said that as long as workers need to generalize their particular interests through the medium of a state they will be subject, as part of the population as a whole, to their own collectivized political will: that 'general will' which forces people to be free. Gramsci's well known comment about the individual governing himself without his self-government entering into conflict with political society (*SPN*, p. 268), needs to be interpreted with care, for it would be wrong to suppose that the working class inhabits islands of 'consent' within a sea of political coercion. As the young Marx reminds us, 'the state pervades the whole of nature with spiritual nerves' (*MECW* 1, p. 306): so long as the proletariat still *uses* the state, it does not use it in the interests of freedom (*SC*, p. 276) for while the proletariat still has adversaries to 'hold down', it cannot itself be wholly free.

In *The German Ideology*, Marx and Engels put the matter bluntly: in order 'to assert themselves as individuals', the proletariat 'must overthrow the state'. Until, it must be said, the concentrated coercion of the state has been dissolved into the organization and discipline of society itself, individuals will 'find themselves directly opposed' to their own 'collective expression' (*MECW* 5, p. 80). Lukacs is therefore right: the proletariat turns its dictatorship against itself (Meszaros, 1979, p. 116) but it does so not as the perversion of a proletarian state built upon morality, but simply because there is no other way, in Lukacs's own words, to 'the true history of humanity, which Marx prophesied and hoped for' (Meszaros, 1979, p. 116).

The dictatorship of the proletariat is 'a contradictory reality' which involves both the replacement of one state by another as well as the disappearance of the state itself (Balibar, 1977b, pp. 121–2). But this contradictory reality can only be grasped if the dialectical unity of coercion and consent in the political process is not mechanically ruptured, with, to cite Lukacs once again, '*the power of morality*' placed '*over institutions and economics*' (Meszaros, 1979, p. 116). Even under capitalism, the working class begin to impose their own collective coercion over the coercion of capitalist circumstances. But before this social logic can prevail throughout the community as a whole, it has to be concentrated into revolution as a '*political* act' (*MECW* 3, p. 206), the proletariat organized as a ruling class. To recall Rousseau: 'this act of association creates an artificial and collective body', 'the total alienation by each associate of himself and all his rights to the whole community' (1968, pp. 60–1) and this illusory community can only disappear when the real community has been established. For political coercion to return to its origins, the new social coercion must be secure and the 'new spontaneity', 'the laws of the social economy of free and associated labour' (*PC*, p. 157) able to exist without the helping hand of the state.

Lenin's argument with Trotsky and Bukharin on the trade unions is instructive in this context. The trade unions in the new socialist society are, Lenin asserts, 'an organisation of the ruling, dominant, governing class', but the discipline which they exercise is of a social rather than a political character. They constitute a 'reservoir' of state power, not an organization of the state (*LCW* 32, pp. 20–1). Indeed, Lenin makes precisely the distinction which he had brushed aside in his attack on Kautsky, between a class and its political rule; 'the dictatorship of the proletariat', he insists, 'cannot be exercised through an organisation embracing the whole of that class' and this is a point which applies universally. In 'all capitalist countries (and not only over here in one of the most backward) the proletariat is still so divided, so degraded, and so corrupted in parts (by imperialism in some countries) that an organisation taking in the whole proletariat cannot directly exercise proletarian dictatorship' (*LCW* 32, p. 21). State power can only be exercised by a vanguard which has 'absorbed the revolutionary energy of the class'.

It is just this 'objective contradiction' between the proletariat and its state which Trotsky and Bukharin in their identically opposite ways, both miss. Each takes only one half of the relationship between state and society, politics and economics and mechanically hypostasizes, mystically abstracts consent 'from below' and coercion 'from above'. Trotsky advocates an administrative 'shake-up', the absorption of the trade union into the state (*LCW* 32, p. 76; Cliff, 1971, p. 40) while Bukharin propagates the need for an 'industrial democracy' which would have the effect of replacing the state by the trade union (*LCW* 32, p. 81). As we noted in chapter 4, the proper relationship between politics and economics can only be grasped through a dialectical understanding of the problem of coercion and consent. Trotsky's view of the state as 'brute force' or pure coercion means that he overlooks the intermediary role of the trade unions as 'transmission belts' between the vanguard and the mass, establishing contact with the people and winning them over (*LCW* 32, p. 23). 'Comrade Trotsky speaks of a "workers' state". May I say that this is an abstraction. It was natural for us to write about a workers' state in 1917; but now it is a patent error to say: "Since this is a workers' state without any bourgeoisie, against whom then is the working class to be protected, and for what purpose?" ' (*LCW* 32, p. 24). Why does Lenin characterize the concept of a 'workers' state' as an abstraction? Partly because the proletarian state is, as he says, 'a workers' and peasants' state' (*LCW* 32, p. 24), but also because 'ours is a workers' state *with a bureaucratic twist to it*' (*LCW* 32, p. 24). Is this then a 'deformed' workers' state, a perversion, as Claudin supposes, of the 'original soviet system' (1977, p. 75)? No, says Lenin, this reasoning is theoretically quite wrong. In marking the workers' state with this dismal tag, there 'you have the reality of the transition' (*LCW* 32, p. 24). In other words, the need to have the workers protected by trade unions against their own political rule arises not because some unforeseen 'degeneration' has occurred, but because there exists a transitional *state* as well as a *transitional* state. It is after all a *political* coercion, an officialdom above the people, which is being translated into the social coercion of 'freely associated' labour. The 'coalescing' of the trade unions and the state implies, says Lenin, 'the existence of *distinct* things that *have yet to be* coalesced'. We 'must use these workers' organisations to protect the workers from their state, and to get them to protect our state' (*LCW* 32, p. 25).

If trade unions are reduced to the state (as Trotsky proposes), political coercion, deprived of the necessary consent to sustain it, simply crumbles; if trade unions are wholly abstracted from the state and cease to function as a 'reservoir' of state power, then social coercion lacks the necessary 'preparing, teaching and training', the political education (*LCW* 32, p. 50) to counter the coercion of circumstances through the process of planning. Bukharin's 'industrial democracy' merely inverts Trotsky's 'administrative shake-up'. Militarized coercion confronts syndicalist consent as the two halves of the same 'abstraction'. Taken not as an abstract ideal, but as a living reality, all workers' states suffer the dismal tag of a bureaucratic twist, from the Commune form to the *Manifesto* model, from the most direct kind of political rule to the dictatorship of the proletariat 'in its harshest form' (*LCW* 27, p. 498). As Meszaros comments wittily: 'The ideas of "degeneration", "bureaucratization", "substitutionism" and the like not only all beg the question, but also culminate in an illusory remedy, explicit or implied: namely, that the simple overthrow of this political form and the substitution of dedicated revolutionaries for party bureaucrats will reverse the process — forgetting that the blamed party bureaucrats too were in their time dedicated revolutionaries' (1979, p. 119). Alas, for the proponents of the 'pure will' and the 'organic divide', the distinction between revolutionary and bureaucrat, whatever the 'political form', remains perpetually blurred.

STALINISM AND THE POLITICS OF FORCE

It has been argued that with Lenin's departure from the Commune model, the basis was laid for developments which culminated in Stalinism. Stalinism denotes not only a 'model of socialism primarily based on force' (Harrison, 1979, p. 25), but in Meszaros's words, a '*self-sustaining* political power' which has yet to become 'a *self-transcending* organ which fully transfers the manifold functions of political control to the social body itself' (1979, p. 111). As the model of the socialist state which refuses to wither away, Stalinism appears to refute Marx's own 'prophecies' and expectations, particularly as it is regarded not merely as an historic system which lasted from 1929 to 1953, but as an 'existing socialism' which can be found in many parts of the world today (Boffa, 1978, pp. 2—3). Stalinism is the 'state socialism' which contrasts with a socialism of 'self-management' and 'participation': it is the socialism which suppresses freedom as opposed to the 'pluralistic, free, democratic type of Socialism' (Radice, 1978, p. 43; p. 47) which Eurocommunists would like to see arise in its place. As the socialism which rests upon coercion and denies consent, Stalinism stands at the heart of the 'crisis of Marxism' for in Rossana Rossanda's eyes, it is living testimony to the fact that 'all the revolutions thus far' have 'come to grief on the key problem of the state and revolution' (1979, p. 8). In Claudin's view, 'the elimination of the initial Soviet democracy until nothing but the shell remained meant that the system could not properly be called socialist' (1978, p. 34) and he thus implicitly endorses Kautsky's argument that since the Bolsheviks created a state which is undemocratic, it is not a socialist state at all (Salvadori, 1979, p. 295).

In order to examine this line of analysis in more detail, I shall say something in this section of the chapter about the rise of Stalin and the character of his political rule and then follow with an assessment of developments in the USSR after his death. This will make it possible to grapple with the problem of coercion and consent as it relates to one of the key questions which have preoccupied Marxists over the past one and a half decades: the question of socialism and democracy.

If Meszaros finds that Lenin tragically set in motion the developments which were to make him 'historically superfluous' (1979, p. 117), for Harrison, Lenin left a 'heritage containing several contradictory, alternative futures' (1979, pp. 22—3). The Russian Bolsheviks had a choice: between rural community development with a gradual, balanced economic growth and the alternative of 'rapid, forced industrialisation' (1979, p. 24). To each of these strategic options, there corresponds, in Harrison's explicitly neo-

Gramscian analysis, the project of building a Soviet 'civil society' and the model of a socialism based primarily on force; the 'coercive struggles and military disciplines' which submerge the elements of community and consent (1979, p. 25). The first point which is problematical about this kind of argument is that it characterizes Lenin's New Economic Policy (NEP) which he developed at the end of 1921, as 'a voluntary, cooperative road to socialism' (Harrison, 1979, p. 23). It is true that Lenin identified his NEP with its stress on co-operatives and incentives to the peasantry, as a 'strategical retreat' (*LCW* 33, p. 63). In arguing for the move away from the rationing and centralized distribution of War Communism, he speaks of the 'frontal attack' which has failed and the need for a 'flanking movement', a method of 'siege and undermining' (*LCW* 33, p. 69) to take its place. If this is Gramsci's war of position, the element of 'maneouvre' is also close at hand, for Lenin made it clear that the NEP had been conceived as a temporary retreat, soon to yield to 'our subsequent victorious advance' (*LCW* 33, p. 116; Tucker, 1977a, p. 92). The NEP was not, therefore, a road to socialism but one of the tactical moments along the way. Moreover, the 'voluntary' and 'co-operative' nature of what Lenin called its 'reformism' (*LCW* 33, p. 109) has to be placed in the context of a struggle for state power (*LCW* 33, p. 85) and the adoption of the 'sternest disciplinary measures' (*LCW* 33, p. 71). Political coercion clearly had a central role to play in making it possible for the workers and peasants to work for themselves. Although we lack, declared Lenin in 1923, 'enough civilisation to enable us to pass straight on to socialism', we do have 'the political requisites for it' (*LCW* 33, p. 501): in other words, the capacity to impose a coercion which commands consent.

Significantly, in the fierce debate within the party following Lenin's death, about a strategy of industrialization as against the continuation of the NEP, each side of the Machiavellian Centaur was grasped in abstraction from the other. As far as Trotsky was concerned, the situation called for 'a dictatorship of industry' (Cohen, 1974, p. 130) and among the Left oppositionists, there was an obsession with discipline (Harrison, 1979, p. 23). Bukharin's position here is particularly interesting. In his *ABC of Communism* (1919) he characterizes the power of the state in terms of 'brute force and spiritual subjugation' (1969, p. 84) and, as Carr has recalled (1969, p. 24), he demonstrates just how easy it is to move from one of these abstractions to the other. Initially hostile to any 'statism' in the socialist order (Carr, 1969, p. 21), Bukharin was momentarily influenced by Trotsky's attachment to 'brute force'. An eulogy of proletarian coercion in all its forms is then followed by a 'dramatic turnabout' (Cohen, 1974, p. 206) and Bukharin champions the methods of persuasion as one-sidedly as he had earlier endorsed the methods of force. With a similar kind of agility Trotsky insists that his dictatorship of industry can only take place in what Deutscher has called 'the broad daylight of proletarian democracy, with the consent of the masses and free initiative "from below" ' (Tucker, 1977a, p. 87). Truly a 'spontaneist' vision of coercive central planning! Cohen argues that Bolshevism after 1921 was a movement bifurcated by two conflicting ideological and emotional traditions and suggests that 'in a limited way, the bifurcation of Bolshevism echoes a duality in Marxism itself, where voluntarism and determinism has been subtly interwoven' (1974, p. 129). But here caution is required. For this bifurcation into the mechanistic abstractions propagated by left and right arose not out of a 'duality of Marxism' but from the antinomies of the Enlightenment. The duality of a fatalistic necessity and voluntaristic freedom passed into the theories of revolutionaries like Gramsci, Bukharin and Trotsky as a legacy of the Marxism of the Second International. For Marx and Engels (as indeed for Lenin) the 'conflicting traditions', the 'evolutionary reformist' and the 'revolutionary heroic', had yielded to a political synthesis of coercion and consent.

But where does Stalin stand in relation to these bifurcations of Bolshevism noted above? Tucker portrays a political

leader concerned to keep all his options open. Stalin's ad-
herence to the NEP, he tells us, was much more 'tactical'
than Bukharin's, drawing 'inspiration from the War Communism heritage that Bukharin had resolutely rejected'
(1974, p. 403), while Stalin's Lenin was the Lenin who had
said when introducing the NEP, we retreat 'in order to draw
back, run and make a greater leap forward' (1974, p. 414).
Indeed, here it must be said that in comparing Stalin with the
other Bolsheviks around him, Lenin's 'testament' is all
revealing. If Bukharin is the 'major theorist of the party', he
has never fully understood dialectics (*LCW* 36, p. 595) – a
point borne out by our observations above. As for Trotsky,
perhaps the most capable man in the Central Committee, he
has 'shown excessive preoccupation with the purely administrative side of the work': the Trotsky for whom politics can
be reduced to the pure coercion of the will. What of Stalin?
He is, of course, the Secretary-General who 'has unlimited
authority concentrated in his hands, and I am not sure
whether he will always be capable of using that authority
with sufficient caution' (*LCW* 36, pp. 594–5).

Between Bukharin's abstract moralism and Trotsky's
'brute force' stands Stalin's organizational effectiveness.
Hence it cannot be right to say, as Kolakowski does, that
'Stalin was Trotsky *in actu*' (1978, p. 42). If Stalin's temperament and personality, his social background and the circumstances of his time all incline him to the moment of force,
neither his tactics nor his pronouncements on theory, which
are often little more than mechanical summaries of Lenin's
texts, employ a simple preference for coercion over consent.
Stalin's strength lay in *organization* and it is precisely in
organization that we see the fusion of the two levels of the
political process. A firmness of will certainly, but linked, as
Deutscher says, to the capacity of 'studiously' cultivating
contacts and 'the art of patiently listening to others' (1966,
p. 276). A commitment to doctrine, but at the same time, a
'unique sensibility to all those psychological undercurrents
in and around the party, the untalked-of hopes and tacit

desires, of which he set himself up as a mouthpiece' (Deutscher, 1966, p. 293). In Gramsci's terms, here was hegemony although clearly, not without force; a 'patient and sustained interest' in detail (Deutscher, 1966, p. 238) crucial to the war of position, but tied to the capacity to mount the sudden strikes of a *manoeuvre*. 'It would be an error', Tucker comments, 'to view the Bukharinists' defeat as a victory of naked organizational power on the part of the Stalin faction. As in the earlier phase of the leadership contest, the outcome also reflected the persuasiveness of Stalin's case and his crude effectiveness in the arena of intra-party controversy' (1974, p. 411). For those who persistently separated out coercion and consent within political theory and practice, Stalin was the kind of Marxist whom it was easy to underestimate.

There can be little doubt that the coercion during the Stalin period was massive, macabre and at times appears almost self-destructive; yet this was a coercion which was political and social in character. The 'revolution from above' can only be understood in relation to the popular enthusiasm 'from below'. Cohen speaks of the substantial support which existed for Stalinist policies 'from the beginning and through the very worst' (1977, p. 28) and warns that this is a 'problem largely ignored and inconsistent with the imagery of a "totalitarian" regime dominating a hapless, "atomized" population through power techniques alone' (1977, p. 27). The drive to collectivize agriculture and industrialize the nation involved in no small measure the concentrated coercion of the state but this political coercion was itself only sustained through a mass participatory response (Tucker, 1977b, p. 324; Harrison, 1979, p. 24). Medvedev comments with great bitterness that 'the longer this tyrant ruled the USSR, cold-bloodedly destroying millions of people, the greater seems to have been the dedication to him, even the love, of the majority of the people' (1972, p. 362): if Stalin was, as Davies puts it, 'a ruthless personal dictator', he was also an immensely popular one (1979, p. 9). What kind of regime then was this?

According to Medvedev, Stain's NKVD, his security police,

arrested and killed during two peak years of the purges in the 1930s more communists than had been lost in all the years of the underground struggle, the three revolutions and the civil war (1972, p. 234). Yet, at the same time, 'Stalin involved millions of people in his crimes', from the thousands of party officials and government representatives who sanctioned arrests, to the masses of 'ordinary people' who demanded severe reprisals against 'enemies' (1972, p. 365). If Stalin occupied 'a unique position' free from control by his Central Committee, the party or the people (Medvedev, 1972, p. 149), he continued, nevertheless, Medvedev argues, 'to rely on the masses which was the chief peculiarity of Stalin's actions and the ultimate determinant of his success' (1972, p. 375). There was massive terror and massive progress. New cities were built; new social groups were created; large numbers of ordinary Russians were educated and promoted to responsible positions (Davies, 1979, p. 9) — 'Soviet society was truly revolutionised' (Harrison, 1979, p. 25). Here, indeed, lies the key to understanding the character of the system, for given the fact, as Medvedev says, Stalin had to take account of 'the ideology and the collective will of the Party, Lenin's heritage, the socialist aspirations of the workers' (1972, p. 371), his 'unlimited personal power was a form, the worst possible form, of the proletarian dictatorship' (1972, p. 556). Harrison argues that under Stalin there developed the 'politics of subordinacy' and this meant that the working class which had constituted itself as the ruling class and 'directly exercised political power' in October 1917, now beat a retreat (1979, p. 24).

Yet, to argue that the working class can only be a ruling class because it directly exercises political power, is to present the proletarian state as an *abstraction*. The 'politics of subordinacy' and 'the subjection of the workers themselves to new coercive disciplines' (Harrison, 1979, p. 24) is not peculiar to Stalinism: as we have noted above, this gulf between the producer and his political rule is inherent in all forms of the proletarian state. With the development of what came to be called after 1956 a 'cult of the personality', there arose in the Stalinist form of proletarian dictatorship all the negative symptoms of the political mentality (*MECW* 3, p. 119) — a belief in the *'omnipotence* of the will' which encouraged a voluntarist style of planning and a tendency to ascribe material difficulties to malevolent 'wreckers' (Medvedev, 1972, p. 351). If one can argue that all transitional workers' states will suffer some degree of 'statolatry' (to recall Gramsci's term), here was a statolatry which did tend to 'become theoretical fanaticism' (*SPN*, p. 268).

Doubtless, Stalin's immense popularity is ascribable to the cultural backwardness of the Russian masses and the 'inability', as Medvedev puts it, of many people to think for themselves (1972, p. 398): a 'petty bourgeois' mentality reminiscent of Marx's French peasants under Bonaparte whose representative appears as an 'unlimited governmental power that protects them against the other classes and sends them rain and sunshine from above' (*MECW* 11, pp. 187–8). The reproduction of such 'patriarchal benefactors' in China under Mao, in North Korea under Kim Il Sung and in its most rabidly self-destructive expression, Cambodia under Pol Pot suggests that what we are dealing with here is a state-form of proletarian dictatorship as it arises in 'exceptional' circumstances. Miliband conjectures that 'some kind of dictatorial rule' would have prevailed in Russia after Lenin's death, whoever had succeeded him and that it is 'very likely' that this would have turned into 'one-man rule' (1982, p. 8).

What might be legitimately said, therefore, in response to the celebrated 'inevitability' problem, is that Lenin (had he lived) would have sought to minimize the abuses inherent in this most extreme version of proletarian state power — its 'worst form' — while Stalin, for example during the years 1936–8 and 1947–53 (both periods of intense international pressure), appeared ready to *maximize* them. The role of personality can only be understood as an 'accidental' response to the wider coercive necessities of society and the state, either aggravating or mitigating the contradiction which exists between the class which rules and the special instrument of coercion through which its interests are represented in general form. 'From how many crimes, wars, and murders, from how many horrors and misfortunes might not any one have saved mankind', declares Rousseau (1913, p. 192) had they prevented the formation of the state! Whether it is the proletarian or the bourgeois state, the 'worst form' merely exacerbates the problems which are embryonic even in the best.

Lane is correct to insist that in analysing Stalin's state, the role of denunciation must not take precedence over explanation (1981, p. 82). To say, as Medvedev does, that unlimited personal power was a 'form of proletarian dictatorship' and yet 'severely checked progress towards communism' (1972, p. 556) is to fly in the face of historical realities, for how do we analytically distinguish between the political coercion which created the basis for an industrialized society from the brutal coercion which decimated the kulaks? Medvedev's voluntarism, as Lane calls it (1981, p. 82), arises from an unwillingness to accept the implications of his own analysis, that even in the 'worst form' of proletarian dictatorship, mass coercion is only possible through mass consent. Before we rush to condemn violence and assert with Boffa that Soviet society advanced not through Stalin's methods, but 'despite them' (1959, p. 63), it is worth remembering that such violence cannot become political unless it is also 'legitimate'. Coercion cannot be sustained without consent. No strategic options exist, as Harrison seems to think (1979, p. 24), which make it possible to 'choose' one rather than the other.

Stalinism as an extreme form of the proletarian state, can only be understood if we grasp the character of politics in general. No state should be presented as 'ideal' for, as we have seen, political idealism arises as the ideological expression of the state's coercive instrumentality. Idealizing politics necessarily mystifies reality by 'mechanically hypostasizing' one moment of the political process at the expense of the other. It is for this reason that Marx and Engels declare that communism is not 'an *ideal* to which reality [will] have to adjust itself' (*MECW* 5, p. 49) and why do they insist upon this point (*MECW* 6, p. 498)? The real movement which abolishes the present state of things has to pass through many phases and since each fluidly interpenetrates with the other, none should be presented statically as an ideal. In the *Civil War in France*, Marx argues that the working class 'will have to pass through long struggles, through a series of historic processes, transforming circumstances and men' and hence: 'They have no ideals to realise' (*PC*, p. 76). For Bernstein, it is not only the transitional state which is an absurdity and the concept of the dictatorship of the proletariat an abomination (1961, p. 146); the notion in Marx that the working class have 'no ideals to realise' is either 'self-deception' or 'a mere play upon words on the part of its author' (1961, p. 222). Since consent is the basis of democracy and coercion the source of dictatorship, are there not self-evident ideals at hand for all socialists to revere? It is not surprising therefore that this tendency to idealize the political process makes it quite impossible to understand the character of Stalinism.

Meszaros argues that under Stalinism, Marx's 'ideal' of the self-determining life-activity of freely associated social individuals is completely transformed into the 'forced association of men ruled by an alien political force' (1979, p. 109). This 'idealizing' of Marx is accompanied by the demonizing of Stalin as the glow of consent grimly contrasts with the dark shadows of coercion. According to Maszaros, a 'double perversion' occurred with the rise of 'an alien political force': | 'Marx's ideal is turned into a highly problematical reality, which in its turn is reconverted into a totally untenable model and ideal' (1979, p. 109). Yet both the moments of this 'double perversion' are misconceived for it is wrong to idealize Stalin precisely because it is wrong to idealize Marx. The Stalinist state can be understood neither as an ideal nor as the perversion of an ideal and therefore the irony is this. Stalin's system tended to present itself in terms of that very political idealism which Meszaros wrongly ascribes to Marx: as the 'worst form' of the proletarian state in which the working class rules less directly than in any other, it was particularly prone to 'theoretical fanaticism' and political mystification.

Stalin's willingness to take liberties with the Marxist classics must not however be exaggerated. As Davies notes, his rule involved a coercion justified by a 'Marxist framework' (1979, p. 9) and it seems incorrect to say, as Medvedev does, that Stalin brushed aside Marx and Engels's idea of the hegemony of the proletariat (1972, p. 515; Stalin, 1954, p. 101). Nor is it quite right to argue that the notion of a stateless communism is 'absent from Stalin's writings' (Lane, 1981, p. 78). It is true that Stalin does present a somewhat 'statolatrous' view of a period of communism in which the state still exists but this, Stalin insists, would only continue until 'capitalist encirclement is liquidated' (1973, p. 387). While Lenin's comment in *State and Revolution* about the 'great abundance and variety of forms' possible for a workers' state is reaffirmed in Stalin's writing (1973, p. 385), there can be little doubt that he tended to take a rather restricted view both of how the proletariat could win power and the form this power could take. He poses the Paris Commune against the democratic republic as 'the most suitable form of the dictatorship of the proletariat' (*CPSU* (B), 1951, p. 542) — an 'idealizing' error he shares with staunch anti-Stalinists like Claudin (1977, p. 72)! — and Lenin's stress on violent revolution, particularly in his polemics with Kautsky, is given a rather absolutist reading so that curiously, there is an inverted Eurocommunist echo to Stalin's argument that the dictatorship of the proletariat 'cannot arise as the result of the peaceful development of bourgeois society' (1973, p. 127; see Carrillo, 1977, p. 149; Seve, 1977, p. 142).

If commentators are right to see in Stalin's theoretical statements an inclination to idealize apologetically the moment of force — (although the quality of Stalin's Marxism is easy to oversimplify) — this can scarcely justify the counter-tendency to present a utopian idealization of the moment of consent. Despite his critique of abstract moralism in Medvedev's view of Stalinism, Lane argues that while the mode of production under Stalin can be described as socialist, this cannot be said of many aspects of the political super-structure. Socialism as 'a system of economy' should not be conflated with 'socialism as a "way of life", as an ideal state' (1981, p. 92). But this argument takes us back to Medvedev's moralism for if practices involving 'the repression of man' (Lane, 1981, p. 92) are considered 'degenerate' and pseudo-socialist, then 'truly socialist relationships' (as Medvedev calls them, 1972, p. 554) can only be those based on consent. Lane is rightly critical of Carrillo's contention that the October Revolution has produced a state which is not, as yet, 'the proletariat organised as the ruling class', a 'genuine workers' democracy' (Carrillo, 1977, p. 157) and he evokes precisely the argument we have outlined above: that the socialist state rules on 'behalf of' the working class, not at its 'behest' (1981, pp. 93–4). Yet it is this gulf between the producer and his political rule which should caution us against assessing *any* form of the state in 'ideal' terms. Although the Eurocommunist *desire* to establish a different form of the socialist state can certainly be justified, given the different traditions, material circumstances and cultural development of Western Europe, it does not follow that a *possible* political model should be converted into the *true* 'workers' democracy'. Indeed, what Carrillo's *'Eurocom-munism' and the State* graphically demonstrates, is that when one form of the state is mechanically hypostasized, then all the paradoxes of vulgar liberalism return with a vengeance.

Carrillo himself quotes Lenin's reference to the 'diversity of political forms' (*LCW* 25, p. 413) and declares that Lenin 'was no more than half right because the essence of all the various political forms of transition to socialism is . . . *the hegemony of the working people*' while the diversity and abundance of forms entails the possibility of *'the dictatorship of the proletariat not being necessary'* (1977, p. 154). But is this working class hegemony in the happy position of having finally abstracted itself from all those 'degenerate' Stalinist features of a 'socialist totalitarianism' which constitute the moment of force (1977, p. 146)? Carrillo clearly considers himself a utopian who has his feet on the ground: in the 'democratic socialist society', he writes, 'it will still be necessary to have functionaries who are specialists in the pursuit of crime, and in safeguarding the security of the population' (1977, p. 57). *Libertas*, it seems, is still to be inscribed on prison doors, for while consent is proudly displayed on the portals, coercion is smuggled in through the back door. The familiar problem: just as the guests are settling in to their consensual feast, the coercive ghost of Banquo returns to disrupt the proceedings! As long as we remain prisoners to political idealism, it is impossible to grapple with the character of Stalin and Stalinism as a politics of force: a proletarian state form which combines exceptional violence with exceptional legitimacy. An extreme form of the dictatorship of the proletariat as a contradictory political reality.

LIBERALISM, SOCIALISM AND DEMOCRACY

At the heart of the 'crisis of Marxism' lies, as we have seen, the question of democracy and it is my contention in this chapter that this problem cannot be properly tackled unless the different forms of the socialist state are themselves correctly interrelated. A dialectical view of the coercion/consent problem in Marxist political theory makes it possible to understand why the Commune form, as the most direct, and the Stalinist form, as one of the least direct, are nevertheless *both* forms of proletarian rule. I want to conclude this chapter with an even more contentious proposition, namely that in both these forms of the socialist state, the proletariat is organized as the ruling class and that therefore both varieties can be legitimately characterized, in Carrillo's words, as 'genuine workers' democracies'. Since 1956, the political system of the USSR has been moving away from the Stalinist model and towards the Commune form and this has involved just that 'self-transcendence' of political power (albeit still in embryo) which those trapped in the metaphysics of a 'crisis of Marxism', have been unable to see.

Marx and Engels in the *Manifesto* unambiguously equate raising the proletariat 'to the position of a ruling class' with 'winning the battle for democracy' (*MECW* 6, p. 504). If this equation seems strange to contemporary liberal theory, it unmistakably evokes the class-based definitions of democracy common to the ancient Greeks and early liberals. For Aristotle, 'democracy occurs when the sovereign power is in the hands of those who have no accumulated wealth' (1967, p. 117); for Plato, a democracy 'originates when the poor win, kill or exile their opponents' (1955, p. 228), while even in the nineteenth century, J.S. Mill could sympathetically echo De Tocqueville's fear that democracy, having destroyed 'the feudal system and vanquished kings', would shatter the power of 'the middle classes and the rich' (Tocqueville, 1966, p. 8; J.S. Mill, 1968, p. 250). As late as the 1920s, a government publication in the USA could define democracy as 'a government of the masses ... Attitude towards property is communistic — negating property rights ... Results in demagogism, license, agitation, discontent, anarchy' (Goldman, 1956, p. 222). Carrillo, as we have seen, is dismayed by Lenin's view of democracy as 'a *state* which recognises the subordination of the minority to the majority' (*LCW* 25, p. 456) and urges socialism to recover for itself, among other things, liberal values and 'respect for dissenting minorities' (1977, p. 98). But if, as Carrillo *also* says, the 'genuine workers' democracy' arises with the proletariat organized as the ruling class, then respecting liberal values and 'dissenting minorities' is easier said than done.

As far as the *Manifesto* is concerned, the political supremacy of the proletariat necessitates 'despotic inroads on the rights of property' (*MECW* 6, p. 504), and this creates precisely the problem of which earlier political theorists were only too acutely aware. For what rights are likely to be more dearly held by minorities in a time of political change than those 'rights of property' which, in James Madison's eyes, have been found ever 'incompatible' with systems of democracy (1961, p. 81)? Medvedev has argued that real democracy cannot exist under socialism unless the rights of both majority and minority are guaranteed, unless there is a place for dissent and opposition and the possibility of forming independent social and political associations (1975, p. xvi). But this position simply collapses liberalism into democracy and ignores the particular task facing the socialist/communist society — that of replacing the 'domination of circumstances and of chance over individuals by the domination of individuals over chance and circumstances' (*MECW* 5, p. 438).

With social and economic *planning*, the 'spontaneous' discipline of the market, reinforced by the capitalist state yields to the organized, collectivist discipline of mass and party organizations, mediated in the first instance, by the concentrated coercion of the socialist state, and this situation undeniably creates potential problems for minority rights and liberal values. For what we have here is, in Meszaros's words, a *politically* determined extraction of surplus labour from society which imposes radically new functions on the proletarian state (1979, p. 122): the 'coercion of circumstances' is to be supplanted by the regulation of society and the role of the state is to ensure that this regulation is effective. Linking state to society is the centrality of the cadre concept — discipline through leadership of a kind which can co-ordinate party and government, the economy and mass organizations, ideology and scientific and cultural institutions (Therborn, 1978, p. 109).

What implications does all this have for liberal values and minority rights, dissent and opposition? The first is that as long as the foundations of the new economy remain heavily reliant upon the 'underpinning' role of state coercion, a premium will be placed on unity over sectionalism, the collective over the individual, and a Rousseauan 'General Will' will look upon 'factions' and 'partisanship' with disapproval and suspicion. The second is that all developments towards decentralization, diversification, 'autonomy', etc., whether in the political or economic realm, can only be implemented, as Meszaros notes, as *'political* principles' (1979, p. 127): they are only likely to be accepted and recognized when they do not endanger the prevailing mode of extracting surplus labour which the socialist state seeks to consolidate. Hence, as Friedgut notes, the subordination of the particular to the general interest is an important part of the Soviet outlook on participation (1979, p. 50). The logic of the process involved is captured well in Rousseau's *Social Contract* where the total alienation of each to the state as representative of the community is a *precondition* for the recovery by each of all that they have lost i.e. power can only be 'returned' to society through the medium of the state. It is therefore not only possible but absolutely necessary that the socialist society should increasingly develop decentralized methods of planning, greater local initiatives, a higher degree of municipal and regional autonomy but in a way in which *strengthens* rather than undermines collectivist discipline and the foundations of a planned economy.

There has, as Churchward observes, been a considerable reduction in the coercive powers of the Soviet state since the death of Stalin. Republican and local government has been extended; police powers whittled down; the rights of the individual citizen enlarged and great stress has been placed on 'socialist legality' as the basis of government. Since government, in other words, has become 'less arbitrary, less personal and more collective in its decisions' (1975, p. 304), it seems only right to conclude that there has been a transfer of power from the state's special instruments of coercion to society at large, not of course, as a dramatic act or 'surrender' but rather as part of the process of making the 'illusory community' more real. But this process of 'transition', of 'self-transcendence' cannot be understood as the triumph of consent over coercion, freedom over necessity: on the contrary, it can only take place through the strengthening of *one kind* of coercion at the expense of another. The social 'transmission belts' like the trade unions and the soviets have acquired more power and the party has entrenched its authority at the expense of the state. Returning the concentrated coercion of the state to society itself can only involve *increasing* the social pressures to participate — in elections as voters, canvassers and personnel for the electoral commissions; in trade unions as administrators of health and insurance services, for example, which in many capitalist countries are the responsibility of the state; in co-operatives and collective farms, comradely courts and fire brigades, street and house committees, pensioners' and women's councils, etc. (Churchward, 1975, p. 270).

Dissolving the state into society necessitates what Therborn calls 'the publicization of private life and the massive political mobilization of the people' (1978, p. 109) and this process of strengthening collectivist discipline only appears inherently oppressive to those who consider the domination of circumstances over people as freedom and the domination of people over circumstances as coercion! The use of 'universal participation' to obliterate the distinction between public and private interests, civil and political society (Friedgut, 1979, p. 314) cannot be grasped if an idealized conception of 'truly voluntary participation' is contrasted with situations in which 'the element of compulsion was ever present' (Unger, 1981, p. 111). What is relevant is not the existence of compulsion within the participatory process, but its individual and social *quality*.

I have argued in an earlier chapter that all social and political relationships involve a recognition by the participant of what has to be done: coercion is only possible through a consensual response. The quality of this consent depends upon the extent to which it becomes a counter-coercion, transforming the social and political realities to which it responds. This is clearly not simply a question of subjective enthusiasm and commitment at the individual level; it is also a question of monitoring changes to reality which occur through mass consent. Hough has argued that the impact on policy making by citizen participation in the USSR is much greater than is often assumed in the West (1976, p. 15); White has recently analysed in detail the 'ombudsman' role of letters in Soviet politics and suggests that 'in some areas at least citizens' letters may yield not just the impression but also the reality of change, particularly when the irregularities or abuses of local-level officials or institutions are concerned' (1983, p. 59). Voting has become more meaningful than in the past; there appears to be some interest in altering the single candidature system and areas of participation are opening up in which the party abstains from using its veto (Friedgut, 1979, p. 120; p. 147; p. 150). Friedgut draws a distinction between a 'mobilized' and an 'autonomous' participation (1979, p. 30) and in evaluating elections to the local Soviets, he comments: 'the people will choose, but the *apparat* will act as a "guiding hand" in making the choice'. Neither 'brute force nor spontaneity are permissible' (1979, p. 137). All this suggests that in the USSR, as in other socialist societies, the 'consensual quality' of political and social participation is relatively undeveloped and that the formation of what Marx refers to as 'the spontaneous action of the laws of the social economy of free and associated labour' (*PC*, p. 157) is far from complete. But is this entirely surprising, given the realities of a *transitional* state?

Medvedev has complained that the overwhelming majority of working people do not participate 'as they should' in the political life of his country (1975, p. 25) and Lane argues that while participation in planning procedures through meetings and discussions are important from 'a mobilising and symbolic point of view', these activities are not 'socialist' in 'the *ideal* way desired by Lenin, and the USSR has failed to produce any really advanced form of direct administration by the masses.' (1981, p. 77). Both these comments, however, miss the point. What is relevant is not the ideal state of affairs but the real movement of a socialist society, the direction in which it is travelling and the extent to which it is still stamped with the birthmarks of the old society (*MESW*, p. 323; White, 1979, p. 48). Any attempt to absolutize one moment of political participation can only obscure the reality of the transition to communism as a process.

Analyses which tend to emphasize consent at the expense of coercion and judge concrete societies in terms of abstract ideals, create a further problem. They make it impossible to get to grips with the proper relationship between liberalism, socialism and democracy. Democracy, I have argued, is best defined as working class power, the sovereignty of those without accumulated wealth. In terms of this argument, capitalist societies can be more or less liberal and the more liberal they are, the greater are the opportunities they offer for the working class to *struggle for* democracy. But strictly speaking, they remain 'oligarchies' in all their political forms — from the most liberal to the most authoritarian — since power is ultimately vested in a minoritarian ruling class. What the index of 'liberality' measures is the degree to which a given ruling class, bourgeois or proletarian, directly controls its own state, the instruments of coercion which represent its particular interests in general form.

This is why Meiksins Wood is correct to surmise that 'the most important question of liberalism has little to do with democracy but is concerned with controlling state power — and here, the earlier *anti*-democratic forms of liberalism may have as much to say as does liberal democracy' (1978, p. 231). In fact, they indicate just how problematic the whole concept of a 'liberal democracy' under capitalism really is. Of course, if democracy is simply reduced to the moment of consent and politics is abstracted from that 'dull compulsion of economic relations' which leaves the mass of the population relatively uninvolved in running their daily lives, then liberalism and democracy appear to encounter one another as benevolent synonyms. In some Eurocommunist accounts, liberal bourgeois societies are considered as close to communism as the countries of existing socialism (e.g. Cornforth, 1980, p. 213) and the idea that the battle for democracy can only be won through raising the proletariat to the position of ruling class, is dismissed as the stale dogma of a reductionist Marxism.

In fact, liberalism is not synonymous with democracy nor does liberalism become democratic simply because workers under capitalism win important social and political rights. Benn has argued that the people in Britain have won in reality, if not in constitutional theory, 'the sovereign rights which belong to the people — which is what democracy is all about' (1982, p. 10), but what does the existence of such rights tell us about the actual exercise of *power*? If the 'political economy' of the working class has made significant advances, its logic is still distinctly subordinate: reforms have been wrested from a ruling class and not without a fight, but the power of that class still stands (as indeed, Benn himself seems to acknowledge, 1982, p. 11). In other words, mass popular consent has not secured *democracy* as long as the capacity of the working class to impose its political coercion on society as a whole, is still to be realized. It is not merely the right to consent, but the power to coerce which is crucial to assessing the character of political rule.

If it is democracy rather than liberalism which is synonymous with the socialist state, liberal values and institutions remain of relevance to socialists for two reasons. The first is the one which we noted particularly in chapter 2. The more liberal the capitalist state, the more directly the bourgeoisie rule; and the more directly the bourgeoisie rule, the more vulnerable they are to proletarian challenge and to radical pressures seeking to 'extend' liberal institutions in a socialist direction. The second reason for the relevance of liberalism is as important as the first. The more liberal the socialist state, the more directly the working class rules. Given the transitional character of the proletarian state, the more directly the working class rules, the greater is the degree to which political institutions have dissolved themselves into the wider coercive process of society at large. What the index of 'liberality' measures, therefore, is not the democratic character of the socialist state, but the extent to which a socialist system has developed into the stateless society of classless communism. Hence it is not surprising that classical Marxism takes the liberal component within socialist thought very much for granted (Johnstone, 1970, p. 244; Medvedev, 1972, p. 425). Indeed, Marx and Engels criticized the Gotha programme in 1875 precisely because it neglected the importance of limiting the power of the state. Rather than strive for some kind of mysterious 'free state', it would be far better, Marx argued, if the German socialists understood that 'Freedom consists in converting the state from an organ superimposed upon society into one completely subordinate to it, and today, too, the forms of state are more free or less free to the extent that they restrict the "freedom of the state" ' (*MESW*, p. 330; *SC*, p. 275). The state under socialism is free (or liberal) to the extent that it has 'withered away'.

Liberal values relate, therefore, not to the question of democracy, but to the problem of limiting the state and, as such, they can only contribute positively to the development of a socialist democracy when the introduction of liberal rights and freedoms serves to *strengthen* the collectivist discipline of a planned society. Attempts either to delay or 'artificially hasten' the implementation of what Shahnazarov has called 'various democratic forms' may be highly detrimental to the task of consolidating socialism (Shahnazarov, 1974, p. 82) for how useful would it be to restrict state power in a context in which the only result was an increase in unemployment, social insecurity and a return to the domination of people by their own anarchic circumstances? The *Manifesto*'s eminently liberal reference to the free development of each as a condition for the free development of all, should not therefore be presented as an 'ideal' (Medvedev, 1975, p. xvi). It presupposes the regulation of social production according to a common plan in conditions under which the concentrated coercion of the state has been returned to the organized bodies of society itself; in a situation in which the 'public power' has ceased to be political (*MECW* 6, p. 505). It is only in a *communist* society that 'the genuine and free development of individuals ceases to be a mere phrase' (*MECW* 5, p. 439). To argue, as Miliband does, that a socialist democracy represents an 'advanced social and political system, of which history so far offers no example and of which there is unlikely to be an example for some time to come' (1973d, p. 391) is to treat liberalism and democracy as though they were indistinguishable and communism as if it was somehow an 'advanced' form of the state. A sober assessment of existing realities is clouded by the mists of political idealism and utopian vision.

In *State and Revolution* Lenin notes Engels's earlier preference for the term 'communist' over 'social-democrat' on the grounds that the 'ultimate political aim' of the Marxist party is 'to overcome the whole state and, consequently, democracy as well' (*LCW* 25, pp. 454–5). If this sounds 'exceedingly strange and incomprehensible', it is only because of a widespread tendency to overlook the fact that democracy is best understood, not as a social principle, but as a form of the state. It is true that Engels also refers to the 'natural' and 'spontaneous' democracy of primitive communism (see e.g. *OFPPS*, p. 150; p. 167) and Carrillo cites these comments as an argument against Lenin's 'restrictive' political conceptions (1977, p. 89). But what we encounter here is a problem of terminology: the problem noted in chapter 2 of what terms to use in characterizing the transition from society to state and the state to society. Lenin's own account is not without its difficulties. At one point he refers to the fact that 'the more complete the democracy, the nearer the moment when it becomes unnecessary' (*LCW* 25, p. 474); at another, he comments that only under communism, will a 'truly complete democracy become possible', a 'democracy without any exceptions whatever' (*LCW* 25, p. 462). The 'confusion', as Carrillo calls it (1977, p. 89), arises out of the use of a single term to account for a dying political form as it changes into its social opposite. Given the ease with which liberalism is collapsed into democracy by contemporary commentators and communism projected as an idealized form of the state, it might be better to tackle the problem of continuity through change by means of a strict terminological differentiation. In elaborating this point in more general terms, I can now bring my analysis of the problem of coercion and consent in Marxist political theory to an overall conclusion.

HAS POLITICS A FUTURE?

It is a commonplace that the classical Marxist tradition regards the communist future as one without a state in which, to cite the time honoured formula, 'the government of persons is replaced by the administration of things' (*AD*, p. 385). We have already encountered in chapter 2 Marx's reference to the performance of common activities arising from the nature of all communities (*C* III, p. 384) and elsewhere Marx raises the question of the social function, 'analagous to present state functions', that will remain in existence in a communist society (*MESW*, p. 331). A planned society is clearly a regulated society with organs of centralized management and administration — what the *Manifesto* calls a 'public power' (*MECW* 6, p. 505). Surely, it might be argued, all this implies a continuing role for politics and that to present a future without the state is to underestimate the problems of accountability and control which inhere in all forms of 'public power' (Benn, 1982, p. 9).

Indeed, this is precisely why, in Hobsbawm's eyes, Gramsci offers Marxist theory something new. By arguing that every person is a 'legislator' and a 'politician' in as much as 'he is active, i.e. living, contributes to modifying the social environment in which he develops' (*SPN*, p. 265), Gramsci expands the concept of politics even beyond the 'extended' state. Politics therefore relates to both the winning of power and 'the core of the new society itself' and this makes it possible, says Hobsbawm, to grapple with the 'continuity between the movement to overcome the old society and the construction of the new' (1982, p. 23).

There can be no doubt that it is important to establish the continuity between the old statist order and the new stateless one, but can this be done by identifying the concept of politics with human activity itself? For this means (as in Gramsci's efforts to develop an autonomous science of politics noted in chapter 4) either arguing that politics is the same as social activity or it is totally different: either class politics and communist politics are indistinguishable (what then of Marxism?), or they are so opposed that the movement from one to the other becomes impossible to explain. The problem of unity and distinction, of continuity through change, can only be tackled if politics is defined as the concentrated expression of coercion and consent. In this way, it can then be argued (a) that politics 'strictly speaking' and 'properly so called' *does* disappear but that (b) in dissolving itself into social organization and administration with its coercion of habit rather than of law, it leaves behind problems which can be described as 'proto-political' in character. Questions of accountability, corruption and abuse would still need attention under communism and Mill's analysis of liberty would doubtless remain relevant in order to ensure that society acts in a manner which is tolerant, fair-minded and generous to the individual. But, and this is the crucial point, these kinds of problems could be tackled through a judicious use of social discipline and without the need to concentrate the diffuse coercion of social relationships into the condensed coercion of the class-based state. Engels was quick to emphasize in his argument with the anarchists that humans simply cannot produce without authority and organization (*MELAAS*, p. 101) and Marx insists that even when people regulate their interchange with nature 'rationally', under conditions most favourable to their human nature, they remain in 'a realm of necessity'. It is only through and beyond this realm, that 'the true realm of freedom' can blossom (*C* III, p. 820). When Lenin therefore argues that people will gradually become accustomed to observing the elementary rules of social intercourse 'without force, without coercion, without subordination, *without the special apparatus* for coercion called the state' (*LCW* 25, p. 462), he makes it clear that these elementary rules of social intercourse imply a coercion of their own (*LCW* 25, p. 474). It is presumably for this reason that McBride complains that the 'various dilemmas' in *The State and Revolution* 'are reducible to the fact that Lenin seems not to have regarded a non-coercive state, in which individuals would act out of free choice rather than out of external compulsion or internalized habit, as a real human possibility' (1972, p. 185).

This is, however, as we have seen in chapter 5, to pose the problem falsely for 'free choice' only exists 'as a real human possibility' because humans enter into relations of production independent of their will. Recognizing necessity is the only way to transform it: consent has to respond to coercion in order to 'negate' it. We have to avoid, as Kann notes, a fatalistic social determinism (which he wrongly ascribes to Marx) *and* a voluntaristic postulation of situations in which 'social pressures are non-existent' (1978, p. 390). This choice can only translate itself into a view of the new communist society as either a libertarian utopia in which consent triumphs over coercion or the uncritical projection of existing social realities into the world of the future. In fact, as the real movement which abolishes the present state of things, communism is neither.

It follows from my argument therefore that a stateless, communist society cannot be meaningfully envisaged through analyses which display any residue of political idealism. Kann presents the case for a 'Dialectic of Consent Theory' in which governments secure legitimacy through policies which would enhance the 'consensual abilities' of all sections of the community — explicitly cultivating a body of citizens able to criticize and challenge government continuously through constructive dissent (1978, pp. 403–5). An admirable idea! But this kind of government could only emerge with the disappearance of the *state* and the creation of dissenting consenters implies not only 'the guarantee of a decent standard of living', but full employment, involvement in the work process, a good education, an absence of anxiety about health care and housing provision, etc. Is any of this possible for all the members of society in a world in which people stand powerless in the face of their own coercive circumstances? The problem of consent cannot really be satisfactorily probed in abstraction from the case for communism for here we encounter once again the need to analyse through synthesis.

April Carter's impressive little volume, *Authority and Democracy* (1979), exemplifies this problem. She defines authority as a relationship of respect which entails 'an automatic tendency to comply with commands' but with a readiness to 'question the reasons for and rightness of specific decisions' (1979, p. 40). What mars however this otherwise persuasive argument is Carter's insistence that this form of consent cannot be part of the world of coercion and power which it negates: authority can only have a distinct identity because it inhabits an autonomous world of its own (1979, p. 51). Yet how could it be possible to sustain the kind of 'free, creative and responsive society' (1979, p. 89) which Carter so rightly favours, if its autonomous acts of consent are not, at the same time, rooted in the coercive relationships of a 'realm of necessity'? Unless consent is conceived of as a moment within the social coercion from which it arises and which it negates, its distinct identity becomes impossible to explain. Analysis without synthesis serves only to summon forth those mechanical hypostases, theological niceties and metaphysical subleties which dominate so much political thought.

Marx writes in the *Grundrisse* that in all forms of society 'there is one specific kind of production which predominates over the rest, whose relations thus assign rank and influence to the others'. 'It is', he says, 'a general illumination which bathes all the other colours and modifies their particularity' (*G*, pp. 106–7). This comment holds also for the pervasive presence of *coercion*, for what is coercion if it is not an ethical expression of the fact that people *have to* produce? It is only *through* the compulsion of circumstances that diversity and autonomy, freedom and authority can flourish. Coercion is the 'ether' which assigns rank and influence to all the other moments in the world of consent and without this basis, these analytically differentiated moments lose their synthetic unity. Methodological distinctions become organic divides and analysis serves only to mystify.

Coercion has first to be *social* before it can be concentrated into class based instruments of the state and it is the failure to grasp this crucial 'unity in distinction' which leaves even Marxist critics of Gramsci like Anderson and Poulantzas, trapped in the antinomies they criticize. Both challenge the imagery of the Centaur (Poulantzas, 1978, pp. 80–1; Anderson, 1976, p. 49), yet both remain the prisoner of its conundrums. One advocates a 'democratic road to socialism' mystically free of all 'statism' (1978, p. 256); the other an inverted Eurocommunism – a leftist insurrection by consent, a spontaneous act of 'brute force' (1976, pp. 77–8)! Unless political analysis is premised on the coercive character of all social relationships, then even if these two levels of the Gramscian couplet are energetically clasped together, they remain all the while mechanically hypostasized and organically spliced apart. What is required therefore is not 'True Socialism', as Marx and Engels called it, but a real socialism which develops from the premises of social realities: 'By "external compulsion" the true socialists do not understand the restrictive material condition of life of given individuals. They see it only as the compulsion exercised by the *state* in the form of bayonets, police and cannons, which far from being the foundation of society, are only a consequence of its structure' (*MECW* 5, p. 479). We conclude with the following observation. Marx's communism as 'the riddle of history solved' (*MECW* 3, p. 297) can meet the challenge of the Machiavellian Centaur. It is 'sound common sense' which has generated the schizoid maladies and errant isms which have plunged Marxism into crisis: it is not the dialectical principles of the classical Marx.

REFERENCES

Reference here is to the date of publication and not to the date of printing.

Adamson, W.L. (1980) *Hegemony and Revolution*, California, University of California.

Althusser, L. (1969) *For Marx*, London, Allen Lane.

Althusser, L. (1977a) 'On the Twenty-Second Congress of the French Communist Party', *New Left Review*, July—August 1977, pp. 3—22.

Althusser, L. (1977b) 'Lysenko: Unfinished History', *Marxism Today*, February 1977, pp. 53—7.

Althusser, L. (1979) 'The Crisis of Marxism' in Il Manifesto (ed.), *Power and Opposition in Post-revolutionary Societies*, London, Ink Links, pp. 225—37.

Altvater, E. and Kallscheuer, O. (1979) 'Socialist Politics and the "Crisis of Marxism" ', *Socialist Register*, 1979, pp. 101—38.

Anderson, P. (1976) *Considerations on Western Marxism*, London, New Left Books.

Anderson, P. (1976—7) 'The Antinomies of Antonio Gramsci', *New Left Review*, November 1976—January 1977, pp. 5—78.

Aristotle (1967) *The Politics*, Harmondsworth, Penguin.

Arthur, C. (ed.) *Karl Marx and Frederick Engels: The German Ideology*, London, Lawrence and Wishart.

Arthur, C. (1979) 'Dialectics and Labour' in J. Mepham and D-Hillel Ruben (eds.), *Issues in Marxist Philosophy*, vol. 1, Sussex, The Harvester Press, pp. 87—116.

Avineri, S. (1968) *The Social and Political Thought of Karl Marx*, Cambridge, Cambridge University Press.

Azcarate, M. (1978) 'What is Eurocommunism?' in G.R. Urban (ed.), *Eurocommunism*, London, Maurice Temple Smith, pp. 13—31.

Balibar, E. (1977a) 'The Dictatorship of the Proletariat', *Marxism Today*, May 1977, pp. 144–53.

Balibar, E. (1977b) *The Dictatorship of the Proletariat*, London, New Left Books.

Ball, T. (1978) 'Two Concepts of Coercion', *Theory and Society*, January 1978, pp. 97–112.

Basmanov, M. (1972) *Contemporary Trotskyism: Its Anti-Revolutionary Nature*, Moscow, Progress Publishers.

Bates, T.R. (1975) 'Gramsci and the Theory of Hegemony', *Journal of the History of Ideas*, April–June 1974, pp. 351–66.

Benn, T. (1982) 'Democracy and Marxism: A Mutual Challenge', *Marxism Today*, May 1982, pp. 6–14.

Berlinguer, E. (1974) 'Reflections After the Events in Chile', *Marxism Today*, February 1974, pp. 39–50.

Bernstein, E. (1961) *Evolutionary Socialism*, New York, Schocken Books.

Blackburn, R. (1976) 'Marxism: Theory of Proletarian Revolution', *New Left Review*, May–June 1976, pp. 3–35.

Block, F. (1977) 'The Ruling Class does not Rule', *Socialist Revolution*, May–June 1977, pp. 6–28.

Bobbio, N. (1979) 'Gramsci and the conception of civil society' in C. Mouffe (ed.), *Gramsci and Marxist Theory*, London, Routledge & Kegan Paul, pp. 21–47.

Boffa, G. (1959) *Inside the Khrushchev Era*, London, Allen and Unwin.

Boffa, G. (1978) *Stalinism*, Rome, PCI Information Service.

Boggs, C. (1976) *Gramsci's Marxism*, London, Pluto Press.

Bogomolov, A.S. (1983) ' "Praxis" of Practice' in J. Hoffman, *Marxism, Revolution and Democracy*, Amsterdam, B.R. Grüner, pp. v–xxi.

Bosanquet, B. (1920) *The Philosophical Theory of the State* (3rd edn), London, Macmillan.

Bridges, G. (1978) 'Western European Communist Strategy' in S. Hibbin (ed.), *Politics, Ideology and the State*, London, Lawrence and Wishart, pp. 123–42.

Buci-Glucksmann, C. (1980) *Gramsci and the State*, London, Lawrence and Wishart.

Buci-Glucksmann, C. (1982) 'Hegemony and Consent: A Political Strategy' in A. Showstack Sassoon (ed.) *Approaches to Gramsci*, London, Writers and Readers, pp. 116–48.

Bukharin, N. and Preobrazhensky, E. (1969) *The ABC of Communism*, Harmondsworth, Penguin.

Burlatsky, F. (1978) *The Modern State and Politics*, Moscow, Progress Publishers.

Callinicos, A. (1982) *Is There a Future for Marxism?*, London, Macmillan.

Carr, E.H. (1969) 'Editor's Introduction' in N. Bukharin and E. Preobrazhensky, *The ABC of Communism*, Harmondsworth, Penguin.

Carrillo, S. (1977) *'Eurocommunism' and the State*, London, Lawrence and Wishart.

Carter, A. (1979) *Authority and Democracy*, London, Routledge & Kegan Paul.

Castillo, R. (1974a) 'Lessons and Prospects of the Revolution', *World Marxist Review*, July 1974, pp. 27—30.

Castillo, R. (1974b) 'Lessons and Prospects of the Revolution', *World Marxist Review*, August 1974, pp. 30—3.

Churchward, L. (1975) *Contemporary Soviet Government*, London, Routledge & Kegan Paul.

Claudin, F. (1977) 'Democracy and Dictatorship in Lenin and Kautsky', *New Left Review*, November—December 1977, pp. 59—76.

Claudin, F. (1978) *Eurocommunism and Eurosocialism*, London, New Left Books.

Claudin, F. (1979) 'Some Reflections on the Crisis of Marxism', *Socialist Review*, May—June 1979, pp. 137—43.

Cliff, T., Hallas, D., Harman, C. and Trotsky, L. (1971) *Party and Class*, London, Pluto Press.

Cohen, G. (1978) *Karl Marx's Theory of History A Defence*, New Jersey, Princeton University Press.

Cohen, S. (1974) *Bukharin and the Bolshevik Revolution*, London, Wildwood House.

Cohen, S. (1977) 'Bolshevism and Stalinism' in R. Tucker (ed.), *Stalinism: Essays in Historical Interpretation*, New York, Norton & Co., pp. 3—29.

Colletti, L. (1972) *From Rousseau to Lenin*, London, New Left Books.

Colletti, L. (1975) 'Introduction' in *Karl Marx Early Writings*, Harmondsworth and London, Penguin and New Left Books, pp. 7—56.

Colletti, L. (1977) 'A Political and Philosophical Interview' in New Left Review (ed.), *Western Marxism A Critical Reader*, London, New Left Books, pp. 315—50.

Cornforth, M. (1980) *Communism and Philosophy*, London, Lawrence and Wishart.

CPSU(B) (1951) *History of the Communist Party of the Soviet Union (Bolsheviks)*, Moscow, Foreign Languages Publishing House.

Cutler, A., Hindess, B., Hirst, P.Q. and Hussain, A. (1977) *Marx's 'Capital' and Capitalism Today*, vol. 1, London, Routledge & Kegan Paul.

Dahl, R. (1976) *Modern Political Analysis* (3rd edn), New Jersey, Prentice-Hall.

Davidson, A.B. (1972) 'The Varying Seasons of Gramscian Studies', *Political Studies*, December 1972, pp. 448–61.

Davies, R. (1979) 'Ruthless dictator or prisoner of coercion', *Times Higher Education Supplement*, 12 December 1979, p. 9.

Della Volpe, G. (1978) *Rousseau and Marx*, London, Lawrence and Wishart.

Deutscher, I. (1966) *Stalin* (3rd edn), Harmondsworth, Penguin.

Draper, H. (1977) *Karl Marx's Theory of Revolution: State and Bureaucracy* in 2 parts, New York, Monthly Review Press.

Easton, D. (1949) 'Walter Bagehot and Liberal Realism', *American Political Science Review*, January–March 1949, pp. 17–37.

Evans, M. (1975) *Karl Marx*, London, Allen and Unwin.

Fabre, J., Hincker, F. and Sève, L. (1977) *Les communistes et l'Etat*, Paris, Editions sociales.

Fazio, H. (1976) 'Analysing the Lessons of the Past in the Interest of the Future', *World Marxist Review*, April 1976, pp. 29–32.

Femia, J. (1981) *Gramsci's Political Thought*, Oxford, Clarendon Press.

Feuer, L. (1978) 'University Marxism', *Problem of Communism*, July–August 1978, pp. 65–72.

Fiori, G. (1970) *Antonio Gramsci: Life of a Revolutionary*, London, New Left Books.

Friedgut, T.H. (1979) *Political Participation in the USSR*, Princeton, Princeton University Press.

Gamble, A. (1979) 'The Free Economy and the Strong State: The Rise of the Social Market Economy', *Socialist Register*, 1979, pp. 1–25.

Gay, P. (1962) *The Dilemma of Democratic Socialism*, New York, Collier Books.

Geras, N. (1971) 'Essence and Appearance: Aspects of Fetishism in Marx's *Capital*', *New Left Review*, January–February 1971, pp. 69–85.

Geras, N. (1975) 'Rosa Luxemburg after 1905', *New Left Review*, January–February 1975, pp. 3–46.

Gibbon, P. (1983) 'Gramsci, Eurocommunism and the Comintern', *Economy and Society*, 1983, pp. 328–66.

Goldman, E. (1956) *Rendezvous with Destiny* (Rev. edn), New York, Vintage Books.

Gollan, J. (1964) 'Which Road?', *Marxism Today*, July 1964, pp. 198–216.

Green, T.H. (1941) *Lectures on the Principle of Political Obligation*, London, Longmans.

Gunn, R. (1977) 'Marxism and Ideas of Power and Participation' in J. Bloomfield (ed.), *Class, Hegemony and Party*, London, Lawrence and Wishart.

Hall, S. (1977) 'The "Political" and the "Economic" in Marx's Theory of Classes' in A. Hunt (ed.), *Class and Class Structure*, London, Lawrence and Wishart, pp. 15—60.

Harding, N. (1977) *Lenin's Political Thought*, vol. 1, London, Macmillan.

Harding, N. (1981) *Lenin's Political Thought*, vol. 2, London, Macmillan.

Harris, L. (1979) 'The theory of value and the value of theory — a reply to Cutler et al.', *Economy and Society*, 1979, pp. 342—64.

Harrison, M. (1979) 'Stalin — A Centenary View', *Marxism Today*, October 1979, pp. 21—6.

Hegel, G. (1956) *The Philosophy of History*, New York, Dover Publications.

Hindess, B. (1977) 'The Concept of Class in Marxist Theory and Marxist Politics' in J. Bloomfield (ed.), *Class, Hegemony and Party*, London, Lawrence and Wishart, pp. 95—107.

Hindess, B. (1980) 'Marxism and Parliamentary Democracy' in A. Hunt (ed.), *Marxism and Democracy*, London, Lawrence and Wishart, pp. 21—54.

Hirst, P.Q. (1977) 'Economic Classes and Politics' in A. Hunt (ed.), *Class and Class Structure*, London, Lawrence and Wishart, pp. 125—54.

Hoare, Q. and Nowell-Smith, G. (1971) *Antonio Gramsci Selections from the Prison Notebooks*, London, Lawrence and Wishart.

Hobbes, T. (1968) *Leviathan*, Harmondsworth, Penguin.

Hobhouse, L.T. (1964) *Liberalism*, Oxford, Oxford University Press.

Hobsbawm, E. (1977) 'Gramsci and Political Theory', *Marxism Today*, July 1977, pp. 205—13.

Hobsbawm, E. (1982) 'Gramsci and Marxist Political Theory' in A. Showstack Sassoon (ed.), *Approaches to Gramsci*, London, Writers and Readers, pp. 20—36.

Hobsbawm, E. (contrib.) (1983) 'Karl Marx: 100 not out', *Marxism Today*, March 1983, pp. 7—17.

Hobsbawm, E. and Napolitano, G. (1977) *The Italian Road to Socialism*, London, Journeyman Press.

Hoffman, J. (1975) *Marxism and the Theory of Praxis*, London, Lawrence and Wishart.

Hoffman, J. (1978a) 'Gramsci on State & Revolution', *The African Communist*, First Quarter, 1978, pp. 92—101.

Hoffman, J. (1978b) 'Politics and "the Will": The Philosophical Basis for a Scientific Approach' in C. Cunneen, D.H. De Grood, D. Riepe and W. Stein (eds.), *Explorations in Philosophy and Society*, Amsterdam, B.R. Grüner, pp. 17–41.

Hoffman, J. (1980) 'Ideology and the Question of "Value-Free" Science', *Dialectics and Humanism*, January 1980, pp. 123–31.

Hoffman, J. (1983) *Marxism, Revolution and Democracy*, Amsterdam, B.R. Grüner.

Holloway, J. and Picciotto, S. (1978) 'Introduction: Towards a Materialist Theory of the State' in J. Holloway and S. Picciotto (eds.), *State and Capital: A Marxist Debate*, London, Edward Arnold, pp. 1–31.

Hough, J. (1976) 'Political Participation in the Soviet Union', *Soviet Studies*, January 1976, pp. 3–20.

Howe, I. (1978) *Trotsky*, London, Fontana.

Hunt, A. (1980) 'Introduction: Taking Democracy Seriously' in A. Hunt (ed.), *Marxism and Democracy*, London, Lawrence and Wishart, pp. 7–19.

Hunt, A. (1983) 'Marx – The Missing Dimension: The Rise of Representative Democracy' in B. Matthews (ed.), *Marx: A Hundred Years On*, London, Lawrence and Wishart, pp. 87–110.

Hunt, R. (1974) *The Political Ideas of Marx and Engels*, London, Macmillan.

Ilyenkov, E.V. (1977) 'The Concept of the Ideal' in *Philosophy in the USSR*, Moscow, Progress Publishers, pp. 71–99.

Insunza, J. (1977) 'Roads of Revolution', *World Marxist Review*, May 1977, pp. 76–86.

Jacobitti, E. (1975) 'Labriola, Croce and Italian Marxism (1895–1910)', *Journal of the History of Ideas*, April–May 1975, pp. 297–318.

Jessop, B. (1980) 'The Gramsci Debate', *Marxism Today*, February 1980, pp. 23–5.

Jessop, B. (1982) *The Capitalist State*, Oxford, Martin Robertson.

Johnson, C. (1980) 'The Problem of Reformism and Marx's Theory of Fetishism', *New Left Review*, January–February 1980, pp. 70–96.

Johnstone, M. (1968) *Trotsky: His Ideas*, London, Challenge Publications.

Johnstone, M. (1970) 'Socialism, Democracy and the One Party System', *Marxism Today*, August, September and November 1970, pp. 242–50; pp. 281–7; pp. 349–56.

Johnstone, M. (1983) 'Marx, Blanqui and Majority Rule', *Socialist Register*, 1983, pp. 296–318.

Kann, M. (1978) 'The Dialectic of Consent Theory', *Journal of Politics*, May 1978, pp. 386–408.

220 *References*

Kautsky, K. (1918) *Ethics and the Materialist Conception of History* (4th edn), Chicago, Charles Kerr.

Kautsky, K. (1964) *The Dictatorship of the Proletariat*, Michigan, University of Michigan Press.

Knei-Paz, B. (1978) *The Social and Political Thought of Leon Trotsky*, Oxford, Oxford University Press.

Kolakowski, L. (1978) *Main Currents of Marxism*, vol. 2, Oxford, Clarendon Press.

Laclau, E. and Mouffe, C. (1981) 'Socialist Strategy — Where Next?', *Marxism Today*, January 1981, pp. 17—22.

Lane, D. (1981) *Leninism: A Sociological Interpretation*, Cambridge, Cambridge University Press.

Laslett, P. (1956) 'Introduction' in P. Laslett (ed.), *Philosophy, Politics and Society*, Oxford, Oxford University Press, pp. vii—xv.

Lefebvre, H. (1972) *The Sociology of Marx*, London, Allen Lane.

Liebman, M. (1975) *Leninism under Lenin*, London, Jonathan Cape.

Locke, J. (1924) *Two Treatises of Civil Government*, London, Everyman.

McBride, W.L. (1972) 'Non-Coercive Society: Some Doubts, Leninist and Contemporary' in J.R. Pennock and J.W. Chapman (eds.), *Coercion*, Chicago and New York, Aldene Atherton, pp. 178—97.

Machiavelli, N. (1970) *The Discourses*, Harmondsworth, Penguin.

McGovern, A. (1970) 'The Young Marx on the State', *Science and Society*, 1970, pp. 430—65.

McLellan, D. (1979) *Marxism After Marx*, London, Macmillan.

McLellan, D. (1983) 'Politics' in D. McLellan (ed.), *Marx: The First Hundred Years*, London, Fontana, pp. 143—87.

McLennan, G. (1981) *Marxism and the Methodologies of History*, London, Verso Books.

McLennan, G. (1983) 'Crisis in Capitalism, Crisis in Marxism', *Times Higher Educational Supplement*, 11 March 1983, pp. 15—16.

Macpherson, C.B. (1962) *The Political Theory of Possessive Individualism*, Oxford, Oxford University Press.

Madison, J. et al. (1961) *The Federalist Papers*, New York, Mentor Books.

Maguire, J. (1976) 'Marx on Ideology, Power and Force', *Theory and Decision*, October 1976, pp. 315—29.

Maguire, J. (1978) *Marx's Theory of Politics*, Cambridge, Cambridge University Press.

Mandel, E. (1978) *From Stalinism to Eurocommunism*, London, New Left Books.

Maximoff, G. (1953) *The Political Philosophy of Bakunin*, New York, Free Press.

Medvedev, R. (1972) *Let History Judge*, London, Macmillan.

Medvedev, R. (1975) *On Socialist Democracy*, New York, Alfred A. Knopf.

Meiksins Wood, E. (1978) 'C.B. Macpherson: Liberalism and the Task of Socialist Political Theory', *Socialist Register*, 1978, pp. 215–40.

Meiksins Wood, E. (1981) 'The Separation of the Economic and the Political in Capitalism', *New Left Review*, May–June 1981, pp. 66–95.

Mercer, C. (1980) 'Revolutions, Reforms or Reformulations? Marxist Discourse on Democracy' in A. Hunt (ed.), *Marxism and Democracy*, London, Lawrence and Wishart, pp. 101–37.

Meszaros, I. (1970) *Marx's Theory of Alienation*, London, Merlin Press.

Meszaros, I. (1979) 'Political Power and Dissent in Post-revolutionary Societies' in Il Manifesto (ed.), *Power and Opposition in Post-revolutionary Societies*, London, Ink Links, pp. 105–28.

Miliband, R. (1969) *The State in Capitalist Society*, London, Weidenfeld and Nicolson.

Miliband, R. (1973a) 'Marx and the State' in S. Avineri (ed.), *Marx's Socialism*, New York, Lieber Atherton, pp. 157–81.

Miliband, R. (1973b) 'Poulantzas and the Capitalist State', *New Left Review*, November–December 1973, pp. 83–92.

Miliband, R. (1973c) 'The Coup in Chile', *Socialist Register*, 1973, pp. 451–73.

Miliband, R. (1973d) 'Stalin and After', *Socialist Register*, 1973, pp. 377–95.

Miliband, R. (1977) *Marxism and Politics*, Oxford, Oxford University Press.

Miliband, R. (1978) 'Constitutionalism and Revolution: Notes on Eurocommunism', *Socialist Register*, 1978, pp. 158–71.

Miliband, R. (1982) 'Political Action, Determinism and Contingency', *Political Power and Social Theory*, 1980, pp. 1–20.

Miliband, R. (1983) 'State Power and Class Interests', *New Left Review*, March–April 1983, pp. 57–68.

Mill, J.S. (1968) *Representative Government*, London, Everyman.

Mill, J.S. (1974) *On Liberty*, Harmondsworth, Penguin.

Millas, O. (1975) 'From Economic Subversion to Fascist Putsch', *World Marxist Review*, November 1975, pp. 33–5.

Moore, S. (1963) *Three Tactics: The Background in Marx*, New York, Monthly Review.

Mouffe, C. (1979a) 'Introduction: Gramsci Today' in C. Mouffe (ed.), *Gramsci and Marxist Theory*, London, Routledge & Kegan Paul, pp. 1–18.

Mouffe, C. (1979b) 'Hegemony and Ideology in Gramsci' in C. Mouffe (ed.), *Gramsci and Marxist Theory*, London, Routledge & Kegan Paul, pp. 168—204.

Müller, W. and Neusüss, C. (1978) 'The "Welfare-State Illusion" and the Contradiction between Wage Labour and Capital' in J. Holloway and S. Picciotto (eds.), *State and Capital: A Marxist Debate*, London, Edward Arnold, pp. 32—9.

Nemeth, T. (1980) *Gramsci's Philosophy*, Sussex, The Harvester Press.

Nove, A. (1975), *Stalinism and After*, London, Allen and Unwin.

O'Malley, J. (1970) 'Editor's Introduction' in *Karl Marx Critique of Hegel's Philosophy of Right*, Cambridge, Cambridge University Press.

Parkin, F. (1979) *Marxism and Class Theory: A Bourgeois Critique*, London, Tavistock.

Partridge, P.H. (1967) 'Politics, Philosophy, Ideology' in A. Quinton (ed.), *Political Philosophy*, Oxford, Oxford University Press, pp. 19—31.

Pateman, C. (1979) *The Problem of Political Obligation*, Chichester, John Wiley.

Perez-Diaz, V.M. (1978) *State, Bureaucracy and Civil Society*, London, Macmillan.

Pilling, G. (1980) *Marx's 'Capital': Philosophy and Political Economy*, London, Routledge & Kegan Paul.

Plamenatz, J. (1954) *German Marxism and Russian Communism*, London, Longmans.

Plamenatz, J. (1968) *Consent, Freedom and Obligation*, Oxford, Oxford University Press.

Plato (1955) *The Republic*, Harmondsworth, Penguin.

Poulantzas, N. (1973) *Political Power and Social Classes*, London, New Left Books.

Poulantzas, N. (1978) *State, Power, Socialism*, London, New Left Books.

Powell, E. (1969) *Freedom and Reality*, Surrey, Elliot Right Way Books.

Radice, L. (1978) 'Communism with a Human Face' in G. Urban (ed.), *Eurocommunism*, London, Maurice Temple Smith, pp. 32—57.

Rattansi, A. (1982) *Marx and the Division of Labour*, London, Macmillan.

Rossanda R. (1979) 'Power and Opposition in Post-revolutionary Societies' in Il Manifesto (ed.), *Power and Opposition in Post-revolutionary Societies*, London, Ink Links, pp. 3—17.

Rousseau, J-J. (1913) *The Social Contract and Discourses*, London, Everyman.

Rousseau, J-J. (1968) *The Social Contract*, Harmondsworth, Penguin.

Roxborough, I., O'Brien, P. and Roddick, J. (1977), *Chile: The State and Revolution*, London, Macmillan.

Salvadori, M. (1979) *Karl Kautsky and the Socialist Revolution 1880–1938*, London, New Left Books.

Sanderson, J. (1963) 'Marx and Engels on the State', *Western Political Quarterly*, December 1963, pp. 946–55.

Schmidt, A. (1971) *The Concept of Nature in Marx*, London, New Left Books.

Schonfield, W.R. (1971) 'The Classical Marxist Conception of Liberal Democracy', *Review of Politics*, July 1971, pp. 364–75.

Schram, S. (1963) *The Political Thought of Mao Tse-tung*, London, Pall Mall Press.

Sève, L. (1977) 'The Leninist Development of the Strategy of Peaceful Revolution', *Marxism Today*, July 1977, pp. 133–44.

Shahnazarov, G. (1974) *Socialist Democracy*, Moscow, Progress Publishers.

Showstack Sassoon, A. (1980a) 'Gramsci: A New Concept of Politics and the Expansion of Democracy' in A. Hunt (ed.), *Marxism and Democracy*, London, Lawrence and Wishart, pp. 81–99.

Showstack Sassoon, A. (1980b) *Gramsci's Politics*, London, Croom Helm.

Showstack Sassoon, A. (1982) 'Preface' in A. Showstack Sassoon (ed.), *Approaches to Gramsci*, London, Writers and Readers, pp. 9–11.

Simon, R. (1982) *Gramsci's Political Thought*, London, Lawrence and Wishart.

Sobolev, A. (1974) 'Chile: Experience and Possibilities of Peaceful Revolution', *Socialism: Theory and Practice*, November 1974, pp. 27–41.

Spriano, P. (1979) *Antonio Gramsci and the Party: The Prison Years*, London, Lawrence and Wishart.

Stalin, J.V. (1954) *Works*, vol. 10, Moscow, Foreign Languages Publishing House.

Stalin, J.V. (1973) *The Essential Stalin*, London, Croom Helm.

Teitelboim, V. (1977) 'Reflections on the 1,000 Days of Popular Unity Rule', *World Marxist Review*, January 1977, pp. 33–40.

Texier, J. (1979) 'Gramsci, theoretician of the superstructures' in C. Mouffe (ed.), *Gramsci and Marxist Theory*, London, Routledge & Kegan Paul, pp. 48–79.

Therborn, G. (1978) *What Does the Ruling Class Do When It Rules*, London, New Left Books.

Timpanaro, S. (1975) *On Materialism*, London, New Left Books.

Tocqueville, Alexis de (1966) *Democracy in America*, vol. 1, London, Fontana.

Trotsky, L. (1961) *Terrorism and Communism*, Michigan, University of Michigan.

Trotsky, L. (1971) *1905*, Harmondsworth, Penguin.

Tucker, R. (1973) 'Marx as a Political Theorist' in S. Avineri (ed.), *Marx's Socialism*, New York, Lieber Atherton, pp. 126–56.

Tucker, R. (1974) *Stalin as Revolutionary 1879–1929*, London, Allen and Unwin.

Tucker, R. (1977a) 'Stalinism as Revolution from Above' in R. Tucker (ed.), *Stalinism: Essays in Historical Interpretation*, New York, Norton & Co., pp. 77–108.

Tucker, R. (1977b) 'Some Questions on the Scholarly Agenda' in R. Tucker (ed.), *Stalinism: Essays in Historical Interpretation*, pp. 320–24.

Unger, A.L. (1981) 'Political Participation in the USSR: YCL and CPSU', *Soviet Studies*, January 1981, pp. 107–24.

Wagner, Y. and Strauss, M. (1969), 'The Programme of the Communist Manifesto and its Theoretical Foundations', *Political Studies*, December 1969, pp. 470–84.

White, S. (1979) 'The USSR: Patterns of Autocracy and Industrialisation' in A. Brown and J. Gray (eds.), *Political Culture and Political Change in Communist States*, London, Macmillan, pp. 25–65.

White, S. (1983) 'Political Communications in the USSR: Letters to Party, State and Press', *Political Studies*, March 1983, pp. 43–60.

Willetts, H.T. (1981) 'The USSR and Eurocommunism' in R. Kindersley (ed.), *In Search of Eurocommunism*, London, Macmillan, pp. 1–22.

Williams, G.A. (1960) 'Gramsci's Concept of *Egemonia*', *Journal of the History of Ideas*, October–December 1960, pp. 586–99.

Woddis, J. (1977) *Armies and Politics*, London, Lawrence and Wishart.

Wolfe, A. (1974) 'New Directions in the Marxist Theory of Politics', *Politics and Society*, Winter 1974, pp. 131–59.

Woolfson, C. (1982) *The Labour Theory of Culture*, London, Routledge & Kegan Paul.

World Marxist Review (1979) 'Revolution and Democracy: International Scientific Conference', August 1979, pp. 46–67.

Zaradov, K. (1975) 'Leninism on Consolidating the Victory of Revolution', *World Marxist Review*, April 1975, pp. 20–4.

Zaradov, K. (contrib.) (1979) 'Revolution and Democracy', *World Marxist Review*, September 1979, pp. 29–47.

INDEX

abstraction 25—6, 41, 67—8,
82, 100—6, 149, 157—8,
166, 171, 184—6, 189,
192, 204
    reflectionist theory of 99—101,
    103, 105—7
    see also commodity fetishism,
    hypostasis, will
alienation 77—8, 81—2, 97,
99, 115, 118—19, 122,
129, 136, 183, 195, 201
Allende, Salvador 158, 162
Althusser, Louis 2—3, 5—6,
8—11, 14, 52, 91
    followers of 21, 34, 93—4
Anderson, Perry 6, 8—9, 15,
54—5, 69—71, 96, 148,
212
Aristotle 199

Ball, Terence 126
base/superstructure 4, 79—81,
92—6, 107, 122—3
Benn, Tony 205
Berlinguer, Enrico 158—60,
163, 165
Bernstein, Eduard 10—11, 14,
16, 103—4, 108, 140—1,
195
Blanquism 59, 141, 144—5
Block, Fred 39
Bogomolov, A.S. 120
Bolsheviks 56, 61, 72, 153—4,
175—6, 187

Bonapartism 21, 33—6, 38—40,
47, 92, 131, 170, 193
    see also state
Bordiga, Amadeo 70
Bosanquet, Bernard 48
bourgeoisie 34—9, 46, 53, 56—7,
77—8, 131, 136, 151, 164
Buci-Glucksmann, Christine 5,
50, 59—60, 63
Bukharin, Nicolai 112, 184,
186, 189—90

Callinicos, Alex 14
'Capital Logic' 93—4
capitalism 41, 44—5, 80, 84,
86—7, 98, 122, 130, 133—5,
137—8
    see also democracy
Carrillo, Santiago 2, 16, 150,
155, 161, 197—9, 207
Carter, April 211
Castillo, Rene 165
catastrophism 2, 4
Chilean coup 159—64
civil society 24—7, 29—31, 40,
82, 88, 97, 109, 188
    and political society 55,
    62—3, 79—80, 96, 148, 150
classes 42—6, 77—8, 92, 118,
133, 173
    see also division of labour
classical Marxism
    coercion and consent in 1—4,
    10, 13—15, 17—21, 46—7,